## ~ For You ~

For you, who yearns for something more,
and reaches to find it.

For you, who dreams,
and never gives up.

For you, who has been set back,
and journeys onward.

For you, who knows we each have a purposeful path,
and leaps toward it.

For you, who believes we can be our greatest self,
and strives to be it.

For you, who knows our greatest life awaits us,
and pauses to see it.

# CHANGE YOUR SHOES

## LIVE YOUR GREATEST LIFE

## KATHY ANDERSEN

# Introduction

I F YOU ARE READING THIS, there is something inside you that yearns for something more—sometimes that yearning is a tiny flicker, sometimes it's a tornado that moves you and unsettles you, sometimes it's a dream that fills you with anticipation and excitement. I believe that yearning is the voice of the most exciting and thrilling gift we have—the voice of our limitless potential. This is the voice that we need to kick us in the pants enough times so that we finally push our pause button!

Welcome to the pause.

I want this book to be a "time-out" for you. A place where you can come, relax, and thoroughly get lost in the journey—through my story, and through the stories, dreams, hopes, and aspirations that I hope are evoked in you.

We have everything we need within us to make the changes we need to step onto a path toward our greatest self, and to live our greatest life. What a wonderful indulgence to pause and unwrap the gift of our limitless potential—explore it, play with it, dream with it—and most of all, turn that potential into a thrilling, fulfilling, purposeful, passionate, authentic … reality!

This book is about changing your shoes—literally and figuratively!

I left Australia to take a "break"—to explore and discover—not only the world, but my *self*. No responsibility to anyone but to me, no expectations, no image to uphold … just to experience.

It took, literally, changing my shoes to do that.

My "break" turned into a journey of more than ten years. Over those years, my journey through the world around provoked a powerful journey within. Throughout my journey, I was able to discover and experience the infinite power we each have within us to transform our lives. I experienced that, despite the worst that happens around us, the best can rise from within us.

We each have our demons and darkness, but we each also have our angels and our light, which are ultimately more powerful. My journey enabled me to step into the darkness that filled me from the abuse and isolation that I had suffered throughout my childhood, and emerge with strength and purpose. Now, I know we are each so much greater than the worst that happens to us.

Throughout my journey, life showed me that when we change our shoes, and step out into the unknown—when it's just you and the universe—extraordinary aspects of life are revealed that are otherwise lost in our darkness, or simply hidden in the busyness we create in each day. Paths emerge that take us on journeys beyond our imagination—beyond our pains, beyond our fears, beyond the limits we set—to places where we chart our own course, we find purpose, we see the possibilities of our greatest self, and we dream dreams that really do come true!

My hope is that this book is a wonderful journey for you.

As you move through the book, there are places for you to pause and to contemplate your journey. At the end of each chapter, you will find *Moments of Pause*—questions for you to contemplate in your own space, and maybe even to share in the space of friends. Perhaps you will have other questions that arise, and perhaps your friends will have more still—there is space for that, too—although you may need more!

The strength of our stories can power our journeys beyond our imaginations. Our stories and our journeys can create connections to our shared humanity where the sum of all of us is greater than the part of any one of us. Through sharing our stories and giving voice to those things that are most meaningful to us, we can become greater together than we can become alone.

Along our journeys, we can find shoes to step into that enable us to not only create change in our life, but also to walk with others to create change in the world. We can take our *self* on a journey to our greatest self. We can live our greatest life!

## A Note to the Reader

Throughout this book, you will notice that I use the word "self"
separate from "my," "your," or "our."

I use "your *self*" and "my *self*" and "our *self*"
to reinforce that we each have a "self" that is uniquely
ours to discover, to nurture, to inspire, to encourage,
to treat with compassion and kindness, to be responsible for,
to love, and to take on a journey to the greatest *self*
that each of us can be, to live our greatest life.

# Chapters

## One

# From Heels to Hiking Boots!

*"Your work is to discover your work ..."*

—BUDDHA

WHEN I LEFT AUSTRALIA with a backpack and a round-world ticket, I had no idea that a single step would turn into a journey of more than ten years. Life in Australia was great—I had a wonderful career that provided a large salary, international travel, and mental stimulation. I was living in a beautiful country surrounded by family and friends. At age thirty, from the outside, everything looked perfect. On the inside, things weren't so perfect.

Do you know that feeling when everything *should* feel right, but it just doesn't? When you feel that you're getting lost in the day-to-day, and there's a voice inside you that is whispering (sometimes yelling!) that there is more for you. But you can't quite put your finger on it.

That was me.

If you had told me a few years earlier that I would quit my job, sell almost everything I owned, and leave Australia with a backpack to go traveling to unknown places without a time frame or an exact plan, I would have said you were thinking of someone else. That just wasn't the way my life operated. I liked time frames and plans, and they had always worked for me.

I had diligently spent my twenties pursuing my career goals and academic plan. I earned my Bachelor of Business degree, started an MBA, and had climbed the corporate ladder from "check-out chick" at the local grocery store in Sydney, to Group Manager at Ford Motor Company in Melbourne. I had purchased a beach-side apartment in the beautiful Balmoral Beach in Sydney. I was living in a chic inner-city apartment in Melbourne, and was already driving an SUV (a goal I had set for much later in life!).

So how did I end up in my mother's living room, packing camping gear into a backpack, and swapping my corporate high heels for hiking boots and flip-flops?

I have to tell you, it wasn't because of a romantic dream to go traveling—I had been too busy pursuing my career and studying to ever think about traveling for anything other than business. It ended up coming down to survival.

Leading up to that scene in my mother's living room, there were a few moments in particular, where all at once, I knew my life was putting me at risk of losing my *self*. Yes! *My* life, which I had artfully crafted, was putting me at risk of losing *my self*.

I remember one moment on the subway in London, when I was traveling for business, visiting the Ford Motor Company headquarters in Dearborn, Michigan, with a five-hour stopover in Heathrow. I had decided to use the time to quickly explore a few places, so I caught the underground metro rail (the "Underground" as it's locally known) from Heathrow to Piccadilly Circus—a busy little central plaza in the middle of London. It was the morning rush-hour, and the Underground was filled with commuters in suits, shiny shoes, and carrying briefcases. Despite the many people, there was a lifelessness to the train that made me feel as though I was in a cemetery.

In particular, in the carriage stood two much older men, not far from me. They looked like grandpas—whitish-silver hair, that soft-looking grandpa skin, a little hunched over, and eyes that were deep with age. I pictured them with their bouncing grandchildren on their laps, with smiles, and baby bottles. *"Why are they on this train?"* I contemplated. My images of them were contrasted with their seriousness. Their conversation was not of grandchildren, but of office matters. I wondered how many years they had been traveling this underground, and how many more years they would travel this underground—carrying their briefcases, wrapped in their gray suits, wearing their shiny business shoes, and talking of office matters. Where were their grandchildren?

I looked around, and the lifelessness and emptiness of the crowded carriage prompted that voice inside me to ask me if this was a carriage on which I wanted to travel through life. My answer shouted back fast and loud—*"No!!!!!"*

The Underground pulled into Piccadilly Circus, and I had a renewed sense of adventure as I explored London in my casual traveling clothes and comfortable sneakers, in stark contrast to the business suits of the morning commuters. These shoes felt good!

On that same trip, I had another striking moment. The first day of my schedule took me to the Ford Motor Company head offices for a day of meetings. The offices were daunting and together formed a bold, high-tech mini-city that made me feel as though I had skipped into a distant future time zone. Inside, the offices were just as daunting—filled with what seemed to be endless cubicles stretching from one end of the floor to the other. I could barely see the horizon. Where are the people? I had to re-focus to find them.

On this mothership, everyone was almost hidden from view in their cubicle, working busily, but without sound or motion.

As I looked beyond the cubicles and through the floor-to-ceiling glass to the outside, I re-focused into the distance. One after the other, like an image infinitely reflected in a mirror, glass buildings filled the view. As I peered closer, I could just make out the shadows of cubicles on every floor in every building, one after the other, after the other. Suddenly, I felt as if I were an anonymous and lost soul, amidst thousands and thousands. Before I knew it, that voice popped up again, *"Is this the mothership on which I want to ride through life?"* My silent answer shook me.

I arrived back at my hotel room, and couldn't take my corporate high heels off fast enough. My bare feet felt great!

One year later, I was packing my backpack in my mother's living room.

Of course, it wasn't just these two moments that caused me to change my shoes from heels to hiking boots. These were just two of many moments in which the universe was giving me a clue—that there was other work to do—but the work was on me. I would come to see that in every moment, the universe is at work, helping us to discover the work that will take us on a journey to our greatest self, and our greatest life.

## MOMENTS OF PAUSE

1. What is the vision for your life? What are your dreams? Your aspirations? What are the things that excite you?

2. How is the reality of your life different from the vision for your life? What is that "something more" for which you yearn?

3. Are there aspects of your life in which you feel that you are losing your *self*? Are there parts of your life in which you feel "stuck"? What are they?

4. In which "shoes" do you feel most comfortable in your life? In which "shoes" do you feel the least comfortable in your life?

5. What would you like to be doing differently in your life?

## MORE MOMENTS FOR YOU

---

---

---

---

---

---

---

---

---

---

Two

# The Great Places You'll Go!

*"You have brains in your head.*
*You have feet in your shoes.*
*You can steer yourself any direction you choose.*
*You're on your own. And you know what you know.*
*And YOU are the guy who'll decide where to go."*

—Dr. Seuss
*Oh, the Places You'll Go!*

OUR GREATEST ADVENTURES ARE OFTEN FOUND, not outside us, but within us, and one ultimately leads to the other. When I left Australia, I had no idea where my journey would take me. It ended up taking me further than I could ever have imagined—not only on the outside, but also on the inside.

From unfamiliar cities, towns, islands, and remote villages in Europe, India, Latin America, and the Caribbean, to traveling through the unresolved, unexplored, and unhealed parts of me, I came to find that you can't escape exploring your own depths when you are traveling alone to new and foreign places. Nor does the journey end when you return (or in my case, when you don't return!).

I know that even the writing of this book will prompt new journeys. For example, I know that I will need to take a very difficult journey with my mother, as I tell her that my father sexually abused me throughout my childhood and teenage years. I have kept that secret from her for not wanting to cause her pain. Yet now, I need to tell her, so I can share my story and help other women and children who have, and who are now, experiencing the same or similar traumas.

I believe that extraordinary "breakthrough moments" come when we are daring enough to put our *self* on the line; when we confront our greatest fears; step into the most uncomfortable parts of our *self*; and simply stand there, experience that space, and feel our own authentic presence in every part of us. I believe that each journey we take starts there—and from there, the places we can go are beyond our contemplation or imagination.

An eleven-year-old girl said to me while I was writing this book, "Don't tell me the sky's the limit when there are footprints on the moon!" I think she is wiser than her years. Among other things, my journey has convinced me that when we dare to change our shoes and step onto new paths, our possibilities are limitless, and our footprints are left in remarkable places—far beyond the sky and the moon.

As I packed my backpack, my mother chuckled and tried to contain her laughter. I may have been extremely capable in the corporate world, but packing a backpack was entirely another story. It didn't seem as though it should have been such a difficult task, especially after I read a few expert guides as to what I should pack, and tips to ensure a lightweight backpack. Clearly, I lost something in translation as I almost fell over backward at my first attempt to mount my pack!

The camping store had been thrilled when I checked out—I bought the complete check-list of items—and it showed in my bulging pack, which looked as if it were about to give birth. My inventory included the "essentials": sleeping bag, camping saucepans and mug, portable gas cooker, bug spray, sunscreen, toothpaste, toothbrush, liquid soap, deodorant, two-in-one shampoo and conditioner (no room for both!), waterproof matches, light-weight rain jacket, hiking socks, essential documents (in a watertight ziplock—including birth certificate, passport copies, travel insurance documents, plane ticket copies, and international drivers license), phone card, writing journal, a pen, address book, and pocket camera. Absent from my pack—my cell phone!

*Lonely Planet USA* would be my traveling companion for the first leg of my trip. The "Facts for the Visitor" and "Getting Around" sections already had me happily contemplating new and foreign scenarios that far surpassed the contemplation of business scenarios to which I had become accustomed.

As for my "wardrobe," I had decided that three days seemed a reasonable amount of time between coin laundromats (which would become a whole new world I would discover during my travels). So in groups of three, I squeezed in hiking pants, shorts, t-shirts, hiking socks, and underwear. I would only take two pairs of shoes with me—my Tevas (flip-flops), and my hardy Australian hiking boots—Blundstones!

I had no idea how much "changing my shoes" would change every aspect of my life—physically, emotionally, spiritually, and professionally. I would come to find that "listening to my feet" was the only compass I needed to make the right steps forward.

I laughed at the things I was leaving behind. I reflected on how much time I had spent acquiring things to create an environment around me that felt cozy and accomplished—the carefully selected sofa, the car, my clothes, shoes, bed linens, pieces of art—everything. These were the things on the outside that created a picture that I wanted to see, but that only tied me down, and filled me with artificial comfort on the inside. When it came time to sell everything, it was apparent what a burden those things had become, and what a short-lived and artificial sense of value and comfort they had provided. Selling everything and watching all of those things taken away was one of the most liberating feelings of my life.

Another breakthrough moment: Too much "stuff" weighs you down. Part of stepping forward is leaving things behind!

At this point, you might be asking, *"Why camping?"* Well, when I was at one of those times that I told you about before—when you pause and simply stand in your shoes and feel what's there (or what's not there)—I felt an overwhelming sense of claustrophobia. I felt as if I were in a straightjacket. *"Where is that coming from?"* I had reflected. Ironically, I realized, during the years I had spent studying and pursuing my career, I had forgotten to live life. I had no balance. It was all or nothing for me. I was on an unrelenting quest. I needed to be the most successful, I needed to be the fastest climber on the corporate ladder, and I needed to be the A-grade student.

People will say that unrelenting quest is about proving "something" to "someone." For me, it was about finding a place when all other sense of identity, worth, and value had been stripped from me. When you're sexually abused over and over, every time you are undressed and violated, you lose a piece of your *self*. It's like a jigsaw puzzle slowly losing all of its pieces.

Over the years, I had lost a lot of my pieces, and I hadn't replaced them with anything that created a beautiful landscape. I had replaced them with whatever I could find that would stop the picture from falling apart.

I filled those missing pieces with work and study after I left school and left home. I could have filled those pieces with very different things and gone down a much more destructive path—drugs, alcohol, and a life that would have led me to the streets or to a jail cell. I think I was incredibly lucky, or maybe I was meant to write this book.

I understand completely why women kill their abusive husbands, and why prostitutes kill their pimps. So why don't young girls kill their abusive fathers? I think they often just can't—at least not until they are older—and maybe it will be their father, or maybe it will be someone else that represents the evil and the humiliation. We can only suppress the bottomless pit of dark feelings for so long until they implode or explode. One way or another, left unresolved, those feelings can destroy us, and they can destroy others around us.

I realized that I was totally exhausted from the struggle within me. Every part of my being was drained to the point of almost being unable to function. I had lost all sense of the next step forward. I had lost all sense of who I was, or of any meaningful purpose. I had spent so much time surviving, so much time fighting my demons, so much time seeking my own security, so much time on a relentless quest to simply feel good about my *self*, but I had no sense of who that *self* was. I needed to give my *self* a break.

Realizing that it was okay to give my *self* a break—to just stop—was one of my most life-changing breakthroughs in those moments of pause. The choice was all mine. Keep whipping my *self*, and driving my *self* beyond reasonable limits, or simply give my *self* a break. Wow! That simple. My choice. My life. In my hands.

Yet what did a break look like? I had never contemplated that. What I did know, was that my sense of claustrophobia had led me to feel that I needed to be in wide open spaces. I felt compelled to be away from the hustle, bustle, noise, and busyness that I had come to know as daily life, and that had kept me from my *self.*

I wanted to explore unknown environments—where I was least comfortable and least familiar. I wanted to experience new things and *feel* what that felt like. I wanted to stay far away from the hotels that were a familiar part of business travel. I wanted to stay away from five-stars, suits, high heels, computers, phones, people, and products. I wanted to live raw, real, and with no regrets.

When I was saying my farewells at the Ford Motor Company head office in Melbourne, Australia, I stepped into the office of one of the senior managers in the customer service division. John was about to retire. He, like many others, wanted to know the job for which I was really leaving. It was more than a little beyond the belief and comprehension of many of my colleagues and "professional" friends that I was simply leaving to go backpacking for an undetermined length of time. As I assured John that there was no other job, he nodded a few times and looked down at his desk. He slowly looked back up at me, and I could see the shift in his eyes and face. I was confused by the sadness in his eyes. "I wanted to do that when I was young," he said slowly, "but I got into the job, and just never found the time."

As I stepped out of John's office, and saw the familiar lines of offices and cubicles, everyone's head down, and the clock ticking away, I couldn't run fast enough. The next week, I was leaving Melbourne for my mother's home in Sydney to say my farewells and set off on my way.

In my mother's living room, it took packing, unpacking, and re-packing my backpack several times before I thought I had a pack that I could carry for any length of time. My adventure would soon begin!

Days later, I was on the plane at Sydney Airport anticipating take-off. First stop, Los Angeles. My mind was abuzz. I had said my farewells to family and friends (most of whom thought I was absolutely crazy, and encouraged me to see a psychologist, which, of course, I declined).

As the engines finally revved up and we started to accelerate down the runway, I felt exhilarated. I felt proud of me. As the plane lifted off the ground, a weight lifted off my shoulders. Just me and my backpack. I wiggled my feet in my Blundstones, and they felt happy. I was off and on my way, full of anticipation of all the great places I would go!

## MOMENTS OF PAUSE

1.  What makes you feel "cozy and accomplished" in your life? Which things on the "outside"? Which things on the "inside"?

2.  When do you feel most "balanced" and in harmony in your life?

3.  When do you feel most tired and drained in your life?

4.  What are the "missing pieces" of your life? Why did those pieces fall?

5.  What would "giving your *self* a break in life" look like? What would be the most extreme "break" that you could give your *self*?

## MORE MOMENTS FOR YOU

Three

# Wide Open Spaces!

*"Afoot and lighthearted I take to the open road.*
*Healthy, free, the world before me."*

—Walt Whitman

To fully adventure through the wide open spaces of the world before us, we often need to leave our plans behind. The tour descriptions of the camping trips I had read with the travel agent before I left Melbourne were a great contrast to the business plans I would normally read. They were the perfect transition from the confines of office buildings, to the freedom of wide open spaces.

When I had first walked into the STA travel office, the agent was so excited to help me leap into the world of adventure travel. She was also quite amused that I was swapping my heels for hiking boots and flip-flops, and couldn't wait to get me started. I felt as though I had walked into a hair salon on a very bad hair day, and the stylist was jumping for joy at the chance to transform me. At that time, I had no idea of the transformation that lay ahead.

As we scoured through the various options, I had very little criteria. I definitely needed something semi-organized to get me started. I was so drained that jumping off a plane somewhere without anything at all to slip into just wasn't appealing. I needed some help to transition, and to get to know the "ropes" of independent travel. I had never travelled "independently" before—always for business, and for a relatively short time. I had always been able to rely on five-star hotels, taxis and drivers, and a generous travel budget.

In contrast, my travel budget for this journey was almost $10,000 in Australian dollars—around $6,000 in US dollars. Unfortunately, I had decided to travel at a time when the Australian dollar was almost half the value of the US dollar, but I wasn't going to wait around for the exchange rate to change. I anticipated that if I wanted to stay away for five to six months, my daily travel budget would be between US$30 to US$40 per day.

It had been a long time since I had been on a budget. My salary during my late twenties had reached six figures, and it wasn't since I was an eighteen-year-old check-out chick at my local grocery store that I needed to watch my spending. At that time, I had moved out of home and was renting an apartment with two co-workers, and we were all trying to make our very low grocery store wages pay the bills. Thankfully, I had been able to save a little during my late twenties. My savings, combined with my unpaid vacation payment from Ford (of course, I rarely took a vacation), and selling my furniture and most other things when I left Melbourne, gave me my travel budget. One way or another, I would make it work!

The descriptions of the camping treks in the Trek America brochures gave me all the encouragement I needed. To start me off, I decided to do three camping treks through the United States and

Canada, which would be a total of forty-nine days. These would take me from touch-down in Los Angeles, up through the Pacific West Coast, into and around Alberta and British Columbia in Canada, then back down to Los Angeles and across to New York City. The tour descriptions had me wanting to jump on a plane right away!

Trek Number One: "Pacific Coast." Fourteen days. Los Angeles to Seattle. *"The Pacific Coast ... famed for its giant Redwoods and volcanic peaks. This incredibly scenic route offers a diverse range of attractions such as isolated, unspoiled beaches, hiking in coastal rain forests and the big city attractions of Los Angeles and San Francisco. See and experience the far western states of California, Oregon, and Washington."*

Trek Number Two: "Canadian Mountie." Fourteen days. Seattle to Seattle Loop. *"Explore the pristine wilderness of British Columbia and Alberta ... Camp in the high Rockies, soak in hot springs, hike across an ice glacier, and canoe on a crystal clear mountain lake. The Mountie will take you into the heart of Canada's wilderness—the perfect outdoor adventure!"*

Trek Number Three: "Southern Sun." Twenty-one days. Los Angeles to New York City. *"Experience the fast paced East, the slow moving South and the laid-back West with exciting activities such as whitewater rafting, horseback riding and hiking on offer— don't forget about the nightlife of New Orleans and Las Vegas!"*

The rest of my travels would be up to me. The round-world "consolidated" airfare the agent recommended was a great option for me because the ticket was completely flexible. I could move travel dates or destinations at any time without penalty and end up anywhere on a whim—just what I needed!

I decided to start with the United States, and travel clockwise around the world from there. The timing of my trip dictated my direction as much as anything—I left Australia in July (winter in Australia), so I figured I could get through the United States,

Canada, Scandinavia, and Europe by the end of December, and then head to Asia-Pacific in January as the Southern Hemisphere was warming up again.

Well, at least that was my plan. As I would come to know, when you throw your *self* out to the universe, the plan of the universe often leaves your plan far behind!

During the flight from Sydney to Los Angeles, my mind was full. I was leaving so much behind in Australia—not only "things," but a life that had been so tormenting in so many ways. I was looking forward to discovery. I was looking forward to breaking away from everything familiar and "safe." I was excited that I had let go of the job, the title, the car, the "things," the expectations, and my own demands. It was one of the most freeing feelings of my life. I think I started to breathe that day.

I reflected on the book, *The Alchemist*, and the shepherd who left his pastures to travel to seek his destiny. Ultimately, after experiencing much along the way, he ends up back at his pasture, and realizes all that he needed was right there, within him. I knew there had to be more—more than just surviving. I couldn't keep running on empty. I couldn't keep chasing false fulfillment. It was so draining. I had lost my sense of identity during my childhood, and the path on which I had put my *self* was taking me further and further away from my *self*.

There was a little girl inside who never had the opportunity to play and who was still very, very alone and very, very tired. She needed my attention. She needed me to give her a break.

I was looking forward to simply placing my *self* into the arms of the universe, and being carried away. That's how I felt tucked into the plane. I had no idea where this journey would take me, but I felt an overwhelming sense that everything would be okay. I sensed the universe would take me where I needed to go, so I could find my *self* amidst the jungle I had created. Along the way, maybe the little girl might get to play, and laugh, and be carefree in the way that all little girls should.

Before I knew it, the plane touched down in Los Angeles. At baggage claim, I waited somewhat anxiously, to see my backpack greet me from its journey in the belly of the plane—this was not a time for my luggage to go missing! As I tried to put nervous thoughts of lost luggage aside, finally my pack popped its head through the black rubber baggage curtains and made its way along the luggage belt to me. I was excited to grab my new companion and be on my way. Funnily enough, I wasn't quite able to scoop my pack from the belt as readily as I had expected. *"Did gravity change between Australia and the United States?"* I'm sure my pack was not this heavy when I left my mother's living room!

I needed to make my way to a small hotel that was the meeting place for the Trek America trip. There, I would meet my fellow travelers, and be briefed on the next fourteen days of camping along the Pacific Coast. I was looking forward to meeting the other travelers in the group. The trek was aimed at eighteen to thirty-five-year-olds who were seeking outdoor adventure. The groups were limited to eight in size, and while there was a schedule, there was a lot of flexibility to explore. The ten-person van in which we would travel was small enough to get to the "off-the-beaten-track" places that we all would be sure to want to explore.

After finding the hotel, the 5:00PM meeting time soon came, and I headed to the reception to meet my traveling companions. Meeting my fellow trekkers was a delightful contrast to the meetings I was used to in the corporate world. Everyone was relaxed, chatting, smiling, and happy to be close to setting off on an adventure.

Our group was young and from several countries—the Netherlands, Sweden, Japan, Belgium, and the United Kingdom. Only two girls from Amsterdam knew each other, everyone else was traveling solo. Most of the group ranged in age from eighteen to twenty-seven, and it was refreshing that everyone seemed to be in the same "groove"—simply looking forward to the adventure ahead, and happy in not quite knowing what that adventure would bring.

Irrespective of our age differences, or from where we came, we were already bonded in our shared sense for adventure and exploration—"no frills" style. What a wonderfully simple agenda (or lack thereof!). Like me, my new friends had swapped their regular shoes for hiking boots and flip-flops and the only mission was to break away and let the wide open spaces be our playground.

The wide open spaces that await each of us are as close as our next step. We can travel far, or we can travel near, to step into the vastness that each moment holds for us. We can each place our *self* in the arms of the universe. We can each be carried away to places and spaces where we can discover all that lies within us through all that lies around us, and all that lies around us through all that lies within us.

## MOMENTS OF PAUSE

1.  What are the roles, expectations, and demands of your life that "stop you from breathing," that keep you "running on empty"?

2.  What experiences in your life have caused some of your identity, your *self*, to be lost?

3.  In which ways do you feel your life is dictating your identity, rather than allowing you to create your identity?

4.  What are the "plans" you have for your *self*? Which of your "plans" feel a part of a "greater destiny" for you?

5.  What are the "wide open spaces" for which you yearn?

## MORE MOMENTS FOR YOU

# Four

# No Matter Where You Go ~ There You Are!

*"It does not matter how slowly you go as long as you do not stop."*

—Confucius

WE EACH HAVE GREAT JOURNEYS ahead of us, waiting for us to embark upon with a first step, and then to simply take each next step, one at a time. The Pacific West Coast was the next step on my journey, and an introduction to the vastness that lay ahead. The landscapes beyond the cities seemed to stretch forever and gave a sense of just how much discovery and exploration lies around us. For sure, leaping off the corporate ladder and out of the board room to land amidst sandy beaches and green hiking trails was my greatest stepping stone to date!

Big Sur, the long stretch of Pacific Coast that runs from north of Los Angeles to just south of San Francisco, was the road that would transport me from the lights and the buzz of concrete cities to the lights and sounds that only nature can create. My *Lonely Planet USA* described this well, "This area is simply awe-inspiring—there are no traffic lights or shopping centers, and when the sun goes down, the moon and stars are the only street lights."

I was looking forward to leaving the rigidity of concrete structures behind and experiencing the flow of windswept coastlines and lush national parks. With every mile we drove farther from the city, the noise on the outside quieted, and the subtle and untouched sounds of the landscape emerged. I also felt something else emerging as the presence of people, traffic, and hurried schedules slipped away—the playful little girl who had been trapped inside was sitting upright and looking out of the windows with eyes wide open, full of anticipation. We were going to have so much fun together!

Confucius said, "No matter where you go—there you are." I knew that as many miles as I might travel on this trip, and as much "stuff" as I had left behind in Australia, what was inside was still there—unmoved and stubbornly packed. I knew already that those experiences in life are not ones from which you can run—they will follow you wherever you go until, somehow, you can stand firmly in your shoes, kick those experiences in the pants, and leap forward.

I knew those embedded thoughts and feelings, which had become part of the way I walked through life, would be much more difficult to shift than any backpack on any terrain that might challenge me on this trip. I wasn't expecting this trip to have the power to move them. I thought the best I could do with those thoughts and feelings was to find new ways to keep packing them down into the black box I had created inside of me. I thought, at best, this trip would give me a break—I never expected it to transform the broken pieces of me.

I would be surprised to find that once I opened up to the universe and stopped trying so hard, once I allowed my *self* to play, when I was just with *me*, when I was able to be harmonious and peaceful with my *self* rather than struggling with my *self*, when I let the expectations slip away, let the roles fade, when I stopped trying to control every outcome and carefully plan each step, when I allowed my *self* to just *be*, and when I started making choices by "listening to my feet," an effortless journey of discovery emerged.

I would find that with each discovery, the worn parts of the jigsaw puzzle that I had forced into place over the years, started to fall away. Old pieces that only made the picture more fragile, were replaced by pieces that created a whole that was greater than the sum of its parts. A renewed sense of being emerged, as vibrant and magical as the breathtaking scenes of nature I would experience throughout my travels.

As we traveled up through Big Sur, the coastline was striking. We could feel the power of the waves crashing against the enormous rocks of the shoreline where the Santa Lucia mountain range rises dramatically out of the Pacific Ocean. The rocky coastal cliffs rise many hundreds of feet from the ocean, with mostly inaccessible beaches scattered along the shoreline.

We stopped along Highway One to take in the magnitude of the view. It is a view, like many we would see, that a camera can't capture. It is more than the magnitude of the scene that eludes the camera—it is the interaction with you that escapes the lens. It is the vibration that resonates through you as the waves create thunder against the rocks, the wind that dances around you, the spray that gently sprinkles its mist on you, the fresh ocean smells that fill you with anticipation of the next sensation. It simply moves you—inside and out. I felt my senses awaken with every touch of the wind, every spray from the ocean, every vibration through the cliffs, and every breath. It was spellbinding, and it captured every part of me. I was happy to release my *self* to those sensations, and I had absolutely no idea how much these experiences would come to move me as dramatically as the cliffs rising out of the ocean.

We continued along Big Sur to find the first campground of our trek. We pulled into the campground around 4:00PM, so we had plenty of time to pitch our tents, prepare for the evening, and enjoy our first camp-side meal together. Cooking was a team effort—we had a roster for those who shopped, those who cooked, and those who cleaned up. Along the way, we would stop to purchase supplies at local supermarkets.

An intriguing part of traveling this way was experiencing each local community through which we passed. From grocery stores, to gas stations, to small diners, from town to town, there were always new characters to see and to meet, and a glimpse into other worlds to be discovered. With those simple experiences came an appreciation, and a sense of humility and reverence, that we are all just guests passing through each other's lives. We stay for a moment, or for a while. We can smile at a stranger, and leave a friendly footprint.

After arriving at the campground, we hauled the tents from the roof of our van, and proceeded to have our first lesson on constructing our tents. Like packing my backpack, I couldn't imagine it could be that difficult—a few poles to put together, a piece of tent material to slip over, and some pegs to pop into the ground—it seemed simple enough. Not so! Maybe it was the adrenalin of experiencing Big Sur that made me as uncoordinated as a drunk person. How could poles look so much the same and be so completely different?! There are only two holes in a pole, right? The holes are both round, yes? I growled at my tent before any bear had the chance. Backpacks and tents, I found, have two significant similarities—it takes several attempts to get them right, and they are never as big as you would like!

Finally, my tent was up, and our trek leader assured us that we would all be tent professionals in a day or two. For now, I was just happy to see my tent standing, and hoped it would stay that way through the night.

As sunset came upon us, we lit our lanterns and citronella candles, and started our campfire. The flames and crackles of the campfire, the smell of burning logs, and the subtle scent of citronella faded any remaining sense of the busyness from which we had come. We were in our own world now, nestled quietly amidst the towering pines and ancient sequoia trees, immersed in the color and the magic of all that was around us—guests in the six-star accommodation of Mother Nature.

Camping provides a refreshing sense of simplicity. For the first time in a very long time, I felt free to just experience each moment as it came, and to experience the moment for just what it was. That sounds too simple, but it was freedom for me. In the busyness of all I had created in my life—the distractions, the work, the "role" I was playing, the expectations I had set, the void I was trying to fill—I had lost the discoveries and possibilities that exist in each new moment. I had weighed down each moment with episodes from the past, and scenes of the future. Before the next moment arrived, I had already predetermined what it would be—there was no space for anything that the universe was trying to reveal to me. I had beaten up each moment as much as I had beaten up my *self*.

The physical space opening around me was a reflection of the space that was opening within me—space that would allow me to simply live in the moment, and to be filled with sensations I hadn't predetermined. The turbulent feelings of "act and react," "fight or flee," had started to be replaced by a gentle ebb and flow.

That night, I was content to simply burrow into my sleeping bag, with the sounds of Mother Nature keeping me company, and the peaceful breaths of the little girl resting within.

The next morning we set off to journey farther north along the Pacific Coast. Yosemite National Park was next on our trek. Yosemite was my first introduction to the immense grandeur of the national parks in the United States. When I left Australia, people were perplexed as to why I would choose to travel to the United States among all other options. It seemed that people thought of the United States as an enormous country of cities, and a vast continent of activity, filled with convenience stores, mega-stores, drive-thrus, and corporate offices. What I would find, was another side of that world—a world of extraordinary natural wonders that stretched farther, deeper, and higher than anything I had anticipated.

My *Lonely Planet* let me know that Yosemite was the first national park established in the United States, starting with a declaration by President Abraham Lincoln in 1864, and officially becoming a national park in 1890. Not only was Yosemite the first national park in the United States, but also the first recorded national park in the world. I felt somewhat as though I was in the belly of a great, great grandfather amidst the huge gray granite glacial formations that rose from every direction. Towering ominously above the valley floor was the extraordinary Half Dome—an enormous granite dome that rises 5,000 feet above the valley.

We had two choices for the day in Yosemite. The first choice was to conquer the Half Dome trail, which was known to be grueling and required a cable-assisted ascent to the peak of the mountain. The second choice was to hike the Panoramic Trail—a beautiful scenic trail that meandered ten miles up to Glacier Point, and then wound back down to the nature center. Normally, I would choose the more challenging of the two, no question—the steep trek up to Half Dome. However, the thought was more exhausting than the challenge was appealing. I realized how thoroughly exhausted I was from the corporate ladder that I had been relentlessly climbing—climbing to the next promotion and the next title, racing to the next meeting, competing to do the best proposal, studying the next acquisition, rallying the staff, appeasing the board, managing futile expectations, and scurrying around on the merry-go-round while still climbing, climbing, climbing.

Climbing Half Dome required physical and mental energy. Much of mine had been consumed without replenishment in the corporate world and in the daily struggles of getting through my childhood. The little girl inside was desperately wanting to stroll a little more lightly and enjoy all there was to see, smell, feel, and experience, rather than running just to keep ahead of the past. It felt safe to be restful here, amidst Mother Nature.

It was time to let my *self* relax, to walk more slowly, breathe more deeply, pause more often, and feel the path upon which my spirit wanted to take me. With those thoughts, I set off on the gentler Panoramic Trail. As beautiful as the trail was, most precious was the choice I had allowed to emerge to take a different path. *"Keep listening to what is within you—that will be your guide. It will grow with each breath and with each pause—and that is all you will need."* I was happy to find the silence to hear in the vastness of Yosemite, and was captivated by the stunning hike along the trail, with nothing to achieve, except to put one foot in front of the other, enjoy each step, and see all there was to see.

The next national park on our trek was Redwood National Park, home to many of the world's oldest Redwood trees. Looking high up into the Redwoods, some of which were up to 2,200 years old and stood hundreds of feet high, I felt adequately inadequate!

The message from the Redwoods was as clear as the trees were towering. It's ironic how much time we spend every day trying to feel so tall, so "adequate," so self-important, and so independent.

In the corporate world, that was just part of the culture—everyone scurrying up the corporate ladder, competing for the next "prize." Yet in our daily lives, for what "prizes" are we competing, for what purposes, for what sacrifices?

Amidst such powerful forces of nature, it seemed that the natural world around us was the perfect and pure reflection of the unlimited potential that is within each of us—remarkable beauty, extraordinary magnitude, hidden wonders, pure perfection—simple, abundant, authentic. So much is lost amidst the technologically advanced concrete cities that we typically call home. Yet here, nestled deep within nature, there is a feeling of home that is distant from any description we would call home in our modern world. Simply being. Letting go. Breathing in. Breathing out.

There are streams of travelers that flow throughout the spaces that Mother Nature provides. These streams, as I continued my travels, would grow more apparent with every new place I visited. Each person, each couple, each group of friends, each collection of strangers, had all set out to experience something beyond the place from which they came. Something more. Something greater.

To travel, I think, is to be willing to be touched. Touched by different people, different places, different feelings as they rise and fall, different perspectives, and different sensations that are beyond definition—that just are. Sensations that defy our notions and mystify our minds. Sensations that assure us there is more. They leave an imprint. They tap into the soul of the traveler when it is free to wander beyond the confines of the daily walls in which we often entrap our soul and our spirit. They are sensations that start to set us free.

The remote and active volcanic mountain, Mount St. Helens, was the next to leave its imprint, just as it had left its mark so dramatically on the surrounding landscapes. The mountain erupted in 1980 and had been the most devastating volcano in the history of the United States. Looking out over the mountain ranges that were victim to the volcano was haunting. I felt as though I was looking over nature's cemetery, but at the same time, looking over nature's nursery. At first glance, the destruction was apparent for as far and wide as I could see. It was as though I was looking at a barren, gray, mountainous planet not our own. Yet as I looked into the gray, nurseries of green emerged—one after the other. The life that had been created through the destruction was striking and captivating. I was moved by how such destruction and devastation could create such beautiful and renewed life.

In that moment, standing and pausing in my Blundstones, I was filled with appreciation for the possibilities that I knew could emerge from within me. The seeds were there, I just needed to let them grow through the destruction. I needed to see beyond the gray that had often consumed me, to the green nurseries that were waiting to be revealed. Within each of us, amidst the gray that invariably finds its way to us, lies fields of green that emerge to create beautiful and renewed landscapes.

I knew that I needed to nurture the fields of green that lay within. I needed my roots to be centered in something meaningful and purposeful that was authentic, and not just filling empty voids.

As I continued to look across the landscape, now only seeing endless nurseries, I appreciated the unique place that each and every tree had in the bigger picture. I was yet to discover my own place, but standing there, I knew and trusted that was the way of the universe, and that all would be revealed, one step at a time. I started to see that was the way of the universe for each of us—to take us on our journeys in our own time, to help us to keep going and not to stop—on our path to something more and something greater.

## MOMENTS OF PAUSE

1.  Which experiences in life are packed deep within you? Which experiences have you tried to "leave behind," but still feel rumbling beneath the surface?

2.  What are the "broken pieces" in you that you would like to repair?

3.  Which experiences have awakened your senses, and resonated harmoniously through you?

4.  Which spaces are you opening each day to let the universe reveal its messages to you? When was the last time you simply paused, and listened to all that is in the moment?

5.  What are the seeds within you that are waiting for your attention and your nurturing?

## MORE MOMENTS FOR YOU

# Five

# Rocky Mountain Spirit Guides

*"Each of us is here to discover our true Self...*
*we're not human beings that have occasional spiritual experiences—*
*it's the other way around:*
*we're spiritual beings that have occasional human experiences."*

—DEEPAK CHOPRA

EACH NEW EXPERIENCE is an opportunity to awaken our greatest self. Arriving in Seattle marked the end of one trek and the beginning of another adventure. The vast wilderness of the Canadian Rockies was the farthest I had traveled into Mother Nature's womb, and from there, an awakening would begin.

The Canadian Mountie trek would take me through the remote wilderness of British Columbia and Alberta. Canada was to be an adventure with many reflective pauses in my Blundstones and Tevas.

It seemed the farther I went from cities, and the closer I experienced Mother Nature, the closer I came to my *self.*

Ironically, many people along my travels asked me if I was doing "that walkabout thing that Australians do." I hadn't thought about it in that way, but in reality, I guess I was on a kind of "walkabout." In Australian Aboriginal culture, a "walkabout" is a spiritual quest that young Aboriginals embark upon. They leave their daily lives and disappear for weeks or months to walk in solitude. In that space of solitude, they seek to find the spiritual powers that will guide them to a state of oneness with themselves and with the world around. For me, the spiritual journey was only just beginning, and I would find many spirit guides amidst the vastness of the Canadian Rockies, and beyond.

My new group of traveling companions was again an international group. All were from diverse places—mostly from throughout Europe and Scandinavia—and all were younger than me. I wondered if I had missed something by not traveling while I was younger instead of waiting until thirty. However, that thought didn't last long—which in and of itself was a nice feeling. I was where I was supposed to be in this moment, and that was all that mattered. In this wilderness, there was no point to comparisons, especially to others—that was something I was leaving behind with my corporate high heels.

To feel the magnitude of the moment would be one of the greatest gifts that the vastness of the Rockies would bestow on me.

Yoho National Park was like nothing I had seen before. With every step deeper into Mother Nature, a scene and experience unfolds that transports you to a more spiritual realm. Your breath is taken away—again and again and again—each time more deeply. There is no part of you that is not consumed in the awe of the moment. Stopped in your tracks, standing alone in your shoes, there is nothing to do but be.

Amidst such extraordinary landscapes, there is a divine presence that is overpowering and disarming. There is no choice but to surrender, to be consumed, to be overcome—to give the universe permission to enter your senses and touch every part of your being. Like thousands of twinkle lights turned on in a dark house, every atom within me started to light up. I felt a sparkle and a warmth from the core of me—an awakening of my soul that had been long smothered.

I had given up on ever feeling anything other than violation. Through the abuse of my childhood, I had become used to my senses misleading me. Now, I was starting to feel my senses leading me to a place closer to home—to a place where I could feel "something more."

Yoho was full of beautiful lakes lined with fir tress, with colorful meadows, thunderous waterfalls, ancient and towering glacial peaks, and seemingly endless plains of flattened rocky terrain left behind after the eldest glaciers had long since disappeared. We set off on a hike that took us through each of these magical landscapes. It was as if we were passing through different worlds, each alien to the other, but all connected by streams that flowed from the same beginning.

It is striking how effortlessly nature reaches out to connect its many worlds, nourishing each of them. There is an intelligence present that eludes anything that can be captured by man. Here, one feels appropriately small and humble, yet welcome to step into the mystical streams of the universe and be taken on an unknown journey into inner and outer worlds.

I reflected on the Aboriginal walkabout, and the journey to find the spirit guides that would lead one to an awakening to discover one's place within oneself and within the world around. I felt the unique power that lies within these landscapes to take us on a journey deep within our *self*. It was as simple as stepping into the stream and allowing the journey to take place—open to the spirit guides that awaited.

Venturing up the steep hiking trail through the thick trees and lush shrubs, I came upon a high clearing that looked out over a beautiful green lake. Fir trees and snow-tipped glacial mountains surrounded the lake for as far as I could see. I stopped and stood silently as I listened to the streams that trickled mystically from every direction.

As I looked out through the trees, I was reminded of the little girl who used to peer out from the tree in my neighbor's front yard. From about the age of five, I remember that tree as a place of refuge—a place of safety where I would hide away from everything. I would climb the thick trunk and the main branches of the tree and make my way out to the farthest, smaller branches that were surrounded by camouflaging leaves.

My favorite part of the tree was nestled on those smaller branches, which curled around me to make a seat right in front of a small clearing of leaves. I would sit on my seat and peer through the clearing, pretending I was in a spaceship. From my captain's chair, the two branches that reached up in front of me became my steering controls, and from there I would explore galaxies. I would stay there for hours—for as long as I could stay safely away from the inside of the house. I felt free there—tucked away in the arms of my spacecraft, high above where anyone could touch me.

The sense of anxiety in my childhood house was ever-present and overwhelming.

It wasn't just the physical part of the sexual abuse that tormented me every day, it was the anxiety of turning any corner or walking into any room, and there he would be. His smug stare always sent chills through me. I wanted to kill him. I *really* wanted to kill him. I wanted to send pain through every part of his body, to see that smirk turn into squeals of unspeakable pain. I had to put all of my energy into suppressing the hate and the anger—as if trying to suppress a volcano. I think if I had let that volcano erupt, I would have self-destructed. All I could do was to lash out when I could, and the rest was packed into a bottomless black box.

Every day the hate grew, and every day I crammed more and more into that black box. Almost every day he would hunt me down and find me, wherever I was.

From the time I was four years old, he would come into the bathroom. I remember being so happy playing with my yellow rubber ducky with its little orange beak, splashing in the bathtub. Maybe it was the sound of my playing and splashing that gave him a reason to come into the bathroom. He would start to play with the bouncing ducky and then he would start to play with me. I was confused. I didn't know why his fingers were going inside me under the water. I just wanted to play with my ducky in my bath. I stopped playing with my ducky. I stopped splashing and laughing with my ducky, but my father never stopped coming in.

He would find me everywhere. He would come out to the small garage in the back of our yard when I was playing with my toys. I would hear his footsteps and then the turning of the door handle. It was so dark when he would close the door behind him and latch the lock. There was nowhere I could go, and no one to hear if I made a noise.

When I was old enough to stay up late to watch television, he would tell me to come and lay next to him on the couch under his blanket to help keep him warm. My older brother would sit in the opposite corner of the television room, oblivious to the movements in the blanket as my father put my hand on his penis and gave himself an erection, and then penetrated me with his fingers. I would freeze and scream in silence.

As I went through school, he would find me in my room while I was doing my homework. I would hear the handle of the door turn and close and lock behind him. I would close my eyes and say in my head, *"I'm not here, I'm not here."* I would think those words over and over again, hoping that if I thought them loud enough and often enough, and if I closed my eyes hard enough to see only black, that I would disappear into the noise and darkness in my head. But it never worked. I would feel him start to touch me and take my clothes off, and one more piece of the little girl would die.

There was nowhere to escape him. Almost every day, somewhere, he would find me. Even when he wasn't physically messing with me, he was messing with my head.

I would find every reason to stay away from the house as often and for as long as possible. I would go to my friends' houses. I would stay late at school helping teachers so often that my friends would tease me for trying to be the "teacher's pet." All I was trying to do was to find places to stay away from him.

To everyone else, he was the perfect, wonderful, sociable father. No one could understand why his daughter was so troublesome, and showed such anger and hostility toward such a "wonderful" father. Poor father, to have such an unappreciative daughter. After all, he had wanted me so much—my father and mother had adopted me as a young baby—so how could I possibly have issues with my generous and welcoming adoptive father? From a very young age, I saw manipulation up close and personal—living and breathing it every day, unbeknownst to everyone except my predator.

There was nowhere to go to find peace.

Yet here, amidst the beauty of endless landscapes of Yoho National Park, I felt peacefulness for the first time. I looked out and saw a view so much more expansive than any view I ever saw from my childhood spaceship. I felt feelings of wonder that a young child should feel many times throughout their childhood.

During my childhood, any good and wondrous feelings were quickly destroyed by violation and humiliation. The feelings that were familiar, the shoes in which I walked every day, were filled with anger, resentment, humiliation, and intense hate. Such strong and horrifying feelings for a child. The thing is, as a child, having such violent thoughts and feelings makes you start to think that you must be the monster.

It was only during my twenties that I saw a very clear picture of just how much anxiety had been in the house for me. I was reading the book, *Reclaiming Your Life*, by Jean Jenson, and started to do an exercise in the book that seemed fairly simple. The exercise asked me to draw a floor plan of my family home showing all of the rooms and surrounding areas. Next, I needed to color different rooms of the house based on the feelings I remember having in the different rooms and areas. Red represented anger, gray represented loneliness, white represented fear, yellow represented happiness and safety, and blue represented sadness. As I colored each room of the house, there was no yellow anywhere—every room was predominantly filled with red, then mixed with some gray, white, and blue. The only yellow was in my tree.

It's amazing how a picture can tell a thousand words. My picture instantly connected me to feelings that were still present. It was as though I carried that house—that container of feelings—with me every day. It's as though you move through life with those feelings as part of your DNA, because you've never known anything different. Each step I had taken, I had taken with those feelings leading the way. Each new situation that presented itself, I had met with those feelings. Each breath that I took seemed to feed only those feelings. Each person I met, I saw through those feelings. Each time I looked in the mirror, only those feelings were reflected back at me. There is no freedom when your being is trapped in a prison of self-destructive thoughts and feelings. There is only a daily struggle to survive and constantly find ways to escape.

Those feelings were ever-present, but now, they were starting to be overshadowed by the sense of awe that the universe was pouring into me on this journey. It's a little like pouring water into poison—as you keep diluting the poison, you get to a point where the poison is so diluted it is barely noticeable. My body was a hazardous container, and I needed much water. Maybe the universe could replenish me amidst these landscapes and flowing streams.

Looking out over the green lake and vast mountain ranges, feeling the trickle of the streams within me, I felt refreshed. The spirit guides had found me and were making a home for my journey.

The campground near Yoho was a restful break after our trek through the glaciers and mountains of the park during the day. My fellow travelers had decided to camp in an adjacent area of the park—a little closer to amenities and to some other campers. While I enjoyed the company of my new friends, I was captivated by the solitude and the worlds that awaited me there. For me, the orange flicker of the campfire and the light of the moon reaching gently through the towering trees were the perfect company.

I had been a loner through most of my childhood—content to be in my own space. I think I felt safe in my own space. There, at least, I could control that space. I could daydream, and feel relaxed that there was no one lurking around the corner, waiting for a time to pounce. My birth sign is Pisces—forever dreamers—so maybe that was an inherent trait that allowed me to escape to other worlds when I was young.

Now, as I sat in the warmth of the flickering campfire, the dreamer in me was doing so much more than dreaming to survive. I was dreaming to thrive.

The next morning we set off to Banff National Park, where the majestic Lake Louise greeted us. Photographs can only capture some of the color, but not the magic, of the lake. The shimmering emerald lake transports one to a scene of Dorothy, Toto, and their companions standing before the fantastical emerald city of Oz. This wilderness land around me, like the Land of Oz, seemed somewhere far over the rainbow. For Dorothy, the Land of Oz was a place where "dreams that you dare to dream really do come true." I had not believed there were such magical places that could fill your spirit with dreams that transcended your dreams. Yet standing in front of this sparkling emerald lake, my spirit guides were telling me otherwise.

*The Wizard of Oz* was one of my favorite childhood stories. I loved all of the characters, I think because, like me, they were searching, escaping, trying to find their way through a maze. Each of them had been discarded, and left to their own devices to find their way. During their journey, each of the travelers—Dorothy, the Tin Man, the Scarecrow, and the Cowardly Lion—found the piece of their self that they thought was missing. It simply took circumstance for those things to emerge. It took an adventure along a yellow brick road, and coming face to face with all that would be revealed, to bring those hidden qualities to life. The Tin Man without a heart found he was full of compassion. The Scarecrow without a brain found he had all of the sense and good thinking of the brightest brain. The Cowardly Lion without "the nerve" found he had the courage of a thousand lions. Dorothy came to find that she had all the power right there within her to realize all of her dreams.

Here, on the edge of the emerald lake, I could feel the glow of its color all around me and upon me. Glinda was the Good Witch of the North, who guided Dorothy and kept her safe on her travels along the yellow brick road—all the way to Oz and home again. Feeling the glow of the lake upon me, I felt the presence of many guides who would be with me through my journey. I knew that with their presence, I would find the heart, the mindfulness, and the courage to open up to the universe, let down my barriers, embrace the discovery in every moment, and release my soul to explore all of what was hiding within me.

As I walked from the lake, I met up with our tour leader, Anna, who seemed mesmerized by the lake, despite the many times she had traveled to it. I think it is like seeing the sunrise every morning of which you never tire, because each morning brings a different light, a different array of color, a different movement, and a different reflection when the beauty of the outer world connects with the beauty that is within. Like magnets, the reaction is to be drawn to the other and allow the natural common energy to quietly resonate.

Anna and I walked along a trail that brought us up to a clearing beside the lake. In places as magical as this, I think one can't help but feel the presence of a much greater energy. Before long, we were talking about James Redfield's book, *The Celestine Prophecy*. *The Celestine Prophecy* was a very special book for me. It was the first book that connected me to a way of thinking, perceiving, and being that helped me to shift my entire energy to a more positive place. It was apt that here, amidst the magic of the emerald lake, two strangers would be "coincidentally" sharing that reflection. Of course, in the world of *The Celestine Prophecy*, there are no coincidences. There are only events with meaning that occur continually until we learn the message that is intended for us, and needed on our journey toward something more—toward a higher evolution.

Central to *The Celestine Prophecy* is the flow of energy systems, and our interaction with those energy systems. It is our choice as to whether we engage or disconnect. Engaging in this "divine energy" is engaging in a spiritual journey toward a greater purpose. Disconnecting is a lack of awareness of the flows that surround us—living, as Socrates would say, "the unexamined life"—a life without the discovery of truth or meaning; a mundane life of conformity that fails to realize one's potential, and ends in a life without significance.

Sitting over the lake, surrounded by snow-capped glacial mountain ranges, one was captured by the energy flow. One could leave or stay. To stay was to experience how significant we can be, how much of an imprint we can leave, how much of a legacy we can create, and how beautiful we can be. Like the magical lake that has captivated travelers for hundreds of years, our lives can be lived with purpose and significance that continues far beyond us, and takes us to a place of magic and fulfillment—a nirvana that is beyond our imagination.

The next morning we set off to the Columbia Icefield for a glacier walk. As we traveled along the spectacular Icefields Parkway, the landscapes became more and more incredible. Each new scene was more alien, more untouched, more surreal. These were dreamlands that existed in another realm.

The Columbia Icelands are a UNESCO World Heritage Site, and the largest mass of glacial ice in the Canadian Rockies. As we pulled into the parking area, we were struck by the enormous shimmering blueish-white Athabasca Glacier that appeared to cascade from the heavens and sit ominously in front of us, almost daring us to come nearer.

We stepped out from our van, each of us in absolute awe of the magnitude of this "tongue of ice" before us. Our guide, Lily, approached and welcomed us. I don't think any of us were sure what was ahead. Lily handed us our liability waiver forms, and started to tell us that our walk would take us three and a half hours across the top of the moving glacier. For some reason, I thought we were taking a casual walk along a scenic viewing walkway that might have run along the side or over parts of the glacier. Clearly this was my imagination at work! Within minutes, we were strapping on our crampons ("shark teeth" that strapped onto the bottom of our hiking boots for traction on the ice), being tied one behind another with heavy-duty hiking safety rope, and being given our safety briefing for walking directly on an active glacier.

As we set off, I was reminded of Mount St. Helens. Here, any "eruption" or meandering onto the wrong part of the glacier could be the end of us. With the wrong step, we could all plunge thousands of feet down into one of the many and vast millwells scattered throughout the glacier. Nonetheless, off we went in our new pair of shoes on another adventure!

We followed Lily's footsteps with intent concentration and focus, one behind the other. This was much too early for the journey to end for any one of us by falling into the icy depths of a glacier. The fear of falling, however, was overshadowed by the awe-inspiring fantasy world that surrounded us. I was content to simply follow the tug of the hiking rope from in front of me, so I could take in every breathtaking moment around us. The glacier itself, Lily told us, was almost four miles long. It seemed to swell over the looming horizon and spill down the mountain like an enormous frozen waterfall. We would be ascending from 650 feet to 2,000 feet during our hike, and traversing up three elevations of the glacial "icefall"—a huge slippery slide of Mother Nature.

Time and space were different here. The gentle whistling sounds of wind across the sparkling ice were like playful angels dancing, their wings glistening in the luminous rays of sunshine. The deep echoes of booming avalanches from afar were like ancient voices telling stories of myths, legends, and gods from dreamtime worlds beyond. The cold air was light and whimsical as I inhaled and felt a magical spell passing through me. The trickling of water rising

out of the millwells was like spirits rising from the womb of Mother
Nature and harmonizing the elements around.

It is here that one feels the existence of multiple realms—the
physical and the spiritual—peacefully coexisting in limitless time.
The spiritual world was as real and tangible as the physical. This
is the place where the presence of the types of energy systems at
work in *The Celestine Prophecy* are as visible as the day. It is a
place where the presence of the gods can be felt—whichever god or
gods embody the higher power in which one believes. It is a place
where you can feel the spirit within you awaken and emerge to be
nourished by the elder spirits that make home in this sanctuary. I
could feel the spirits within me awakening, emerging, and reaching
out to play in this new paradise of space, unfettered and uninhibited
by any confines of thought or reason, free to dance in the sky. The
little girl inside was awake and alive. For perhaps the first time, she
was also dancing like a child with the spirits in the sky.

Our coping mechanisms are extraordinary things. They are
powerful means to get us through whatever comes our way. But just
getting through in life is not fulfillment, it is simply survival—the
minimum passage one can take. As intelligent and spiritual beings,
there must be more. There must be the ability for our spirit and our
soul to take us beyond the physical and mental obstacles that are
an unavoidable part of the human experience. We must be more
than the bad things that happen to us.

My coping mechanisms had enabled me to survive—but just
barely. I had daily thoughts of ending my life through my teenage
years and into my early adulthood. You see, when there is simply
no one who notices the pain, no one who takes the extra moment to
see what's behind the angry child, no one who cares to look beyond
the troubled teenager, no one who sees the sadness in empty eyes,
and no one who notices that so much is wrong, then you simply feel

invisible, inconsequential, and insignificant. You feel nothingness. You feel pointless. You feel discarded, and not worth anyone's care or attention. There is simply no point to your existence, and nothing to be lost or gained by it—just an end that might bring peace.

Here, in the company of ancient spirits, I felt more. I felt the peace that I had imagined in death, but it was peace in life. Walking atop the glacier, letting my spirit be free, letting the little girl dance, I felt a peace that I had never felt before. I felt renewed—as if I were just beginning the life of a child that was ended with the first violation by a father.

As we traversed back down the glacier, the three and a half hours of hiking seemed to be timeless—I felt as though I was waking from an all-consuming dream. The presence of the dream resonated through me—a calming vibration that continued to awaken my senses and comfort my soul.

I was so happy to be immersed in this world, full of welcoming spirits that reached into my soul, lifted my being, connected me to "something more," and let the little girl dance.

We arrived in Jasper late in the afternoon after our glacier hike and pulled into Whistlers Campground. I was looking forward to lighting the campfire and nestling into my sleeping bag for the night. My sleeping bag had become a cozy cocoon to tuck myself into each night. I loved the simplicity of my sleeping bag and tent under the stars of the Rockies. I loved feeling the warm blanket of Mother Nature gently upon me, and the deep comfort of feeling a oneness with "the universe." Solitude, sanctitude, and simplicity. Perfection.

As we entered the campground, we saw what had become the familiar bear warning signs that greeted us at each of the national parks and camping areas. Our tour leader had briefed us on bears as part of our orientation. Over the past days, the frequency of bear warnings reminded us that we were in someone else's backyard, not so much our own (despite feeling the nurturing arms of our common Mother Nature!).

One of our greatest abilities is our ability to adapt, and the ability of our instincts to take over for survival when needed. Knowing there are bears lurking just through the bushes, puts one's antennas to a higher sensitivity. I think we all felt our antennas propped up at full attention. The options for dealing with a bear are limited, and it seemed that one would need to be on full alert to assess the options and to act appropriately, instead of doing what would seem to come instinctively—run!

There are two types of protection from a bear. The first (and preferred) is the preventative type—that is, making a *lot* of noise as you walk through the campgrounds and trails so the bears hear you and run before you run into them. The second (not preferred) is the reactive type—that is, what you need to do when you wander into a bear.

So far, we only had indirect contact with bears—hearing them moving through the bushes around our camping area, in search of any scraps we might have left behind. Several times, late at night, they had come so close as to brush by the outside of our tents. On those occasions, I would follow one point of advice—freeze, which also meant to stop breathing! These were the times when I was glad I had double zip-locked my toothpaste, and securely stored my snacks and anything else scented in the van for the night. One sniff of peppermint toothpaste or trail mix is enough to start a bear salivating and set off on a quest to find its feast. Not in my tent, Mr. Bear!

The early evening colors were once again settling in around us, as we all looked forward to a camp-side meal after the day's trekking. The campground also had the luxury of shower facilities, and that was to be the first priority after dinner.

Rain came soon after we finished our much-needed showers. I was happy to once again nestle into my tent, and listen to the rustling and pattering of the rain through the trees and against my tent. I had always loved rain storms—there is something deeply relaxing and meditative about the rhythm of raindrops and the sounds of storms. It is as though the heavens are touching the earth—a gentle reminder of the nourishment from beyond.

The day had been intense for me. My senses were inspired, my soul felt elevated, my spirit felt exhilarated, and my mind was full of contemplations. These sensations were very different from the type of "excited" sensations that I had experienced before.

The corporate world had "excited" me for a time—the next promotion had always been stimulating, getting the next new company car had been a buzz, each bonus was a thrill, each merger and acquisition was energizing. Yet there was an emptiness, a void, something very intangible that was simply missing. There was something that made the excitement feel artificial, contrived, temporary. That was it—temporary. Mostly, it seemed temporary. One thing, then another, then another—an ongoing game of finding the next thing that would feel good, that would be a "buzz," a highlight, an "achievement."

It was an endless and trivial pursuit. It was all driven by external "things"—so many things on the "outside"—pushing and pulling, rising and falling, expanding and contracting, stretching and compressing. Where was the core? Where was the center? Where was I? Who was I? Where did I belong? What was I?

I came to see that "I" was inside, but "I" was buried alive.

The next day we were expecting to heli-hike in the Rockies just outside of Jasper. A helicopter would drop us at the top of one of the glacial peaks, and we would hike our way down. The heights of some of the peaks were such that the best way to explore them was to let the helicopter do the hardest part—getting up. Unfortunately, when we woke, the rain from the night before had left a thick blanket of fog around the mountains that made the helicopter flight impossible. I always think that when something like that happens, it happens for a reason. So a few of us gathered to come up with other options for a rainy day, and decided that laundry and Internet would be the perfect alternative.

We headed into Jasper with our very smelly laundry bags. First stop, the laundromat. Second stop, the Internet cafe. Laundromats become an entirely unique part of the backpacking experience. There are people passing through, stories that are told, journeys that are in progress, new friendships that are made, dreams contemplated, life observed, and life reflected. An entire world exists within these unlikely places, with time passing effortlessly with the tick-tock of buttons clicking as they tumbled in the dryers, and the whirling back and forth of washers filled with clothes that were getting ready for their next adventure.

Our laundromat experience in Jasper was to prove one of the longest experiences in laundromat history, thanks to a malfunctioning washer that left all of our clothes smelling like gasoline. The anticipation of opening the washing machine and smelling the fresh scent of just-washed clothes rise as if from a bouquet of flowers was always a thrill at the laundromat. It was a delicious and eagerly awaited treat. However, this morning, we all sputtered a cough as the smell of pungent gasoline filled the air as soon as we opened the top of the washer. Sadly, our clothes had smelled better in our very smelly laundry bag.

It took washing our clothes three times before the smell faded to something that didn't make us feel nauseous. Then, as if seeing an oasis in the desert—in the far back corner of the laundromat—we saw a vending machine cradling a wonderful orange packet of Bounce fabric freshener that beamed across the room like a beacon. We were like little kids who had seen the very best Christmas present ever. It wasn't quite as exhilarating as heli-hiking might have been, but at that time, it was quite exciting. Bounce became our new favorite thing, and no visit to the laundromat was the same unless we had our little orange friend. Five hours later, after three wash cycles and two drying cycles with Bounce, our clothes were the cleanest smelling in the laundromat. Hopefully the bears in our campground wouldn't like the smell as much as we did!

During the time we were re-washing our clothes, we had wandered through the quaint main street of Jasper to the local Internet cafe. Internet cafes, like laundromats, were their own little world for the backpacker. They were filled with travelers from all over the world sharing their journeys with friends and family, searching for the next destination on their travels, checking itineraries, looking up train schedules, finding accommodations, and checking on news that was so nicely distant.

As we took a break from email, and enjoyed our coffees on one of the sofas in the cafe, we reflected on life. Laundromats and Internet cafes will invariably do that to you. We were all on a journey of discovery. None of us, it turned out, were traveling to simply see the sites. We wanted to find that "something more," but we didn't know what that something more was. We didn't know what we wanted to discover. We simply felt that we were in the right place, in the right flow, in a stream of curious travelers moving through a different space and time than the worlds from which we had each come. We had each "changed our shoes" for different reasons, but we had all changed them to step into a place that was different to the "everyday." We each wanted to pause to hear the voice that was hinting that change was needed, even though we couldn't quite put our fingers on what that change was. How precious to be in this space!

My dreams that evening must have taken me to places of further contemplation. *"If I died tomorrow,"* the thought came to me as I woke the next morning, *"... and went back to my higher self, my higher realm, and re-united with the spirits, would I be proud of the way I have acted in this life? The way I have treated others? Treated my self?*

*"Would I know the spirits there? Have I spoken to them often in this life? Have I been open to them or shut them out?*

*"If I died now, would the spirits be happy with me? Would I be happy with me?"*

I paused. The voice inside rose softly, *"I'm not ready to die at this point in my life. I don't think I'm ready to die because I haven't done enough. I haven't given enough. I haven't been purposeful. I've closed my self away and shut people out, consumed with my own survival, getting through and keeping control.*

*"How do I look beyond and within? In others and in my self? To the spirit and soul within? We are all connected by the one spirit, one humanity. So why be so fearful?"*

One of the books that I had brought with me and was reading day by day was the Dalai Lama's, *Transforming the Mind*. The Dalai Lama reminds us that we are all connected by a string, and that the consequences and reactions to what is sent out along that string will return. Calling our attention to the words of Shantideva, the Dalai Lama encourages us to be "other-centered," not "self-centered," "The source of all misery in the world, lies in thinking of oneself. The source of all happiness, lies in thinking of others."

I reflected as the Dalai Lama continued his teaching, "The seeds of kindness of a Buddha, and the compassion of a Buddha towards all living beings, and therefore the potential for enlightenment and for perfection lies in each one of us." For me, with so much of me still believing that deep inside was the monster that wanted to kill my father, still haunting the little girl every day, so full of anger and hate tucked away, I needed to believe there was something more, something good inside me—the seeds of something sacred. I needed to believe there was something more than the false "I" that I had created. I needed to let the seeds of "something more" grow.

"*I need to ask each day,*" I thought, "*What did I give today? What did I share today? How was I compassionate today? How did I nurture the seeds that are within me today? What did I send out along the piece of string that connects us all? How am I closer to "I" than I was yesterday?*"

I needed to discover the purposeful, spiritual being that had become trapped inside a body that had only known harm, yet that held the potential, as we each do, to heal and become so much more.

## MOMENTS OF PAUSE

1. What experiences have brought you closer to your *self*? When have you felt your soul "awakened"?

2. When you think about your place in the world, how do you see it?

3. What anxieties exist in your life that are rooted in your childhood? What "safe spaces" have you created for your *self*? What are your coping mechanisms?

4. What are the qualities hiding within you that are waiting to be explored—the qualities that you need for your journey? These are the qualities that are more than coping mechanisms, but are the core of your unlimited potential.

5. What are the external things in your life that give you temporary fulfillment, and only end up pushing and pulling you into highs and lows?

6.  What "coincidences" and patterns recur in your life? What meaning do they hold for you?

7.  How connected do you feel to a greater purpose, to that "something more"? What "yellow brick road" is guiding you through life? What do you think the universe is leading you toward?

8.  How far beneath the surface is your "I" buried? How can you get closer to your "I"?

9.  If you died today, would you be happy with what you have done in your life? How true are you being to your *self* in your life?

10. What legacy are you creating through your life?

## MORE MOMENTS FOR YOU

# Six

# Sleepless in Vancouver

*"The secret to my own happiness,
my own good future, is within my own hands.
I must not miss that opportunity!"*

—His Holiness The Fourteenth Dalai Lama

OUR CHOICES IN EACH MOMENT, in each step along our journey, are in our hands. As we take each step, our conscious choices can lead us closer to our greatest future. Even amidst uncertainty, when our path is not clear, each mindful choice can illuminate the opportunities that lie before us. We start to feel the paths that resonate with happiness.

As I watched the trek van drive away after I chose to leave the group the day before our final stop, I felt happy to be making simple choices just for me. I had decided to leave the trek a day early in Vancouver, so I could explore Vancouver and its surrounds. I had two weeks to go wherever my feet felt like taking me, before heading back to Los Angeles for my next cross-country camping trek. With my backpack beside me, my shoes were ready to journey onward.

The Jericho Beach Hostel came highly recommended on the Hosteling International web site, and so that was my destination for the day. As I hauled my backpack onto my back, I nearly ended up flat on my butt on the sidewalk! Clearly, there was a big difference between hauling my backpack on and off the van from camp site to camp site, and hauling it onto my back and preparing to walk a few miles. I pondered whether a bear cub might have had time to sneak into my backpack—it sure felt like it! Task one at the hostel—downsize my pack.

As I wandered through the streets of downtown Vancouver trying to follow my map to the hostel while balancing my backpack, the thought did cross my mind to take the easy path—head down to Santa Monica on a train and soak up the sun on the beach for a few weeks before my next trek. With my backpack loading me down, that sounded like a good idea. I had to end up there anyway, so why not just cut short the journey and do it now? *"Bah Humbug!!!"* sprung that little voice from inside. You know that voice that would kick you in the pants if it could? There it was. *"Are you kidding?!! Don't be a lazy pants! Adventure awaits! Get to it! Jump into the unknown! Don't be a wimp!"* So eliminating the option to "wimp out," onward with my backpack I went.

In my journal that afternoon I had written a little side note, *"Should I just go home, get a job, an apartment, and a puppy ... ???"*

Bah Humbug!!! That could wait!

Sleeping at the hostel that night was a dramatic change from my tent, of which I had grown very fond. I already missed sleeping amidst Mother Nature. The sounds of the rustling leaves and wandering bears were replaced by mechanical sounds of the city. The fresh smells of fir trees were replaced by the smells of restaurants, car exhausts, and people. The silence and the solitude of the mountains was replaced by people passing in and out and through and up and down. I was struck by how out of sorts I felt. The activity was like a disorienting storm.

It took hours to go to sleep that night. My mind was full of vivid images from my journey so far, and thoughts of what was ahead in the weeks to come as I explored alone. It didn't matter that I had no idea where I would end up, day by day or night by night, over the coming weeks. Now that the weight of my backpack was off my back, I was simply excited at all the unknown would bring.

I woke the next morning to a soft orange glow coming through the windows—the delicious warm light of the early sunrise. I jumped out of bed and headed to the beach that was just a few minutes away, eager to see the ocean and feel the sand under my feet. I briskly walked through the park that led to the beach, knowing that minutes made the difference between seeing the sun rise over the horizon or missing it for another day. As I walked through the clearing in the park, I smiled an enormous smile as I saw the sun emerging from the horizon and the water sparkling in the morning light.

I walked along the beach, and that wonderful tranquility that comes with every sunrise followed me with each step. The beach ran along a beautiful quaint cove, and in the distance at the far end of the cove, houseboats swayed quietly with the current of the gentle ocean. There was a strange familiarity to the beach. I had never heard of the beach before, so I assumed it was just one of those moments in which you feel an undefined familiarity—the light, the landscape, the smells, the sounds. As I turned to walk back, it struck me from the other direction—the beach reminded me so strongly of a beach scene in one of my favorite movies, *Sleepless in Seattle*.

How funny to be reminded of the strangest things in the most unlikely places. It's as though wherever you go the things that have meaning to you will pop up at the most unexpected times. Often they pop up at the most appropriate times, but we just don't pause to find out why. Luckily, I had all the time in the world to pause.

*Sleepless in Seattle* was one of those movies that opened my heart and jumped right in. I think the quest for "happy ever after" captured me. The hope of a "happy ever after" had always been the core of my survival. But to date, the trust and self-esteem that had been taken through my childhood, and been replaced with fear and caution, had kept me at a safe distance from people and relationships. For sure, I had work to do before I was going to be standing atop the Empire State Building with my soul mate.

For me, being abused and being adopted, relationships became a terrible, horrifying, and tormenting dilemma. On one hand, I was absolutely starving for love and affection, and so desperately wanting to feel those things. On the other hand, all I knew from relationships was abandonment, manipulation, deception, aggravation, and humiliation. What was worse—taking what I could get, or not feeling love at all?

I had taken what I could get from my father, sadly enough. You see, when your abuser cuts you off from all other sources of love by making you out to be the bad person, isolated from the rest of the family through fear and guilt, all you have are the scraps of love from the person you hate the most, in whatever form that comes.

Your standards for love become so low, that you take whatever you can get. In addition to that, you also bear the responsibility of breaking the family apart if you disclose the situation. Even as a child, you know that if you tell what is happening, it will destroy your family. You are conditioned into secrecy from the earliest age. The emotional burden is overwhelming. You have nowhere to go. It is a psychological prison as tormenting as the physical abuse. No love. No escape.

I think women in bad relationships must go through a similar experience. Why do we stay in relationships that wear us down, hold us in fear, and keep us prisoner, rather than seeking those that help us to grow, thrive, and be free? Is it because we believe we are unworthy of anything more, or that we are fearful of cutting the only ties to love that we know?

Surely we must be more than that. Surely what we have inside us can rise above those things that can happen outside of us. Surely there is a happy ever after where love is liberating and not a liability. Love should help us soar to our greatest heights, not capture us behind bars.

The thing is, the search for love can be so misplaced that it becomes damaging. It becomes a dependency rather than an enabler. It becomes a search for the person who is going to solve our love issues, or it places happiness in the hands of our children to love us, or in the arms of our parents. We start defining our *self* by the love that we get from others. Without it, we feel empty and feel that we are nothing. We fill our lives with things to compensate—food, clothes, alcohol, drugs, work. We become our own captors, yet blame everything else around us.

We miss that love needs to start at home—not the home on the outside—but the home on the inside. We all have the seeds of love inside us—every religion and spiritual philosophy has that notion at its core. We are all children of a higher god. We are all the result of good karma. We are all the result of the creative forces of the universe. In Buddhism, we can all become Buddhas if we generate the compassion that enlightens our *self* and others. In Judaism, Christianity, and other religions that believe in one God and a Heaven, we each can find home in the Kingdom of God if we allow the good in us to emerge and the "evil" to be overcome.

Each of us has within us the potential to experience love in abundance. But we need to be our own gardeners. We need to know where our seeds lie within us and spend the time to nourish them. Only with our own care will we blossom. Then, when our roots are strong and nourished, and our colors are vibrant, we can attract others and share our soil. We can create lush gardens, towering forests, and endless mountains. From a simple seed that is nurtured from within, we can create beauty all around.

Ironically, through my abuse, I had been forced to go within my *self* to find something that could keep me going. I think that is where our survival instincts kick in—our determination to reach deep within us to find something that we feel *must* be there—if only we can discover the path. For me, the bitter irony was that I gained something tremendously valuable through the experience of my abuse—I gained a determination, a resilience, and a confidence to get through anything that life throws at me. I also gained the belief that we can each find our path—we just can't give up looking for it.

I had experienced the impact of giving up on that "something more"—friends who had taken their life, who just couldn't see a way through. Neither left notes. Both hung themselves. One in a forest, the other in his garage. I had found my second friend hanging from the rafters in his garage. I was twenty-two at the time. The image of his lifeless body stays with me. He looked so sad in death—there was no peacefulness, no dignity, no restfulness. Only anguish. It struck me because, in my heart, I knew that could easily have been me. I didn't want to give up like that. I didn't want my father to destroy me so completely as to end up like that. He had no right to do that to me. What he did was bad enough. I wasn't going to let him take what was left. That was mine. He had abused me enough. I wasn't going to abuse my *self*. There was a little girl inside who still wanted to live.

I found that I continually needed to tap into that place inside to keep going. I needed to keep that garden alive. It was work, every day. But again, ironically, it ended up being a source of power that

I can now channel to create good things for me and for others. Thankfully, I was able to gain strength from what happened and find ways to empower my *self*. I do believe that the universe works in ways that are not at all apparent to us at the time. I believe we are each here to grow, and that life is a journey full of opportunities to grow—to expand or contract with each experience. It's up to us how we respond, and sometimes it takes something dramatic to happen to jolt us to the realizations we need to have, and the growth we need to experience on this journey.

There is also a humility in surviving, because too many don't. There is a deep appreciation for every moment, for every breath of freedom, for every opportunity to choose. Life becomes illuminated.

I feel as though I was given two chances in life. The first was that my birth mother chose to give me an opportunity for life, rather than to abort me. The second was that I came so close to ending my life and giving in to abuse, but wasn't quite able to.

I had more often than not, felt lucky to have been adopted, rather than to have been aborted. As a child, my mother would often read me the book, *Mr. Fairweather and his Family*. The book would reinforce how wonderfully grateful Mr. and Mrs. Fairweather were to have the opportunity to adopt children.

Some people will say that my father did truly love me, but that he was simply sick. I personally don't accept that thinking. For me, I don't believe you love someone when you put your own needs above the needs of, and responsibilities for, that other person. For me, loving someone is not only about the thought of loving someone, it is how that thought translates into actions.

For me, "love" is a verb.

Figuring out the contradiction between the "notion" of love and the "action" of love is an insight that has become central to the love in my life. I try my best to be open to receive love based upon it, and to give love by it. For sure, sometimes we fail in the way we give and receive love, and for sure we keep learning through those experiences. But our ongoing learning does not translate into continuing excuses. More often than not, our actions of love should far outweigh the mistakes we make. If not, we need to take stock of why. Most of the time, it is not because of the things that are right or wrong around us, it is because of the things that are right or wrong within us. We react to what is outside us, but we evolve based on what is within us.

If you have seen the movie *28 Days* with Sandra Bullock, I'm sure you will remember the scene in the movie describing how you know when you are ready to love someone. The lesson was, first, start with a plant. If the plant survives, you can think about getting a pet. If the pet survives, you can start to think about having a relationship. This may be somewhat simplistic, but I think it's a good analogy that *we* need to be ready to give and to receive love. *We* need to do the work.

As a child, I believed I needed to give and receive love in the way it was being dictated to me. I wasn't capable of realizing the distinction, or making the choice. Now, that is one of the most important realizations I have—that love isn't dictated by others, it is decided upon by us. Love is not an entitlement, it is earned. We can choose, based upon what we know is good for us, and what we know is bad for us.

Shockingly, sometimes the abuse from my father felt physically good. It was a physical reaction to physical stimulation. Sometimes, you take the only thing that feels good—even though it also makes you feel even more like a monster—because it is all that you have. It completely messes you up, physically and mentally. Your ability to find the distinction, or to make a choice, is paralyzed.

Which feelings do you trust? When you feel sick in the stomach while you are being violated, but feel pleasure in the same moment because your body is instinctively responding, your whole state of being gets thrown into confusion about sensations and feelings.

Most of the time, I would want to throw up when my father was violating me. The worst times were when he would follow me into the small bathroom at the back of the house. It was barely large enough for one person. He would come in, and close the door behind him. He would pull out his penis, hold my head hard between his two hands, and put his penis in my mouth. He would start thrusting and thrusting until he ejaculated down my throat so that I almost choked. I could hardly breathe as he pushed himself against me and his semen ran out of my mouth. As I coughed and sputtered, he wiped himself off, put his penis back in his pants, and walked out.

Then, we would all sit around the family dinner table in the evening, my father directly across from me, staring me down.

It was an experience that continued week after week, year after year. I think that continual abuse maintains you in a state of shock and trauma so that you can't even respond—at least not directly. You just take each day as it comes, get through it, and get up the next day to get through it again.

I tried to draw attention that there was something wrong. I tried misbehaving at school, but that didn't make a difference—no one asked why. I remember yelling one time at my third grade teacher that my father put his penis in my mouth, but the teacher just looked at me and walked away. I told some school friends in the fourth grade one time, but they laughed at me, and then thought there was something wrong with me. I ran away from home several times, and I told the people I ran to why I was running, but although they allowed me to stay for a few days, they would ultimately send me home.

There were signs throughout my childhood of which I wasn't even aware, but that I have since come to find out are possible warning signs that suggest a child might be experiencing some type of abuse, stress, or trauma. I constantly wet my bed and sucked my thumb well into my teenage years, but those were the types of behaviors that didn't seem to be highlighted as warning signs in any type of forum that made a difference.

As a teenager, I told one of my family doctors what my father was doing, but he only decided to stop seeing my father as a patient. I cut my wrist one time, and I can't even remember where I was, or who put the bandages on. I just remember sitting at the dinner table that evening, and my mother seeing the bandage popping out from the long sleeve I was wearing. She asked what it was, and I remember telling her that I just hurt my wrist. My father, sitting across from me, said nothing, and simply kept eating his dinner.

It seemed that time after time, the efforts that I could make to send a message, to try to put words to something that was so terrifying to speak of, were just not loud enough. It was like trying to scream, but the scream wouldn't come out. I wanted to hear my voice explode from deep within, filled with all of the hate, anger, and desperation that consumed me. But it was as though my father had penetrated every part of my being, and was there inside me, waiting to strangle and silence any words that tried to escape.

During my high school years, I tried to disappear into another world by drinking too much at parties. I thought that might bring some relief, but it only made me feel like I was losing control of my senses, and that felt like the same loss of control that would happen to my body when my father would touch me. I thought that if I drank too much, someone might wonder if something was wrong, but people seemed to think that was just a "normal" part of high school years.

Sometimes you feel that you just can't put the effort into trying anymore. That it doesn't make a difference. You feel that the consuming hole of life just isn't worth the tiring struggle. You feel that ultimately, you're on your own. I was brought up Catholic, and my mother took us to church every week. I certainly didn't believe there was a god who cared, or who was there to offer any help.

The effects on how I viewed people in general were overwhelmingly negative, and my thoughts about relationships were equally negative. All of my experiences told me that people didn't care, and they certainly weren't going to do much to help. I had learned that relationships were about manipulation and deception. I had seen they were self-serving, and I had come to know them as something you couldn't count on.

My experience meeting my birth mother reaffirmed that thinking. I contacted my birth mother when I was about twenty-one through the Department of Youth and Community Services. The department matched records of adopted children and their birth parents. Although I didn't want to acknowledge it at the time, and I didn't want to put any expectations on it, I did hope that there would be some connection that filled a void. I wasn't looking to fill a void in a mother figure, because I loved my mother who had adopted me—I wasn't looking for another mother.

I just wanted to experience that someone who I thought should feel some sense of care for me, might just do that—I just wanted some small validation of that. I wanted something that might give me some confidence that I wasn't just something that was dispensable and inconsequential. I wanted to believe that my birth mother gave me up because of the reasons I had read in the story of Mr. Fairweather and his family—that she loved me and wanted the best for me—as opposed to it being a transaction of convenience. If the story were true, I would expect that she would open a small part of her life and have just a little space for me.

It was a sunny summer afternoon when I stopped at my mail box to collect my mail. As I saw the envelope sitting there from the Department of Youth and Community Services, I was filled with apprehension and nervousness. I knew the envelope would probably contain information about my birth mother. Butterflies ran through me, and I knew whatever was in the letter would impact my life in some way. *"Should I even open this?"* I thought about simply throwing the letter away without reading it. *"Maybe it is better not to know the reality, and simply fantasize about my origins. Is the knowing, the reality, worth the risk of finding out a story that could be an 'ugly truth'?"*

Figuring that life can sometimes just be an "ugly truth," but truth nonetheless, I opened the letter. I felt as though I was opening a door into an unknown abyss.

"We are pleased to inform you that we have located your birth mother on our birth register, and are therefore able to introduce you," the letter read. "Your birth mother's name is Patricia. She was twenty-seven years of age when she gave birth to you. She named you Vanessa at birth."

That was more or less the letter. A few more lines about how to contact the department to set up a meeting with "Patricia," but otherwise, there it was—my story in a letter—black and white. Matter of fact. It was a very bizarre feeling. I wasn't expecting that information in a letter. For whatever reason, I was expecting an acknowledgement of whether or not the department had a record of her in their registry. I was expecting a contact number at the department of someone who would give me the next step in the process—a slower process that would gently introduce me to the facts and then the story of my coming into being. I chuckled a little chuckle—the missing piece of my life—an executive summary on paper in the mail. And my name was Vanessa. Strange.

The next day I called the Department of Youth and Community Services. The woman wished me luck and told me they would have Patricia call me in the coming days. Patricia had been advised that I had been contacted by the department, and that I was awaiting her call. A few days later, the phone rang, and there it was.

"Hello, this is Kathy." I answered.

"Kathy, hello, this is Patricia."

I paused, not knowing quite what to say, and with a few butterflies nervously fluttering in my stomach. "Hi Patricia, how are you?"

"Good," she replied. "So, uhm, how has your life been?"

Pause!!! It was a striking question—so innocently forthright—but a question that had an answer that a thousand words couldn't capture. How do I answer that from one end of a telephone conversation? I chose the easy option, "Fine. My life has been just fine."

I think this must be one of the most isolating statements we make. *"Things are fine, just fine."* In other words, *"You couldn't even begin to comprehend what is happening in my life, and you certainly can't do anything about it, so don't worry about it. I'll make it on my own."*

I had come to think that isolation was better than another let down. This time, I hoped for something different.

The conversation was awkward. I had wondered if there would be a familiarity to my birth mother's voice over the phone, but no, just the voice of an older woman who was probably feeling just as strange and awkward. We chatted for a few minutes, and I can't even recall much of the rest of the conversation after, *"How has your life been?"* We ended the conversation agreeing to meet. It turned out that she lived just two hours north of where I lived. I would catch a train to meet her at a local train station just near her house.

The next week, on the train, I wondered all the way whether I would recognize her, and whether she would recognize something in me. I wondered about the story I was about to hear. I anticipated finding out about my natural heritage. What were my birth origins? From which countries? How did we come to be in Australia?

The train finally pulled into the station. As I walked from the train, and along the platform, I looked for someone that would jump out as being that "presence," that "connection." Nothing. I continued across the bridge that went over the train tracks and down the stairs to the street level. As I was halfway down the steps, a woman moved to the center of the stairs as the stairway met the sidewalk. She had silver-gray hair and looked at me directly—an unfamiliar stare. "Kathy?" she queried. "Yes. Hi. Patricia?" I queried back. "Yes," she replied. An awkward hug followed. It wasn't a hug of familiarity, or a hug of a long lost mother and child. It was just an unfamiliar hug from a stranger, filled with anticipation and curiosity.

We wandered to a park just across from the train station and sat on the grass on a picnic blanket she had brought. She pulled out some photos of her sisters, her two children, and my birth father. That was such a strange experience for me—seeing people for the first time whom I looked like. My mother, at my age, had my same nose, smile, and cheekbone structure. Her sisters also had the same nose and facial structure. My birth father was taller, a narrower face, slimmer. I could see me in both of the photos. Yet looking across at my birth mother, there was no sense of connection. There was just the face of a stranger, so different even, to the photographs. It was as though with the years, the familiarity had faded.

She told me how she fell in love with my birth father, a married man, when she was about twenty-seven. She thought that he would leave his wife for her. However, after telling him that she was pregnant, he didn't want anything to do with her or her pregnancy.

More than giving away her child, it was clear that she felt that she was giving away her chance at a life with a man with whom she was in love. She turned to me and said, "You know, by seeing you, I feel like I am getting a piece of him back." I remember thinking, *"No, it's me you're getting, not your hopes from your past of a lost love. Me."* She didn't seem to realize that she had made the conversation about her and her past love, rather than about me and her. It seemed she hadn't closed that chapter of her life after all of these years. That should have been a signal that this was not going to end up with me as a consideration, yet I still held hope.

During the conversation, I learned that my natural history came from England, France, and Scandinavia on my birth mother's side, and from Ireland on my birth father's side. My birth father had several children at the time I was born, and had since remarried and had more children. My birth mother also had two girls, so between both of them, the "family" tree was more extended than I imagined.

Patricia was excited for me to meet her sisters and family. She was also looking forward to my meeting her two girls, and for her girls to meet their "big sister." She said her girls always wanted to have an older sister, and she was never able to say that they did— until now. She was going to find a time to tell them about me, and for us to meet. We left each other that day after relatively small chatter about work, future plans, hobbies, family, and the kinds of everyday things two people meeting each other for the first time would talk about. We agreed we would talk by phone and she would let me know when I could meet my younger "sisters."

A few weeks passed, and I decided to call Patricia—I hadn't heard from her since our meeting, and I was looking forward to meeting my half-sisters. Patricia answered the phone and immediately seemed cold at finding me on the other end of the line. It had turned out, she said, that her current husband didn't want her or anyone else in the family to have any contact with me. I was a reminder of a part of her life that he didn't want to exist, and that he certainly didn't want in her life now. So she simply told me not to call her again, and hung up. That was that.

That experience reinforced everything I had experienced of people, relationships, and parenting. It reinforced that ultimately, people didn't care, were only interested in themselves, and clearly didn't have any sense of responsibility if that meant personal inconvenience. It reinforced that if a situation were likely to cause difficulty, people would walk away in an instant. Family and blood didn't mean a thing. Being a parent didn't mean a thing.

If you can't count on your birth parents, and you can't trust those who have been entrusted with your care; when doctors don't report abuse in the family; when friends laugh at you; and when teachers turn a blind eye, the world around you is not a place of care and nurturing. It is an empty place to fear, and to want to flee.

Every encounter is met with the presumption that you will be left alone and injured. Walls go up. Resentment and loneliness settle in, and they become your company. Your mind becomes trained to see people as enemies. You are always on high alert, ready to do battle. But you are an army of one, ill-equipped to fight every day, tired from the struggle, pessimistic about seeing only constant enemies coming over every horizon. Waiting to explode. Ready to fall.

Rising above those feelings was a constant struggle, and a very lonely and isolating one. What was absolutely clear at that time was that I was on my own, in every respect.

All I had was me.

In that space of isolation, that thought is either defeating or empowering. The irony is that the worst that happens to us, I believe, gives us the opportunity to gain power that we otherwise might not have ever acquired. Luckily for me, there was a survival instinct that had become an embedded part of my being.

*"All I have is me. What do I mean 'all' I have is me?"* I remember thinking after some time. "Me" is a lot. "Me" is a survivor. "Me" is better than being defeated by my father. "Me" is a gift. "Me" cares about "me." "Me" wants to feel purposeful. "Me" wants to discover. "Me" wants to feel fulfilled. "Me" wants to be free. "Me" wants to be happy. "Me" wants to thrive. "Me" is a force and an energy that is just waiting to be tapped!

I could be my worst enemy through my thoughts and sabotage my *self*, or I could be my best friend and encourage my *self* at every opportunity—not out of the need to just survive, but out of the desire to be "something more." I could release and nurture the *self* that had been trapped, in shock, surviving. Or, I could let that *self* continue to drown in my own negative perceptions and thoughts.

I could choose either. If I chose the latter, I might as well slit my wrists and be defeated.

I could still feel that little girl inside who hadn't had a chance to play. She wanted to play, not to die. She wanted to make friends and to laugh, not to cry in the darkness. She wanted to feel a warm hug filled with love, not touches filled with violation. She wanted to dream extraordinary dreams in a peaceful sleep, not have nights filled with demons and nightmares.

I was the only one who could set my *self* free. Some of the reading that I was doing at the time was helpful in allowing me to understand the power of transforming our thoughts. At the core of the reading was the power of the mind, and the energy that flows around and within us. We can channel that power and energy to positively transform all that is around and within us, or we can channel that energy to destroy each moment.

Several years later while traveling through India, I would read a quote in the Deer Park in Sarnath where the Buddha gave his first teachings, which would summarize our self-destructive powers. The Buddha said, "Whatever harm an enemy may do to an enemy, or a hater to a hater, an ill-directed mind inflicts on oneself a greater harm."

My mind was the one thing that could completely destroy me. I was no longer struggling physically with my father, I was struggling with all that he had left in my mind and in my being. As long as I let my mind run wild, untamed, and ill-directed, my mind and my thoughts would become my greatest enemy. They would keep inflicting pain and hold me prisoner in a very dark world.

I was also reminded of the Dalai Lama's *The Art of Happiness,* which places the mind and our own responsible thoughts and choices at the heart of happiness, "Without cultivating a pliant mind, our outlook becomes brittle and our relationship to the world becomes characterized by fear."

Whether we speak of karma, or of universal energy, or of the spirit of God, at the core is seeing the good, feeling compassion for our *self* and for others, and having faith and trust that we can achieve happiness. In *The Art of Happiness,* the Dalai Lama reminds us, "The secret to my own happiness, my own good future, is within my own hands. I must not miss that opportunity!"

I had survived. *"I've made it this far. I'm going to go as far as I can go,"* I remember the encouragement from within. *"I'm going to take every second and turn it into something positive. I've had enough of feeling bad. Enough! I'm not going to allow my thoughts to trap me in that dark place! I'm not going to let others set me back or take me down! I'm going to transform every moment. I'm going to take care of me. I'm going to choose to seek happiness and goodness in each day. I'm going to trust that there is a higher purpose and that I will find it."*

I was however, more than ever, aware of my limitations. Standing on the beach in the warm light of the sunrise, I knew I was far from ready for the happy ending in *Sleepless in Seattle.* Thinking back on the scene from *28 Days,* I was not even at the stage of keeping plants alive, let alone a pet or a relationship. Before I was going to be atop of the Empire State Building with my soul mate, I needed to free my mind, open my heart, and find and fall in love with my own soul.

Despite our limitations, no matter what we have experienced, we each have paths to happiness that lie before us. Our challenge is often pausing to see the choices that are in our own hands in each moment. Then, our task becomes to choose to take a first step that simply "feels right," that resonates with happiness, that opens our heart to finding and falling in love with all we have within and around us. Once we take one step, the next becomes clearer, and the next clearer still. Soon enough, we are far along our journey, and filled with the momentum of endless opportunities that keeps us traveling farther and higher.

## MOMENTS OF PAUSE

1. What are your standards for love that you want in your life? What is the ultimate love of which you are worthy?

2. How are your love relationships helping you soar?

3. How are your love relationships holding you prisoner?

4. What is the love that you have for your *self*?

5.  What are the sources of power you draw from within? What are the experiences in your life that have given you the greatest sources of power?

6.  What are the greatest parts of your *self*—the greatest forces and energy within you?

7.  How can you start to uncover the secret to your happiness that you are holding in your hands?

## MORE MOMENTS FOR YOU

# Seven

# The Compass Within ~ Finding Your True North

*"Do not go where the path may lead,
go instead where there is no path and leave a trail."*

—Ralph Waldo Emerson

WHEN WE ALLOW OUR compass within to guide us, unlimited paths emerge. We can let go of what we know. We can go wherever we choose—beyond paths that we see, to those that take us higher and farther—to our greatest places.

Back in my room at the Jericho Beach Hostel, I started the task of once again downsizing my backpack so I could make it through the next weeks with my back intact! Downsizing my backpack was like a cleansing. With every item I pulled out and left behind, I felt the weight lifted from within me. It felt refreshing. Rejuvenating.

The more I let go of the things I was carrying with me, the more I could be moved by the things within me. Funny how the outside world will slap you in the face to give you a message. *"Hello! Lighten up! Relax! Leave the 'stuff' behind you and walk onward. All you need will be found along the way, but you need space to re-load. Let it all go and move on!"*

Letting go can be a difficult thing to do. Sometimes, even if we feel only pain, at least we feel. It is familiar. We come to know it. We accept it as part of our being. We integrate it into the way we walk through life, even if it weighs us down with every step. It becomes a companion. It protects us from harm by keeping us on high alert. We rely on it to keep us "safe." We make it our friend. We start to think that it is more reliable than happiness because it is always there. To let it go creates a space of nothing. Is emptiness worse than pain? What will fill the void?

I could hear the universe telling me to leave the baggage behind, unload, walk forward. Unpacking my backpack and leaving things behind was easy—the benefit was obvious, and I would immediately feel the relief. It simply became a choice. What will help me as I walk forward? What will hinder me as I walk forward? What do I need given what I know now? What can I leave behind knowing what I know now?

What became apparent, was that I couldn't just keep cramming things inside, and expect my pack to become lighter, and my journey easier. Impossible.

Unpacking my internal bundle didn't seem quite so black and white. Or was it? If everything within me was packed into a backpack, how would I choose what to keep and what to leave behind? Ironically, such simple questions that I instinctively used to decide what I needed in my physical pack, were probably good starting questions for me on my inner journey.

*"What will help me as I walk forward?"*

*"What will hinder me as I walk forward?"*
*"What do I need given what I know now?"*
*"What can I leave behind now that I know what I know?"*

I had packed my "inner" pack full of a whole lot of things that I needed over the years—full of things I needed to survive. I became so used to the weight that I just continued to carry it. I never stopped to take an inventory. It was my survival pack, my safety gear, my essential tool kit.

As I so easily chose what I needed and what I didn't need in my physical pack for my travels ahead, I realized that I didn't know for sure, and that was okay. I still made the choices I felt that I needed to make. I was confident in my best guess, and I knew I would adapt as I went.

What I did know, was that circumstances had changed since I was in my mother's living room only months ago, packing what I thought I needed. Things were so different now than what I thought, or what I could possibly have known. And here I was in life. Knowing more, feeling more. In a different place. More capable in every moment of knowing what I needed and what I didn't need to travel forward. My choice. To pause and to unpack.

Just feeling that sense of choice from the simplest act of downsizing my backpack filled me with a sense of lightness. The feeling that I could simply make changes based on what I knew now in my life felt empowering.

In this moment of pause, I realized that I had never stopped to take stock of the things I had packed in my tool kit to survive. Could it be that simple? Stopping. Pausing. Making the choice.

Do we forget so easily that we have the choice in every moment to make the changes we want to make for our *self*? Do we allow our *self* to be pushed and pulled so far, in so many directions, that we don't pause and contemplate the choices—the possibilities of new paths? Paths guided by that for which our soul is yearning, paths upon which we can walk lightly without the excess weight of things that no longer serve us well?

As the sun shone through the window of my room and fell upon my backpack, I felt warmed with the thoughts of discovery that lay ahead. I felt open to thoughts of change that would come in that space of pause.

The warmth of the sun and the brightness of the morning drew me outside. It was a beautiful, sunny, crisp day in Vancouver. I wandered through the local shop-lined streets and eventually happened upon the island marketplace of Granville Island. Street performers danced, parades of costumed musicians burst through the streets, and artists performed in colorful theatrical shows on every corner. The marketplace was a vibrant festival in every direction—art studios and jewelry stores filled with colorful creations from local artists; fresh produce markets filled with local cheeses, fruits, vegetables, and pastas; florists abundant in stunning local flowers; small playgrounds filled with the giggles of children—all surrounded by the beautiful aqua-green waters that glistened around the island. The air was filled with fresh aromas of roasted coffee, fresh produce, pastries, and breakfasts. A particularly quaint little bookstore called to me as the aroma of fresh coffee caught me and drew me inside.

As I wandered through the bookstore with my coffee in hand, the face of an old, contemplative, and wise-looking woman popped out at me from the cover of a book, *If I had my life to live over, I would pick more daisies.* The eyes of the old woman on the book cover seemed to follow me with humor as I approached. You know when you feel as though a book is almost reaching off the shelf and dragging you toward it? That was it—the arms of the old woman had grabbed me and sat me down, like a grandmother does to a grandchild as she is about to impart words of wisdom. I opened the book—it was a collection of poems and verses by various women.

The editor, Sandra Martz, described the book in the inside jacket cover, "… this absorbing collection is about women making choices." Ironic at this time.

I turned to the first poem. It was the poem that had inspired the book, and was titled, "If I Had My Life to Live Over" by Nadine Stair.

> *I'd dare to make more mistakes next time. I'd relax. I would limber up. I would be sillier than I have been on this trip. I would take fewer things seriously. I would take more chances. I would climb more mountains and swim more rivers. I would eat more ice cream and less beans. I would perhaps have more actual troubles, but I'd have fewer imaginary ones.*

> *You see, I'm one of those people who live sensibly and sanely hour after hour, day after day. Oh, I've had my moments, and if I had it to do over again, I'd have more of them. In fact, I would try to have nothing else. Just moments, one after another, instead of living so many years ahead of each day. I've been one of those persons who never goes anywhere without a thermometer, a hot water bottle, a raincoat and a parachute. If I had to do it again, I would travel lighter than I have.*

> *If I had my life to live over, I would start barefoot earlier in the spring and stay that way later in the fall. I would go to more dances. I would ride more merry-go-rounds. I would pick more daises.*

As I turned back to the cover of the book, the deep brown eyes of the old, wise woman gazed at me. I was grateful to the universe for conspiring with her to bring those words to me at this time. It is the constant reinforcement—sometimes it's a subtle message, sometimes it's a "kick you in the pants" message—that we receive along our path that I was beginning to see, more and more, gives us what we need to put the next foot forward. Despite the uncertainty of the outcomes, despite not knowing where the path will take us, we take the next step forward. We step forward believing that if we open our *self* to hearing and feeling the direction in which we are compelled to move, that is the only true path onto which to step—a path where we can pick more daisies.

Thinking of daisies, I remembered being told of a beautiful botanical garden in Vancouver that was "a must see." Believing in the "clues" we are often given to guide our next step, I let the thoughts of daisies set me on my way to find the botanical gardens.

A nearby Internet cafe gave me an introduction to the gardens— the Van Dusen Gardens—just several miles from the marketplace. A quote from Hanna Rion on the web page of the gardens called to me as had the wise old woman in the bookstore, "The greatest gift of the garden is the restoration of the five senses." Restoration. Growth. Connecting to those senses long since lost and buried within. At this time, those words couldn't have been more apt. As I Googled Hanna Rion, her words resonated deeply with me, "Each year that passes, brings another spring in which to grow young, another fall in which to harvest our riper dreams."

I think we so often forget the simplest truth in life—that every day *is* a new day—a new spring, full of color and magic. We need to pause to see that truth. There is a new day right here and now, and another tomorrow, and another, and another—our lives are full of new opportunities that come with every sunrise. Like daisies waiting to be picked, our dreams await our attention every day. They are colorful and compelling, if we can see them beyond all of the things we keep busy with every day, and through all of the things we carry that hinder us, rather than help us. We have a different pair of shoes we can put on with every new day. We can deliberately choose to take the steps we dare to take to follow our dreams.

For now, my dream was to simply live each day picking the daisies—as simple as that. In this day, I will have almost 65,000 seconds in eighteen hours of time to be awake—not *just* awake—*consciously* awake. Each of us has that. We each have 65,000 moments to choose which places within us will help us rather than hinder us as we take each step, 65,000 moments to be inspired—and to inspire our *self*, 65,000 moments to see the color and the magic, 65,000 moments to discover new moments, 65,000 moments to take chances, 65,000 moments to eat more ice cream, 65,000 moments to be sillier, 65,000 moments to pick more daisies, 65,000 moments to grow younger, and 65,000 moments to be the master of our own destiny.

I sprung up from the computer at the Internet cafe, and made my way to the Van Dusen Gardens, so happy to have met Hanna Rion. I felt as though I had met a new friend, but in reality, I was becoming more and more introduced to me. The little girl within was playing. My soul was feeling free. My "I" was emerging from the depths. The universe was constantly tapping me on the shoulder. All I needed to do was pause and follow the instinct, from the smallest inkling to the most powerful urge, to where my next step should be. That was beginning to be my only guide—my only compass.

The Van Dusen Gardens were, indeed, "a must see." Stepping into the gardens was like stepping into another realm—full of vivid colors, the chirping of birds, and the smells of fresh fauna. After reading some of the words of Hanna Rion, the gardens took on new significance. "Garden making is creative work ...," continued some of Hanna's words of wisdom, "... It is a personal expression of self, an individual conception of beauty ... even in the most unimportant parts of my garden are little secret treasures."

We each have such extraordinary gardens within our *self* full of secret treasures, waiting for us to wander our paths and discover them. We need to be our most diligent gardeners if we are to clear our way and reveal the secret paths and treasures that have grown over with time. We can choose what we clear from our gardens and with what we fill our gardens. We can clear all that interferes with our sights and steps forward. We can create our most personal expression of our *self.*

With my instincts as my compass to set me on a path to discover all of the secret treasures that lay ahead, I quietly sat amidst the gardens and rested. There was a calming comfort to knowing that all I needed was within me. Wherever I went now would be guided by that inner compass, 65,000 awakening moments each day.

The next day I was ready to leave Vancouver and embark upon new adventures. I decided to start by heading to Vancouver Island. After spending a few days in Vancouver, I was craving a return to quiet solitude. Vancouver Island was nearby and had been described to me as a quiet and relaxing island. For over a month now, I had been camping for most nights nestled amidst fir trees and surrounded only by the sounds of nature. I missed the solitude and the spiritual space Mother Nature created, and was looking forward to once again being cradled in a realm where spirits seemed to dwell so peacefully.

As the ferry from mainland Vancouver arrived at Vancouver Island, I saw and heard the sights and sounds of a small city—far from the quiet peacefulness I was seeking. My heart sank. I pulled my backpack onto my shoulders and disembarked the ferry onto the bustling sidewalk. The only thing to do was to make my way to the hostel I booked from Vancouver and hope that it was in a more remote part of the island.

Arriving at the hostel, I felt my heart sink further. The hostel was in the middle of downtown Victoria. Now, don't get me wrong, Victoria seemed to be a quaint and vibrant city, but a city, nonetheless, full of cars, traffic lights, buildings, people, and all of the bustling sounds of movement and busyness. I felt so out of place—so much like I was just in the wrong place. You know that feeling when you're not quite sure where you want to be, but you just know that where you are is *not* where you want to be? Well, that feeling was wrapped around me like a straightjacket!

Fortunately, one of the things that you learn when you're traveling, especially traveling solo, is that sometimes you are just going to end up in the wrong place. There is no escaping it. So you can either stay where you are, and be miserable, or you can kick your *self* in the pants, stop dwelling in misery, and tell your *self* to move on.

Confucius said, "Our greatest glory is not in never falling but in rising every time we fall." We have that opportunity every time we end up in the "wrong" place, every time we stray from our truth, every time we feel lost, every time we fall. We can get back on track, we can rise up, we can find our way. The first step is simply acknowledging that feeling, that "compass within," which is telling us that where we are is not quite right.

The next step? Define the simplest aspects of where you want to be. For me, standing amidst the noise and bustle of downtown Victoria, I knew I just needed to be in a quiet place, with few people, nestled amidst only nature. I also wanted to fly fish. Yes—fly fish! Weeks before, I had learned to fly fish nestled amidst snow-capped Rocky Mountains in Jasper with some local fly fisherman who had taken me to some of their favorite "local" streams. I figured that if I found somewhere to fly fish, I might find the place of natural solitude that I was seeking. So I decided to find a fly fishing store in Victoria, and ask the locals for the "inside scoop" on places to go.

The fly and tackle store in Victoria felt like a sanctuary from the hustle of the streets. I knew from here I would be set in the right direction. Sure enough, the store owner was an avid fly fisherman full of local knowledge that no travel book would have been able to impart.

"Salt Spring Island is the place for you," said Jim, the owner, without hesitation. "St. Mary's Lake has all the trout you need and is away from everything!"

Jim called his friend who owned some small rental cabins on the lake and set me up to stay for a few days. The only thing I needed to do was get to the town center of Ganges on Salt Spring Island. From there, Jim's friend would come and pick me up.

"There's no public transport on the island," Jim said, "so you need to hitch a ride from some locals as you get off the ferry, and they'll get you to Ganges."

I must have given Jim a slightly perplexed look, "Don't worry," he smiled, "folks are pretty friendly there—you'll be fine!"

Now, before I left Australia, I would have thought twice about this venture, but that was then and this was now. I paused, sensed my inner compass, and it felt perfectly aligned. I bundled up my fly fishing kit that I rented from Jim, and headed back to the hostel to sleep a night, before waking early to catch the ferry to Salt Spring Island.

The next morning I set off to the ferry terminal with my substantially lighter backpack and the black cylinder that contained my fly fishing rod and tackle. I was so happy to be at the ferry terminal—there is something about setting off on the next part of a journey that is always rejuvenating. I think it is the feeling of freedom and adventure that comes from launching into uncertainty, and knowing in your heart that only good things await.

"Boundaries and limitations fall as we surge towards new frontiers. We are propelled towards freedom's frontier. Freedom's journey. We delight in freedom's uncertainty." This was a reflection by Steve Zikman, in his book, *The Power of Travel*—a small book I decided to keep in my backpack, despite my determined downsizing. I was happy to be propelled into the uncertainty of my adventures, even if it did require hitching a few rides here and there with the locals on this little-known island!

The ferry soon loaded up with passengers heading to the various islands that make up the San Juan Islands off the southeastern coast of Vancouver Island. The first stop would be Swartz Bay on Vancouver Island, and the next would be Fulford Harbor at the southern end of Salt Spring Island. There was one very obvious distinction between me and most of the other passengers—most of the passengers were in cars.

I remembered Jim's words from the fly and tackle store about hitching a ride with the locals, but most of the cars seemed filled with visitors from the mainland. I decided to relax and enjoy the view of the passing islands and worry about the ride when I disembarked, where I assumed I would come across the friendly locals of Salt Spring Island.

Pulling into the ferry wharf at Swartz Bay, most of the cars disembarked, and all of the passengers without cars left also—except, of course, me. There I was, with a handful of cars remaining on the ferry. I wanted to go somewhere quiet and remote, and from the look of those remaining on the ferry, that was exactly where I was headed.

As the ferry approached the dock on Salt Spring Island, car engines started, and I moved to the passenger walkway. Don't ask me why I didn't ask for a ride while I was on the ferry—one of those obvious oversights that I can possibly only blame on being immersed in the beautiful scenery of the San Juan Islands and the deep blue waters of the Strait of Georgia—the whale-filled waters between Vancouver Island and the shores of British Columbia. Maybe it was the romantic notion of "thumbing" a ride by the roadside that led me to wait to seek a ride until the cars had started to depart the ferry. Either way, before I knew it, the cars were passing me as I walked down the gangway to the dock, and by the time I was off the boat the last two cars were passing me, oblivious to the pathetic thumb I tried to throw them.

The ferry departed as quickly as the cars, and I looked around me. There I was—standing with my backpack and fly fishing kit gazing up a small deserted road that led away from the dock. I smiled and considered the only thing to do was to start walking. Yes, this was definitely solitude!

Luckily for me, not far along the road was a small gas station. A white van by the gas pump was the only car in sight, so I headed over to see if I might be met by some of those friendly locals Jim told me about. Peering into the side door of the van, I was greeted by three middle-aged tradesmen sitting on milk carts in the back of their van having lunch. This was not a scene I would readily tell my mother about, who was already worried about my solo traveling.

"What's up little lady?" said one of the three.

I put on my best smile and told the trio I was looking for a ride to Ganges.

"Lucky for you, we're headed there in about ten minutes. You can ride with us," came the reply from inside the van.

At this point, my options were very limited, so putting aside thoughts of "the worst that could happen," and remembering Jim's promise that all the locals were friendly, I kept my best smile and graciously accepted the ride (another thing I would never have done before this journey!). Not long after, I was bundled up in the back of the van. Soon enough, I arrived safe and sound in Ganges. I thanked the universe, and said farewell to the trio as they headed off to their job in town.

The town center of Ganges was refreshingly simple and quaint. A small parking lot, a few local stores, a post office, and a phone booth. The phone booth was the most significant for me—it was my one means to contact Jim's friend, Ray, to ask if he could pick me up and take me to his cabins. Before long, Ray's old green pick-up truck was pulling into the parking lot, and I was on my way to the cabins.

"Not many people make it out here," said Ray, "it's a pretty local place that not too many people know about."

He was slightly perplexed about why I would travel alone to the island. From what he said, however, he knew his fair share of eccentric people on the island, so I was not that strange in comparison.

Arriving at the cabins felt like arriving "home." Three small rustic-looking pine cabins nestled under fir trees lined the edge of a beautiful, expansive, glistening lake. Each cabin was set apart from the other by a large distance, and each had its own sandy inlet, with a row boat resting on the sand ready to explore the lake.

I couldn't have found a more idyllic place. My cabin was absolutely charming. A little kitchenette was all I needed to cook the fish that I would catch, a small wooden table and chairs made a perfect dining suite, and a small couch that looked through windows out to the lake provided the perfect reading spot. A loft sat above the living area, and was just large enough for the double bed, and high enough for a small window that looked over the lake. No television. No noise. No hustle. No bustle. Nirvana.

I was so excited to get out and onto the lake on my row boat to catch my first fish. The images of cooking my fish over the camp fire I would make were so vivid, I could already taste the fish and smell the campfire. Ray said any time was good fishing on the lake, and that it was full of trout, so I had no doubt I wouldn't have to rely on the canned salmon, nuts, and crackers I picked up in Victoria. I laid my backpack down on the couch and excitedly unpacked my fly fishing kit, with all of the tackle and flies, and prepared to conquer the trout in the lake.

Hours passed. The trout were certainly not as friendly as the locals, and they definitely weren't cooperating with my visions of my camp-side dinner. I rowed all over the lake that first day—nothing!

A few teases here and there by trout that must have known my intentions, but that was it. I tried every type of fly that Jim had given me, and none made a difference. My visions of deliciously cooked trout were changing to visions of wresting with a can opener to get to my canned salmon. Oh well, it was a beautifully sunny afternoon, and the rhythm of casting my line and the sounds of the gentle "plop" of the fly entering the water and spreading circular ripples that danced over the lake were more than fulfilling for me.

As the sun started to set, the insects came out to play around the water. There were all types of insects—probably the type that should have been on my fishing line to attract the trout! Soon enough, little mouths emerged from below the lake wherever an insect had decided to rest on top of the water—it was like a symphony of little ripples all over the lake. Here were all of my trout friends that I had been waiting for all day. Except now, I had more competition than ever—and it seemed that the trout knew the difference between the rubbery flies on my fishing line and the juicy little flies resting atop the water. The trout were now having a wonderful dinner—and I could see I was going to be enjoying canned salmon for mine.

After a few minutes of watching the trout feast on their unsuspecting insects, birds started appearing around the lake. Soon enough, the birds were diving into the water wherever the ripples were appearing—trying to catch my fish. It seemed the cycle of nature was happening right in front of me—I was trying to catch the fish, the fish were trying to catch the insects, the birds were trying to catch the fish, and I was certainly losing out in the cycle. Nature often has it all figured out, I thought, well beyond our competence.

Sitting on the lake, I saw the perfect working order that surrounds us—a harmonious cycle—full of activity, and creating sanctuaries of life. I felt serenity amidst this natural system where everything is created to support its environment, to maintain equilibrium and balance. Undisturbed and untouched, the harmony continues.

"In the midst of movement and chaos, keep stillness inside of you." I was reminded of the quote by Deepak Chopra as I felt the stillness settle throughout the lake. Here, all over the lake, nature was showing me that was the very essence of this cycle of life—to find the stillness in the movement, and experience the harmony and balance that lies within. From there, a sanctuary of life emerges— lush and abundant.

I rowed quietly through the waters and watched the ripples from my oars spread through the lake. I felt part of this sanctuary and saw my ripples becoming part of the gentle movement of the lake. As the darkness settled in, the distinction between my hands connecting to the oars, connecting to the water, connecting to the shore, connecting to the trees, connecting to the star-filled sky became indistinguishable. In the midst of the stillness, I was holding hands with the universe. My compass was resting on its true north as the North Star, Polaris, shined brightly above me.

After enjoying the quiet of the lake for several days, I decided to explore another part of the island. The trout in the lake were not cooperating at all, and I was fully relaxed and ready to discover another environment. Ray was kind enough to tell me about other cabins tucked away on a beach about half an hour by car. It was a fairly straight road that meandered only a little from the lake to the beach, and Ray said there were plenty of locals traveling along the road who would pick me up and give me a ride. I would have yet another opportunity to try my "thumbing" skills, and to meet more of the locals!

I wandered out to the road, and looked expectantly to the horizon. It wasn't too long before a car emerged. This time, I was sure to put my thumb out in plenty of time to be seen. I added a wave and a smile, hoping that would add some character and appeal. As the car slowed beside me, I was excited at my success. Two older women peered through the window at me, and I smiled as they welcomed me into their car.

The car was out of a movie scene—an old cherry-red colored Ford Town Car. The interior was burgundy velvet—everywhere—over the seats, the roof, the doors—everywhere! Behind the back seat along the window, was a collection of small saucepans, for what purpose, I had no idea. Possibly, these two locals were some of those eccentric characters of the island to whom Ray had alluded. Yet the two women had a certain magic about them—they seemed surreal, with their whitish gray hair, softly wrinkled skin, their gentle smiles, and their eyes rich with simplicity. They said they had been on the island for as long as they cared to remember—it was their home and their happiness. The peacefulness in their energy was immense. They had all they needed on this small island, and they were supremely content.

As we continued the drive along Bennis Road that led to the cabins, Mavis and Nida chatted about the island. This certainly seemed to be a place where everyone knew everyone and helped each other out. It shouldn't have been so striking, but "simple acts of kindness" seemed to fill this place.

Throughout my trip, I had met strangers who offered all sorts of "simple acts of kindness"—from a young couple offering pancakes for breakfast at a campground, a store owner including something extra in my grocery bag, a bus driver ensuring I arrived at the right destination, and of course, locals who picked me up by the side of the road to give me a ride, to mention just a few. Those small, simple acts of kindness had helped me move from place to place, like small stepping stones atop an endless ocean.

I started to experience that it is those small acts of kindness that we give and receive every day that fill our path with goodwill—good karma. It seemed that each act of kindness led to another.

It is the simplest things—small acts of kindness—that can change a person's life, that can turn a bad day into a good day. You know those days when you just feel out of sorts, sometimes for a reason, and sometimes for reasons you just can't put your finger on? Then, someone passes through your day—a random stranger—and does the smallest act of kindness that can "tip" your mood completely. In those moments, the smallest act can "tip" our day.

Imagine the difference if there were thousands of moments in every day to help tip our days toward smiles, and to help lift each other up. What I saw, was that there *are* thousands of moments to make simple gestures of goodwill—to put good karma out to the universe, to smile at a passing stranger, or to make a simple offer of help.

What if all we are measured by are those simple, anonymous acts of kindness?

How much difference could we make if we paused to sense where help was needed?

What if the things that brought the most back to us were the simplest things we gave?

Mahatma Gandhi said, "Be the change that you want to see in the world." I started to see, from the smallest deeds, that not only do we start to change the world around us, but we also start to change the world within us. With each act of kindness we receive and "pay forward," with each thought of doing good things, the darkness within us starts to turn to light, and the light starts to shine outward and guide us forward.

Soon enough, we arrived at the cabins. I said farewell to Mavis and Nida, and watched the red car disappear at the far end of the road. I was grateful as much for the contemplation they brought to me, as I was for the ride, and I think the universe was at work again.

Through the trees by the road, I could see a small cluster of rustic timber cabins. I threw my backpack over my shoulder and headed toward my new home. The narrow clearing that led to the cabins was lined with beautifully constructed tree houses, draped with lush foliage flowing down from the robust fir trees from which they hung. The distinct smell of nature filled the air, and once again I felt instantly at home.

The main cabin was somewhat larger than the other cabins. Walking into the cabin, I was greeted by the young woman to whom Ray had spoken, and who had my room ready and waiting for me. Her warm and friendly smile was the perfect welcome, as was the smiling face of Winnie the Pooh that sat in the window adjacent to the reception, enjoying the rays of the sun upon him. "Rivers know this: there is no hurry. We shall get there some day," were Winnie's words of wisdom that hung beside him. I smiled as Winnie smiled at me, his head resting on his hand, his elbow resting on his knee, his foot on a pot of honey, butterflies around his head, blue sky and sunshine behind him, and Piglet at his feet.

With each day, I was getting the message that life need not be as complicated or hurried as I had made it. *Fill the moments with simple things. Relax. Take it easy. Let the burdens go. Come and enjoy. Let life in. Invite it in. Make your home in it."* These were the words that filled me as Pooh's smile seemed to grow.

I had never felt "at home" in life. Life had always felt like a constant struggle of survival—a marathon, an endless jungle. I felt like an intruder, not welcome, being chased out of life, and without a place. Here and now, with the spirit guides of my journey ever present, and with my soul open to hear and experience a different space, I started to feel at home in life for the first time. The day was quiet, and I was content to read in the sunshine surrounded by tree houses, and nestled, once again in the belly of Mother Nature and her melodic sounds.

Awaking early the next morning to the new rays of sunshine breaking through the window, Pooh Bear smiling, and the sounds of birds chirping, I felt peaceful and refreshed. The air was crisp, and I was eager to feel the ocean spray from the nearby beach that ran along the southeastern edge of the island. I bundled up in my fleece and set off through the surrounding trees. Wandering along the narrow dirt road that led to the beach, I felt as though I was the only person on the island. Complete silence surrounded me, except for the wind occasionally rustling through the trees, and the birds playing among the branches and leaves.

The beach was a deserted stretch of coastline that seemed untouched. The vibrant and deep blue waters from the Georgia Strait splashed about the shoreline. I was hopeful to see one of the many Orca whales that inhabited the waters burst into the air. Even without seeing the Orcas, the beach held its own grandeur and mystical charm. This place seemed so quiet and hidden, nestled away from everything, yet home to some of the most powerful creatures of the ocean, looming just off the shoreline.

The morning was chilly, with the winds whistling along the sand, and swirling through the spray of the ocean. More than an hour passed, and I was content to be a part of this playground of nature. As I gazed down the beach, I noticed distant figures on the sand close to the water's edge. As they came closer, I couldn't make out the large objects they were carrying, but there seemed to be a group of one woman and five men. I was tucked away from the wind at the top of the sand, hidden from the view of these strangers. As I watched them pass below me, I could make out the large objects to be instruments—drum cases, guitar cases, speakers, video and photography equipment. *"A band?"* I contemplated, feeling the confused creases in my forehead set in. *"Here? On the edge of a hidden coastline, on an island that is islands away from other islands?"*

The band proceeded to set up on a small rocky peak that protruded into the ocean from the shoreline just down from where I was sitting. It was an odd scene—drums, stereo boxes, guitar stands, and microphones carefully balanced on the rocks. Soon enough, the musicians were in their places, the videographer was ready to tape, and the woman of the group held the microphone and started to sing into the ocean and up to the sky. Her voice carried through the wind—harmonious and haunting, deep and from the soul. It felt as though she was touching the heavens and penetrating the ocean with her words.

After more than an hour, the group packed up their equipment and started to head back down the beach. As the woman climbed down from the rocks, she caught my eye. Possibly, the sight of me sitting on my own on this hidden beach was as strange to her as she was to me.

She smiled, waved, and headed toward me. It turned out that Sherrie and her band were recording a video to bring attention to the logging that was affecting the ocean life along the Gulf of Georgia. She was a mesmerizing and mystical woman—young, but with a depth and age that was beyond her appearance—an "old soul."

Sherrie asked me what I was doing on this deserted coast, and we started talking about living the unordinary life—pursuing dreams beyond the everyday churning of "mainstream" life. We instantly "clicked" and soon enough I was loading up with Sherrie and her band members in their pickup truck and heading into the town center of Ganges for lunch.

The band's name was "Sulk," and Sherrie had a dream to create music to help change the world. Over lunch, dreams were the topic of conversation. Dreams of music, dreams of creating change, dreams of purpose in this lifetime.

As we were finishing lunch, Sherrie wrote her dream on a brown paper bag, folded her music CD into it, and gave it to me to take on my travels. In the small parking lot in the town center, as we were getting ready to load up in to the truck, Sherry opened the tailgate.

She pulled out a guitar, handed it to Brian, and started singing one of her tracks, "If I Love You All Night Long."

Sherrie's voice was one of those penetrating voices that ran through you and gave you goosebumps. Her eyes looked deep into me as she sang—it was surreal and magical. Captured by the music, we were taken to another space—another realm—of passions and dreams and sensual connection where the moments are timeless and bind you like a spell. Sherrie gently moved us through that space, and then returned us as her voice softly brought us back to the present, like a hypnotist brings subjects out of their hypnotic state. And there we were—in a simple parking lot, all moved by a presence much more complex.

As Sherrie and the band dropped me back at the beach, the sun was still bright and glowing on the sand. The beach was as quiet as we had left it, and felt even more mystical and magical for the experience it brought us all that day.

We are all so many peoples, living so many different lives, in so many different places. Searching for our happiness, pursuing our dreams, aspiring, seeking that higher purpose, stepping out, exploring the paths to which we are drawn. Changing our shoes to find the ones that feel just right.

As I walked through the main cabin that night, I passed by a verse that I hadn't noticed earlier above one of the book shelves in the lounge. It was credited only to "An Indian Woman," "May the warm winds of heaven blow softly upon you, and the sun rise with joy in your heart."

With each day, I was feeling those warm winds upon me, and with each day and each experience, a happiness and peacefulness was growing in my heart and rejuvenating my soul. Seeds that had been buried for so long, so deep, unable to grow in a soul that was dark, were starting to feel warmth from the sunshine, and a light in which to grow.

Salt Spring Island was a place where time paused and allowed depths to be revealed. The "I" that had been buried inside was not only emerging, but also becoming my most authentic guide as "I" became connected to the universe—to a True North.

The travels that had brought me to this place seemed to me like waypoints on a map—points that help us find where we are, and allow us to set a path to the next destination. These waypoints are present in every moment, if we pause long enough to see them. They connect us with our dreams. They open new dimensions in our lives that can guide us to our True North. They connect us with a light that lets us know we are not alone wandering in the dark on this journey.

The waypoints along our journey can lead us to our most purposeful paths—paths filled with giving and receiving simple acts of kindness—paths that can lead us to change our *self*, and maybe even to change the world. But we must pause to see them, before we can follow them.

*"Shoot for the moon—you may miss, but you'll land amongst the stars!"* With the thought of the moon and the stars as my company, and guided by my "I" as my compass, I let the warm winds carry me onward, beyond the paths that I knew.

## MOMENTS OF PAUSE

1. If all of the things that happened in your life that most helped you, and that most hindered you, were packed into a backpack, what would be the contents?

2. Knowing what you know now, which things would you unpack from your backpack and leave behind—those things that no longer serve to help you, that only hinder you?

3. Knowing what you know now, which things in your backpack would you be sure to take with you? Which new things would you need to help you on the journey ahead?

4. With your newly packed backpack, which new paths would you choose to walk in your life?

5. What does your distinctive "I" look like? What does it feel like? What things tell you that you are getting closer to your "I"? What things tell you that you are moving further away from your "I"?

6.  As you walk forward in your life, what do you dare to do? Which daisies do you dare to pick? Which dreams do you dare to follow?

7.  If you contemplate your *self* as a garden, filled with secret treasures, which are those most treasured parts of your *self* that you would nurture into the most creative, vivid, and colorful display?

8.  As you pause and contemplate your dreams and roads ahead, where do you feel your compass resonating? Where do you feel your True North pointing? What are the "paths of purpose" to which your "I" is leading you?

9.  Into which new shoes would you step to walk closer to your "True North," to walk along your "paths of purpose"?

10. What are the changes you want to see in the world? How do you step closer to help create those changes?

## MORE MOMENTS FOR YOU

### Eight

# In Search of What?

*"All this searching ...*
*And all we really know is how little we know about what it all means ...*
*... so maybe we should stop trying to figure out the meaning of life*
*And sit back and enjoy the mystery of life."*

—"Trudy the Bag Lady"
Jane Wagner's "The Search for Signs of
Intelligent Life in the Universe"

THE WORLD AROUND US is filled with infinite awe-inspiring
moments. As we pause in each moment of awe, we are connected
to even more moments of awe. Each pause reveals unimagined new
insights into our *self*. With those insights, we can take our *self* on
an exhilarating journey to our greatest self, filled with mystery and
flowing with endless discovery.

I arrived in Seattle on the ferry from Salt Spring Island on a
beautiful late afternoon as the setting sun cast an orange light over

the waters of the Georgia Strait. The islands disappeared into the horizon, as if melting into the sunset, vanishing as surreally as they had appeared. They were like a magical, mystical lost city emerging and then sinking back into the depths until the time they should rise again to greet the next traveler. The energy and mysticism of the islands remained with me as a cherished companion.

I was drawn to Seattle to see one of my favorite actresses, Lily Tomlin, performing Jane Wagner's, *"The Search for Signs of Intelligent Life in the Universe."* I had found out through the Internet that the show was playing at the Seattle Repertory Theatre before it moved to Broadway. I loved Lily Tomlin as an actress—hilariously funny, quirky, warm, and timeless. She seemed to be one of those women who was front and center, bold and charismatic, and distinctively "her."

The title of the performance was apt, and very appealing to me at the time. Certainly I was on a journey of discovery, and was keen to enter what was sure to be a satirical and humorous interpretation of our "search" for the meaning of life. Of course, I was not disappointed!

Jane's writing and Lily's performance created a universe of colorful characters, all played out by Lily, and all experiencing the mystery of life from all walks of life. Maybe the characters represented the many lives of different people, or maybe they represented the many aspects of the one human life, with all of its complexity, confusion, diversity, paths, experiences, triumphs, and opportunities.

There is Trudy, the "certified crazy" New York City bag lady who acts as a "tour guide through humanity" to aliens trying to find out about the human race in search for signs of intelligent life in the universe. It turns out that Trudy the bag lady may just have more insights to the mystery and meaning of life than anyone. She is the "wise fool" among us. What drove her to "craziness" was her "ah-ha" moment, coming face to face with humanity while working for "Mr. Nabisco" and having the remarkable idea to make mega-profits by marketing snacks to the billions of people in the world without food. Her excitement for the idea was overcome by the obvious conflict with humanity—we're making mega-profits from whom?

I couldn't help but contemplate. Who is crazy? Who is not? Why? Why not? Why do we judge, value, respect, disrespect one life, one person, more or less than another? From whom do we get our insights on the "meaning and mystery" of life? How do we come into contact with our own humanity, with our collective consciousness that is so deeply connected to our collective survival?

There is an angry runaway punk-rock teenager, Agnus Angst, whose motto is "Evolve or Die." Agnus has seen her friends give up on life and commit suicide. She is full of fear, but deals with her fear by building an outer shell so strong, and a skin so thick that she can't be penetrated. She pretends not to mind or care about anything around her. She believes that if she can trick herself for long enough, she really won't mind or care. Yet despite all of the tears she tries to hold back, she can't escape that she really does care. She really does mind.

What shells are we creating around us, and what skins are we thickening, so that we don't hear, so we don't feel, so we don't mind, when really, there are many things that we do mind? Are we evolving in each moment, or dying in each moment?

There is Kate, a lonely rich woman who has come to see that having everything has made her stop wanting anything. Kate relies on her looks, on her quest for perfection on the outside, to "elevate" her above everyone else. Her armor is her coat of high fashion in which she struts through life. Yet ultimately, all that Kate experiences through her "perfection" is isolation, not admiration. Despite her wealth, Kate craves the essential things that money can't buy—the authentic connection to another, the simple shared experiences of laughing, crying, and the fullness of experiencing life through people.

Do we fill our lives with so much, that we lose sight of the essential? Do we exhaust our *self* on things that are inconsequential, so we have no energy for those things of greatest consequence? Do we create so much armor around us that our only enemy becomes our *self*, closing us off from the warm and wonderful experiences of our shared humanity?

Then there is the "new-age, trend-seeking" Chrissy, who jumps from one latest trend to the next seeking identity. Chrissy is lost chasing the next identity that society advertises and is filled with the false hopes of fulfillment that the next latest trend offers. She is so caught up in perpetually *chasing* that she never gives herself the opportunity to pause and *be*. Without all of the fads and trends, Chrissy realizes that she has no identity, no substance, no authenticity. Yet in a world around her that thrives on an economy of selling trends and identities, she remains lost.

How much do we stifle our authentic self with the latest fad, or those things to which society and culture lure us, rather than being lured by our authentic self? How often are our deepest desires lost in our *chasing*, rather than in our *being*? How much energy do we consume day after day jumping from trend to trend, false hope to false hope, rather than pausing and being still to hear and feel our deepest and most authentic dreams and desires?

We are so many peoples, so many lives, but really just one. We are part of the same evolution, the same collective consciousness, the same humanity. Trudy the bag lady contemplates our evolution, and comes to the conclusion that there must be some kind of "cosmic crazy glue" that connects everything—that binds every particle to another particle across the universe. The "crazy" bag lady has the "crazy" notion that there is more that we can *be* as a collective humanity, as she wears her badge that reads, "Let's be a no limit species!"

Ironically, I reflected, the Dalai Lama would agree with Trudy. The essence of Buddhism is that everything is interdependent. There is no state of existence that exists in isolation. There is little compassion or empathy that can be felt for others unless each of us feels interdependent—unless we feel bound to each other by some kind of "cosmic glue."

"I think the mistake we make," says the Dalai Lama, "is that when we're grown up, we start to think we're independent. We think that in order to be successful we don't need others—except maybe to exploit them! This is the source of all sorts of problems, scandals, and corruption. But if we had more respect for other people's lives—a greater sense of concern and awareness—it would be a very different world. We have to introduce the reality of interdependence. Then people would discover that, according to that reality, affection and compassion are essential if anything is ever going to change."

So too, Martin Luther King Jr., would agree, "We are caught in an inescapable network of mutuality, tied in a single garment of destiny. Whatever affects one directly, affects all indirectly."

It seems that many of us believe we are all connected—and interconnected. Our connection to each other can be the path to something much greater. It is through our interconnectedness that we experience what Trudy the bag lady refers to as the "goosebumps" of life. These are those magical moments that fill us with awe, and bring us more in touch with humanity and with our *self*. We see how, together, we can bring about those magical moments for the greater good of the many—for our collective whole.

In our busyness, it is easy to miss those magical moments—to constantly move so quickly that we don't pause to feel the connection to all that is around us and within us. I know I did that for so many years. Chasing. Avoiding. Running. Denying.

Yet in every moment, we have moments of awe all around us. We simply need to pause to *be* in them. All we need to do is look up to the stars each night, or out to the ocean, or up to the sky, or simply to the grass, or into the eyes of a friend, to feel the goosebumps.

Trudy the bag lady had a term for this—"awe-aerobics." When we create the space for pauses every day, we feel the goosebumps flow through us. They connect to our authentic being and give us that sense of "something more." We feel the awe of our wondrous self and all that we have the potential to be.

As Trudy wandered off into stars, and the theater faded to black, the concept of "awe-aerobics" resonated with me deeply as I reflected on my journey since leaving Australia. That, right there, gave me goosebumps. How lucky we are to have the opportunity for "awe-aerobics" in every moment. It is, I think, the key to unlocking the heart and the soul—to open our *self* to the universe, to experience the mystery. To feel. To be. To live. To be able to change our shoes in any moment, and walk the path driven by our deepest desires and our greatest self.

I left the auditorium, and on a chance, I asked the security guard if I could meet Lily. He looked strangely at me as I told him of my journey that brought me to Seattle to see Lily. With a smile, he asked me to wait and he would see what he could do. About thirty minutes later, he returned, and to my surprise and delight, he said that Ms. Tomlin would see me. *"You never know until you ask!"* I thought with a smile.

As I walked along the corridor to the dressing room, out came Lily in a wonderfully elegant white flowing jacket and pants suit, with her black and white canine companion. Her smile was infectiously larger than life, and she embraced me with such a warm hug. She didn't know, and I don't know why I didn't tell her at the time, but that was my first hug since I left Australia. One hug can tap into that shared humanity in a single moment. Goosebumps.

I could understand if Lily was bemused by this Australian backpacking around the world who had stopped along the way to see her. I felt like a character from her play—or, more so, I felt pieces of each of the characters in me. I told her about my travels and of not knowing what I would find along the way, or where my journey would take me. Being here to see Lily in such an apt performance was one of those moments of coincidence that *The Celestine Prophecy* would say was not a coincidence at all, but the energy of the universe at work.

Lily gave me much more of her time than I expected, which was a gift. As I thanked her, she gave me another gift—a message that she wrote in my journal, which has stayed with me and resonated since.

> *Kathy,*
> *When you get "there"—there will be a there there.*
> *Love,*
> *Lily Tomlin.*

The next leg of my trip was soon to begin—the "Southern Sun" camping trek—twenty-one days from Los Angeles to New York City. I was looking forward to the cross-country exploration and to allowing the mystery of each day to further unfold, and experiencing all of the "there's" along the way.

I left Seattle on a train and headed to Santa Monica to spend a few days before starting my trek. I found my next hostel through my trusty *Lonely Planet USA*, and looked forward to a new bed in another new place. My backpack was finally down to a manageable size, and I was happy to feel the vibration of the train tracks along the beautiful West Coast.

It was a perfectly sunny afternoon when I arrived in Santa Monica, and I decided the best way to explore was on roller blades— it seemed an ideal way to experience the oceanside like a local. It also seemed to be one of the most popular ways, with roller blade rental kiosks abounding along the sun-drenched, sandy oceanside.

As I roller bladed along the beautiful oceanside path, known as Ocean Front Walk, I became less and less sure that I wasn't in the middle of a movie set. It was as though my train had mistakenly dropped me off at Universal Studios, *"Is this real, or a stage for the next Hollywood movie?"* I thought.

The beautiful Santa Monica Pier was somewhat of an icon from so many movies and television shows that had been shot on location there. Exercise parks furnished with colorful gymnastic and acrobatic equipment ran alongside the ocean walk, which was filled with blonde-haired bronzed bodies that looked right out of an episode of *Baywatch.* I hadn't seen anything until I explored farther south and arrived at the famous Muscle Beach, where aspiring Mr. and Miss Universes were so pumped up they looked ready for take off!

After a few days of exploring the local scenes around Santa Monica, and, of course, taking a ride on the famous Santa Monica Ferris wheel, I was ready to meet up with my new traveling companions for my final Trek America expedition.

The morning brought our new group of travelers together, ready to set off across country. Once again, I was in the company of others whose only goal was to experience each day and enjoy all that arose. That feeling was as refreshing now as it was on my first trek—simple, pure, almost naive—and we all delighted in it.

As a tourist necessity, we did *the* tourist thing in Los Angeles— the sightseeing bus tour. The past days seemed like a constant movie set, and the bus tour was no exception. *"Is this place real?"* I thought as we traveled along. The sights and scenes weren't like any reality I had experienced—from Hollywood, to Sunset Boulevard, Rodeo Drive, Beverly Hills, Bel Air, and to, ironically, the doors of Universal Studios.

I felt as though I was in the movie *The Truman Show* with Jim Carey, in which Carey plays a salesman who realizes his life is taking place inside a film studio made to look like real life. Reality is eventually revealed when the sky opens up to reveal that "real life" is actually a film set.

As I looked around, I was waiting for the sky to separate at any moment and reveal the film set behind all of this. *"Is this the real Universal Studios that we have pulled into, or a created Universal Studios within the "real" Universal Studios?"* I contemplated. To this day, I'm not sure. Reality? Fantasy?—Fantasy? Reality? Which is which? I started to see some of the real-life scenes that I was sure must have provided some inspirational material for Jane Wagner and Lily Tomlin!

The next stops on this trek would take our small group to a contrast of places where we would be sure to experience the different flavors of the United States—from the Grand Canyon, to Las Vegas, Zion National Park, Monument Valley, San Antonio, New Orleans, Tennessee, Washington D.C., and finally New York City. Once again, I was looking forward to experiencing those awe-inspired "goosebumps" in out of the way "wide-open spaces."

Arriving in Las Vegas was quite a scene. Once again, I wondered in which movie set I had landed. For a girl from "Down Under," who had only seen these types of scenes on television or in movies, these places seemed far from reality. They were Disneyland for adults—full of lights, camera, and action. You could be anyone or no one, someone or everyone. It didn't seem to matter, because everything seemed to get lost in the flashing lights and the glitz, like infinite colorful static on a larger-than-life movie screen.

Amidst all of the static, I felt a quiet serenity. It was as though a peaceful "home" had been nurtured within me during my journey. The spirit guides had settled deep within. The North Star held my hand. My compass was steady. I felt protected, as if I were in a bubble under the ocean, with everything around moving in slow motion. The noise and frenzy of activity didn't disturb me. Instead, it was transformed into a gentle humming vibration as it reached me. It was a peacefulness that I had not felt before, and I felt the little girl within smiling at a newfound tranquility.

I settled into my hotel room that afternoon, and was happy to relax. I continued to read some of my books that were now contributing to most of the weight of my backpack, and to write further in my journal. As I turned to the next new page in my journal, I smiled at the full page Lily had taken to write her note to me, *"When you get "there"—there will be a there there!"* In that moment, I was reminded of the rhyme my traveling companions and I had created on one of the earlier treks, "This is where we are, 'cos this is where we've come, and that's what we're here for!" In other words, *be* where you are, live in the moment, see all that is within you.

I started to write in my journal, *"What do I want from this time away, now that my mind is in its own company, now that I am 'here'?"*

I continued writing, *"I want to discover people—I have always been closed to people, untrusting, seeing the worst, but there must be good within if we are all part of the same whole. I want to go to places every day that give me goosebumps—to see amazing national parks, enormous flowing waterfalls, horizons that never end. I want to discover unfamiliar places and explore new places in me. I want to find hidden places and walk on the edge of comfort!"*

My writing continued, *"All we really have is what we hold within us—the thoughts we keep, the 'goosebumps' we experience, the mindfulness that we have, our intentions, our memories, our dreams, our hopes, our aspirations, our desires. What we hold within us and what we let go become the fibers of our being. How we weave these together, determines if we create a tangled mess, or a piece of art. I want to create art!"*

With almost 3,000 miles to cross ahead of us, I decided I would approach each day, each new mile, with a simple mindset, *"Pause in awe. Feel the goosebumps, enjoy the mystery, create art, let the search reveal itself."*

## MOMENTS OF PAUSE

1.  What are you searching for in life? Are you searching so much that there is no time for the mystery to emerge?

2.  From where and from whom do you gain insights into the meaning and mystery of life? What have been your greatest insights into life?

3.  What are the things in life that you "mind," and would like to speak of, but about which you remain silent?

4.  How do you make each moment an opportunity to evolve?

5.  What are the essential things in your life? What are the things of greatest consequence in your life?

6. What are the things you are holding onto that may only be false hopes, distracting you from your greater purpose? What are your deepest and most meaningful dreams and desires?

7. What are the things that bring you closer to others? What are the things that make you feel "connected" to a greater humanity?

8. What are the moments that have filled you with the greatest awe? What are the moments that have given you goosebumps? How often do you pause to do "awe-aerobics"? Can you pause more often?

9. Which things in your life send you fleeing to a fantasy world? Which things in your life keep you grounded in a purposeful reality?

## MORE MOMENTS FOR YOU

_____

_____

_____

_____

_____

_____

_____

_____

_____

_____

_____

# Nine

# We Don't Have to be Just Sheep!

*"It takes courage to grow up and become who you really are."*

—E.E. CUMMINGS

THE MOMENTS THAT GREET US on our journeys give us precious choices to determine our own unique path. We can leap courageously, uninhibited and unconfined, to become all that we can be.

Zion National Park in Utah was the next stop along our trek. The thought of being once again amidst vast open spaces filled me with a wondrous excitement of a child. The national park was known, in particular, for its breathtaking towering orange-black canyon gorge called Zion Narrows.

According to our trek guide, some of the canyon walls in the Narrows rose fifteen hundred feet, and some were only twenty feet apart. The hike through the canyon was said to be spectacular, with the entire hike being done by wading through the river that runs through the gorge. The biggest danger of the hike was unanticipated flash flooding, but apparently, the weather forecast was clear for our day in Zion.

We had the option to hike Zion Narrows, or to explore some of the other paths through the park. My choice was the Narrows, despite everyone else opting to walk the dirt paths rather than wading through a river with the slight possibility of an unexpected flash flood. I had come all this way—my spirit guides were not going to abandon me now!

The van dropped me at the entrance to the trail that led to the Narrows. Surprisingly, there was no one in sight, and as the van drove off, I smiled as I felt a familiarity to the scene when the ferry had left me on Salt Spring Island.

As I made my way along the trailhead that led to the Narrows, I had that wonderful sensation of being completely alone in a new world. The sounds around seemed to bounce off the canyon walls in the near distance and fill every step with the whistling of hidden birds, the brisk movements through the bushes from unidentified creatures, and the rustling of leaves through the surrounding trees.

Soon enough, the trail turned into a more structured path leading through the canyon walls that now surrounded me in every direction. After about half an hour, a few people appeared, and as the number of people continued to grow, there seemed to be a congregation ahead halting my free-flowing pace. As I approached, I realized why—this was the beginning of the famous Zion Narrows. The picturesque Riverside Walk led to the viewing area that enabled visitors to watch the river as it flowed down through the massive canyons. The scene was one of those moments of awe that brought goosebumps at the size and grandeur of the vibrant orange canyons, and the splashing aqua waters that flowed through them.

As beautiful as the canyons were from the viewing area, I couldn't wait to jump in and make friends with this world-renowned feature of nature, and feel its currents flow all around me. I picked up a long branch by the side of the path that had been left behind as a walking stick by an earlier hiker, and climbed down into the river.

The chill of the water was immediate and took me by surprise, but it was a refreshing and exhilarating surprise. The water at that point was only about two feet high, and the pebbled canyon bottom and splashing current, made each initial step more than a slight challenge. But I was determined to explore the gorge, and soon enough, I found my rhythm and I was off and around the first winding wall of the canyon. Around the first turn, I stopped, completely still and silent in my tracks.

In front of me was a scene of grandeur that struck me with so much awe that I literally couldn't move. My breath leapt away. Every ounce of energy and movement was sucked out of me. As I finally gasped a breath, I felt energy fill me that was like a thousand stars bursting into light. It was a kind of energy that penetrates every atom in your body—every fiber, every molecule—and sets off a chain reaction that flows through you and transforms every cell.

Looking up at the vast sky-scraping orange-black walls of the canyons bursting with lush greenery and watery falls, the milky turquoise water cascading around the emerging rocks and now rising to my hips, I was captured by these forces and content to be held there. The warm embrace of the universe was as real and secure as any embrace I had felt. The canyons and rivers had a life to them as real as any living being. In places of the greatest solitude, I was finding moments of the most extraordinary and uplifting company.

With the canyons rising far above me, I felt my capacity to feel expand beyond limits. I felt my emotional barriers overpowered—like a powerful spirit holding me in limbo, imparting its essence into my soul and moving my being into a heightened state of sensitivity, able to absorb every aspect of magical awe. I felt humbled at the interaction with the forces of the universe that, in a moment, had transformed every sense in my being. I felt the strength and power of the canyons find a home in my soul.

I reflected, *"If every atom in our universe is connected, if we are one with all things, stemming from the same creation, then the potential of those atoms of creation that lie within each of us, is there—latent potential beneath our surface, just waiting for that catalyst to spark a chain reaction and unleash an energy that can transcend us beyond our limits. Maybe there is a reason we cannot determine the outer edges of the universe around us. If we are a microcosm of all that is around us, maybe therein lies a simple message—there are no limits.*

*"Each of us is a vast and infinite abundance of transformational energy, waiting for a connection to trigger that 'big bang,' that gasp, those goosebumps, which take us beyond our current self and on a path to our greatest self—to our greatest life. The mystery unfolding."*

I wandered the trail for about two hours before turning and heading back to the trailhead in time to meet the trek van. The entire gorge was filled with unbelievably grand scenes that one would normally only see in a National Geographic photography book. In these moments, I was walking through the midst of the book, turning each winding corner like turning another page to reveal the next awe-inspiring scene. By the time I reached the trailhead, the book of images and the moments of awe were imbedded timelessly in my consciousness. So too, was the embrace of the universe amidst the solitude of the canyons that once again reinforced that we are constantly in the presence of our own infinite and ultimate self, just waiting to be unleashed, with the arms of the universe ready to hold us steady.

Our next stop, the Grand Canyon, was to be literally an "on the edge of comfort" experience. One of the seven natural wonders of the world, images of the vast Grand Canyon stretch around the world, and that was evident from the range of tourists visiting the site.

We arrived at the Grand Canyon in time to see one of the most magical moments in the canyon—the sunset. I was looking forward to arriving at the rim of the canyon and finding a place of solitude to enjoy this wonder. As we pulled near the parking area of the rim shortly before sunset, one might have thought that a rock star was about to perform a concert—there were cars and people everywhere—hardly the serene and peaceful scene I envisioned. I sighed, not wanting at all to be surrounded by thousands of bustling tourists trying to gain access to the same best vantage point to watch the setting sun. Unfortunately, there was no obvious alternative in sight.

After eventually finding parking, we made our way through the busy lot to the rim that was filled from left to right, as far as I could see, with people six to ten deep. Our group of eight finally found a spot through which to squeeze. We jostled together to create a small clearing in front of the rope that was the barrier between the rim and the rocky descent out to the edge of the canyon.

In that moment, a flash of a *Far Side* cartoon came to me that for many years had sat on my corporate office desk back in Australia. The cartoon showed one sheep leaping up out of a flock of sheep, his hoofs outstretched in the air, shouting, "Wait! Wait! Listen to me! ... We don't HAVE to be just sheep!"

I felt uncomfortably like a sheep standing along the rim with the stretch of rope keeping us all herded together. It's quite remarkable how programmed we sometimes become to do what we are told to do, without question. One small line of rope, thousands and thousands of people, content to be herded.

Now I'm not advocating anarchy, by any means, and certainly many barriers are put in place for our own protection. However, the gift of being sentient beings and not merely sheep, gives us the wonderful ability, in any moment, to choose for our *self*.

With that in mind, my senses overcame me, and over the rope I jumped! I must say, it did become clear why the rope was there. The hard-packed trail along the rim quickly turned to loosely packed dirt and rubble on the other side of the rope, and started to descend fairly rapidly to large boulders below that led out to a peak of one of the canyon walls. That was the spot that had called to me to jump the rope. Luckily I was wearing my sturdy Australian Blundstone outback boots, and I was able to get my footing with some concentrated effort.

As my traveling companions called me back, I kept focused on the peak of the canyon, which was now only about fifty feet away. However, there was some obviously challenging navigating to be done with careful footing, in order to reach that idyllic spot at the peak. As pebbles fell beneath me and rolled down the side of the canyon wall, I became quite aware that I was probably doing something quite dangerous. Nonetheless, the adventure drew me onward, with a sense that I would make it just fine, and the thought that the sunset was going to be spectacular from my place of solitude!

The peak where the canyon walls converged was only about six feet wide, and as I approached, I could see the peak was like an inverted nose that returned sharply inward below the ledge of the peak. There must have been only about ten feet of rock below the ledge before it jutted back into the canyon wall below.

Finally, I was almost there. I crouched low to navigate the final few feet to the edge—knowing, despite my positive mental self-talk, that a little slip would end my journey very quickly, and the mystery of life would soon become the mystery of the afterlife! With my butt firmly on the ledge, I inched out farther and hung my legs over the edge. As I tilted my body forward, tingles rang through me like thunder, and my head was as light as air. Vertigo took over as the vast drop of 7,000 feet hung below me.

Tilting my head back to the upright position, I felt my blood start to circulate more smoothly. The vertigo dissipated, and I felt as though I was sitting next to the clouds, ready to feel the sunset from a place that seemed as if it were an alien planet. The canyons spread out in front of me for as far as I could see—as though this canyon world was once again stretching out to meet the setting sun, as it had done for almost two billion years. Yes, I was sitting on two billion years of the earth's existence. If ever I had felt humbled, it was now.

I couldn't even fathom two billion years. It certainly puts our lifetime into a different perspective—a flash of time. As I was engulfed in the yellow, orange, and pink light of the sunset reflecting off the canyons all around, I couldn't help but wonder what type of light we cast in our flash of time on this earth. The warm light of the sun reached far in every direction, revealing so many aspects of each canyon that were otherwise hidden in the shadows of the walls. What was revealed in the mystery of the walls was beauty and complexity, resting quietly, waiting to emerge and add further awe to a scene already filled with awe. Endless awe—just waiting to be revealed.

I recalled the badge that Trudy the bag lady wore, "Let's be a no limit species!" As I looked out over the canyons, I contemplated, *"With so many moments of endless awe that have existed for billions of years, that surround us now, and that will continue past our lifetimes, we are already part of a no limit species. We just need to let the light reveal that within us, and live like a no limit species! We don't HAVE to be just sheep!"*

Ironically, we are often our own herders. We too often stay safely tucked into the flock. Our protection mechanisms are like cattle dogs that come to herd us back to the flock if we start to move to the edges. Yet it is at the edges that we start to experience our individuality, our uniqueness, our creative distinctiveness, our outer limits. We can pull away from the flock and step onto our own path that can enlighten us, rather than enslave us.

On the edges, there is imminent danger, but there is vast discovery. The danger can be overcome by care, by awareness, by consciousness—by making sure we have solid footing. Is there greater danger to our soul by stepping out to the edges with care and consciousness to discover our unlimited potential, or by staying tucked into the flock, being herded to the next destination, unaware?

Why do we seek the "safety" of the flock? Ironically, when we step out to the edge, we are in our own hands, and the arms of the universe. When we stay in the flock, we are in the hands of others. Who do we trust more to provide "safety"—our own self, the universe, the higher powers and spirits that surround us; or those that maintain the herd?

Stepping out is uncomfortable, but it is also exhilarating. It is unknown, but it is a gateway to freedom. We each have our pain, and sometimes the first step is simply stepping away. We can't begin to find our *self* if we are lost, consumed, and paralyzed by pain and fear.

When I left home at seventeen, I was full of fear, but I needed to break free from the fear that had paralyzed me throughout my childhood. I didn't know what would be next. I just knew that I needed to do something to break free. All I could do was take that first step, knowing that it would get me away from my father and the physical and mental pain that was a part of every day.

At that time, I didn't have any money put aside. I was a "checkout chick" at a local grocery store, and earning the minimum wage. A few months prior, I had dropped out of the university course I had started after finishing school, so I could work full-time at the grocery store to support living away from home. I could pay my rent, I could save some money. I could be in my own space. I could breathe.

I remember the first night I slept in "my own space." There was a calmness. For the first time, I didn't have to worry about the sound of the door handle turning, knowing it was my father coming to get his prey. I didn't have to feel his stare across the dinner table.

Whatever uncertainty lay ahead, it wasn't worse than what I was leaving behind. That step was the only step I felt I could take to set me on a path to freedom.

When I left Australia at thirty, likewise, I didn't know what lay ahead. I had a plane ticket that took me from continent to continent, but no time frame, no specific destinations in mind, no specific experiences I was seeking. In a way, it was similar to when I left home at seventeen. I was trying to break free.

This time, I was trying to break free from a world I had created, but which only kept me prisoner. I managed to create a world away from my father, but I ended up filling it with meaningless things in order to fill it with "something" that would make me feel some sense of "living"—whatever that was.

I had climbed the corporate ladder in various organizations to try to feel "accomplished." I had my choice of company cars in which I could try to feel "clean and new." I had been able to save and buy an apartment to try to feel secure. But I had become trapped in a world full of things that I had pulled together to hold my world together. I had become my own herder.

By creating a world where I felt "safe," I had created a world where there was no *me*. I felt like a sheep in a flock. I felt like a "cog in a wheel," despite the six-figure salary, despite the company car. Once again, I felt the need to step out in order to find freedom, and to find my soul—to find something that felt *real*, that felt purposeful, that felt like I was here for a reason. I needed to feel that I was something more than someone else's "tool." I wanted to discover something more unique "on the edge," rather than surviving in the flock.

The only option was to once again, step out into the unknown, to leave the flock, to leave the certainty and the "security" behind, to venture into unknown spaces—no matter how uncertain and fearful it felt—and to see what the universe would reveal. It would end up revealing so much more than I could have ever imagined, and the fear would be left behind as something much more powerful filled its place.

Arriving at Monument Valley was a surreal experience. It was like a place lost in time. The vast red desert stretched to the horizon, filled with rich orange sandstone rock formations reaching to the heavens in a grand array of shapes and sizes. Each monument seemed to have a life and story of its own after surviving more than fifty million years of land shifts, weathering, and erosion. It was like a forest of enormous sculptures rising up from the red earth. The late afternoon sun cast a deep yellow light through the valley, coating the monuments in liquid gold as though dressing the ancient stones in royal robes.

With evening near, the choice for the night was to camp at a remote and primitive camping area that overlooked the canyons, or to have an evening with cowboys at a local cowboy-themed campground, complete with a rib barbecue, and a lasso and whip demonstration. The choice was easy for me—the quiet campground overlooking the canyons. The rest of the group was attracted to the barbecue and amenities at the cowboy camping ground rather than the canyon camping site that had no amenities whatsoever. I would be having crackers and canned tuna again for dinner tonight, and was more than happy with that simplicity.

It was about 5:00PM when the van pulled up to the camping site—a wonderfully deserted semi-cleared area at the end of an unpaved dirt road that overlooked the valley. The primitive and empty camping area was a stark contrast to the surrounding endless stretch of desert filled with monuments in every direction. I couldn't wait to jump out of the van and pitch my tent. The awesome scene lured two Polish girls from our trek to stay for the evening, and we all leapt from the van, eager to experience a night of magical solitude under the stars.

As I looked around for a place to pitch my tent, there were several spots on the edge of the clearing that provided an uninterrupted view of the monuments rising through the valley. My Polish friends pitched their tent about thirty feet away. Soon we were joined by Sam, an older gentleman, traveling alone; and then by a middle-aged couple, Ellen and Larry. The clearing was perfectly sized for us to be far enough apart and in our own space, while also enjoying the quiet company of strangers in this magically remote and deserted place.

The sunset was spectacularly beautiful with all the colors of the red and yellow spectrum cast over the valley and reflecting off the monuments that rose hundreds of feet from the valley floor. The East and West Mittens and Merrick Butte, three of the most well recognized monuments, stood directly in our view, and were kept company by surrounding monuments, each as ominous as the next.

The intense spirituality of the valley was striking. It was immediately apparent why the valley is a place of immense reverence for the Navajo people, who believe the valley is a place touched by Holy Beings. The monuments are believed to be trails left by the gods, or are themselves, gods frozen in time, rising each day to talk and pray to the gods of other realms. Some say The Mittens represent hands left behind by the gods, symbolizing that the gods will one day return and rule from this place, hence why it is sacred land.

To the Navajo people, life is a learning experience for each of us to reach a higher state, and the land and nature are full of opportunities to gain insight and knowledge. Each day is an opportunity to search one's surroundings for knowledge of life, and to acquire balance and harmony with all that is around. These monolithic monuments were an obvious testament to the Navajo beliefs—seemingly individual and independent structures abrasively breaking through the valley, yet interdependent parts of a whole, each a part of a journey, each with its own distinctiveness.

The learning to which I had become accustomed, was learning through books, removed from the direct experience of a life that I was fearful to experience. The books from which I had gained insight such as *The Celestine Prophecy, The Alchemist*, Buddhist literature, and other "self awareness" reading, had opened my mind to new mysteries. Yet here, I was directly immersed in those mysteries. The touch of the energy was as real as the touch of the pages of a book. Like Alice in Wonderland, I felt transported into a dream-like place filled with mysterious creatures and surreal experiences. There was no fear here.

As the darkness settled in and the stars emerged in the sky, the monuments seemed to move with the light, as though they were stretching from the stillness of the day and coming to life. The valley filled with an energy as living as each of us watching the scene.

An enormous full moon started to rise above the horizon, and with it, the winds picked up without warning. Within minutes, the wind had built into a fierce windstorm, whirling through the camping area. The force was so strong that I was sure my tent was going to be uplifted and carried off into the night sky. As the moon seemed to find its place casting its full light over the valley, the winds subsided—as though they had finished their work of helping to lift the moon into its proper place. It seemed as though we had witnessed the day giving birth to the evening, and now all was still and in awe of the creation that had emerged. The light of the full moon cast a pure white blanket across the valley, as it hovered like a protector over its children.

Reflecting on "the search," it seemed that we didn't need to search for the mystery to be revealed at all—it is present and right in front of us, flowing all around us, and filling us with experiences of grandeur and insight. To be filled with the powerful uplifting of the winds and the peaceful light of the full moon was transforming. It was beyond the pages of any book. No words necessary. No pages to turn. No meaning to consider. Just to feel. Just to be.

I turned to see my tent, to my delight, still intact. However, staying inside my tent was suddenly no longer appealing. The magic of the valley and the light of the full moon led me to find a sleeping place in one of the rock shelves that led down to the valley floor. The rock shelves looked like nature's perfect beds.

I climbed a little way down the side of the cliff, and packed my sleeping bag into one of the small shelves that was just long enough for me to stretch along. As I nestled into the crevasse, I felt like a butterfly wrapped in my own little cocoon. The white blanket of the moon cast another layer over me. I felt a sense of breathing in time with the monuments, and as at home as I had ever felt. Once again, I felt in awe of all that was around that reminds us that we are part of such an extraordinary state of being with the universe, with so much magical potential.

I knew I couldn't come to such extraordinary places every day, but I did know that I could create extraordinary spaces in each day to experience the magic of the moment.

We each have the opportunity every day to create those magical spaces. We can pause and feel our potential and our divine connection with the powerful energies that are flowing around us and through us in each moment. We can pause and allow the winds to penetrate us, absorb the glow of the moonlight, radiate in the light of the stars, and know that we are intimately a part of those forces. We have unlimited ability to transform that energy to become our unlimited self. We have the ability to step out and to choose our own path. Therein lies the journey—the journey to our greatest self, the journey to live our greatest life.

As I looked out at The Mittens cloaked in the white blanket of the moon, and still reaching up to the stars, the two monuments reminded me of the outstretched hands of the sheep reaching into the air, *"We don't have to be just sheep!"*

The paradox hit me as I looked at the monuments, which seemed lonely in the night. *"How do we step away from the flock, find our unique distinctiveness, walk our own path, while not ending up isolated, like a lonely monument in the night?"*

My journey was bringing me much closer to "me," and more connected to the "universe," but the thought of connecting to people still felt foreign, superficial, and untrusted. Away from "the flock," I was finding my *self*, but I knew I ultimately had to find a connection back to people. I didn't want to remain isolated, but it was all I knew, and it was the only space in which I felt safe.

I had discovered through my journey that there is a connection that flows through everything. There is awe emanating from all things. We just need to pause long enough to feel it, and stay long enough to experience it.

Maybe I would find a space along my journey that would cause me to pause to find that connection with people—a space that would somehow enable me to find a way to exist in peace with my *self*, and exist in peace with people. Maybe there was a path where I could not only step away from the flock to continually discover new outer limits, but also to find a purposeful connection to humanity.

That possibility seemed to be one that was universal as I looked across the monument-filled valley. Imagine a world where we could all reach our greatest heights, thriving in our own uniqueness, yet feeling part of a connected and purposeful whole. That possibility awaits us in each moment. We just need to draw on the courage within us, and step onto our most authentic and purposeful path that takes us to all that we can be; on a journey to our greatest self, to our greatest life.

## MOMENTS OF PAUSE

1.  What latent potential lies beneath your surface?

2.  What images do you have of your "ultimate self"? What does your "ultimate self" look like?

3.  What experiences have pushed you to the edge of your "comfort zone"? What did you discover there?

4. When do you feel as if you are part of a flock, herded by others? When do you feel you are breaking away from the flock to discover your own "authentic" path? What has that path revealed to you? What unique and unlimited potential did you discover?

5. What would being a "no limit species" look like to you?

6. How do you exist in peace with your *self*? How do you exist in peace with others? What is your most purposeful connection to your *self* and to humanity?

## MORE MOMENTS FOR YOU

Ten

# The Darkness and the Light Within

*"Faith is the bird that feels the light and sings
when the dawn is still dark."*

—Rabindranath Tagore

THE DEPTHS WITHIN US can be the source of our greatest and most exhilarating desires, but also home to our deepest and most hidden fears. If Zion Narrows, the Grand Canyon, and Monument Valley were insights into all of the awe and spectacular wonder that exists around us, the next stop on our trek, Carlsbad Caverns in New Mexico, was to be an insight into the mix of darkness and light that lies beneath our surfaces.

Oscar Wilde warned, "Those who go beneath the surface do so at their peril." When we search deep within, we may come face to face with the worst of our experiences. We may unlock memories that we have buried so that we might never need to confront them. Yet in order to see the light, one must know the darkness. If we are not brave enough to see the deepest and darkest parts of our *self*, we can never be daring enough to take our *self* beyond our farthest outer limits.

I believe it is one of those inevitable aspects of the sentient human condition—that opposites must exist for either to exist. Like *yin* and *yang*—the seemingly opposite forces that are, in fact, interdependent and interconnected, giving rise to each other, effect after effect. Like jumping on a trampoline, the deeper one can create a downward spring, the higher one can catapult upward. If there is no depth, there is no height. Like Newton's third law of motion, for every force in nature, there is an equal and opposite force.

Without the honest and uninhibited search for that which is deep within us, the search for that which is around us can only be superficial and frivolous—an endless pursuit of the next "thing" that takes us nowhere. Answers cannot be found around us, because we haven't yet discovered the answers that lie within us. We cannot be catapulted toward our highest self, because we run in the same circles, on the same plane. We keep our *self* in shackles in our self-made prison.

We crave safe spaces in order to avoid the pain that is hidden in the depths. But spaces that only create a fragile and temporary false reality are not safe—they are shattered by the smallest pebble.

As Buddhist monk, Pema Chodron, tells us, "What keeps us unhappy and stuck in a limited view of reality is our tendency to seek pleasure and avoid pain, to seek security and avoid groundlessness, to seek comfort and avoid discomfort ... We're in this zone of safety and that's what we consider life, getting it all together, security ... We fear losing our illusion of security—that's what makes us anxious ... We spend all our energy and waste our lives trying to re-create these zones of safety, which are always falling apart. That's the essence of samsara—the cycle of suffering that comes from continuing to seek happiness in all the wrong places."

According to Buddhist philosophy, the only path to happiness is through the brave exploration of the depths of our inner being. We find peacefulness by letting go of emotions that constantly pull us between highs and lows.

As I stood in front of the entrance of the cavern and looked into the depths below, I felt tingles of anxious exhilaration run through me. These are the tingles that come when we are on the edge of the unknown, about to step into the darkness, poised for discovery. More and more, I felt the universe leading me to explore the depths in order to discover my light. Each day, each of us have the opportunity to discover all that lies in the depths within us. The step is ours to take.

The dark descent into the caverns was lit only by small dim yellow lights along the pathway. The light from the world above quickly dissolved as the path wound steeply down between massive gray wrinkled canyon walls. The transition into another world was immediate. As the path flattened and widened, a huge opening revealed the breathtaking "Big Room"—a cavern chamber hundreds of feet in every direction, filled with dozens of smaller caverns, each filled with hundreds of glistening yellow and white stalactites and stalagmites of all sizes. The piercing "mites" rose from the cavern floor and fell from the ceilings, like teeth of a giant prehistoric dinosaur. Carlsbad Cavern is one of more than 300 limestone caves as part of an enormous fossil reef created by an inland ocean almost 280 million years ago, and is scattered with artifacts dating back to the ice age. One felt within the belly of an enormous, ancient dinosaur.

As I looked out across the vast chamber, loneliness seemed to linger in this dark place, coexisting with the beauty of the glistening "mites" and yellow light reflecting from the various chambers. So many thousands of formations, but all existing in isolation, without interaction or communication—static and frozen in time.

Here, the loneliness was even more striking than that which I had sensed amidst the monuments in Monument Valley. Suddenly, I felt a huge appreciation for the sentient human condition—filled with all of our senses, able to interact and grow, able to make individual choices, to explore beyond boundaries, to express, to love, to touch, to feel.

Who would be an isolated "mite," rather than a fully conscious, awakened, expressive sentient being? Yet sometimes, we live like "mites" in dark caves—isolated, cut off from our *self* and others—scared to breathe, scared to live.

I spent a great deal of my life living like an isolated "mite." It felt safe, away from any further threats. It was dark and isolated, but the darkness made me feel invisible, and I liked that because I thought it would hide me from harm. If I stayed as still as I possibly could, pretended not to exist, maybe my father would not notice me and would pass by me like a predator unaware of his hiding prey. There was no protection amongst people—they had never helped, but the darkness provided a place to hide.

The problem with existing in darkness, is that little grows, and what does grow is stunted by the darkness. The scene that lay in front of me in the cavern was once filled with life, light, color, and movement, but now it seemed like a graveyard—beautiful—but a graveyard, nonetheless. A large part of me had felt like a dark graveyard for so long.

I think we all come into this world filled with life, light, and color, but the things that happen to us can create graveyards within us. Somehow, we need to rise from the death and despair that can exist in that space. But if we don't know that space well, we can't transform it.

The evidence of those spaces within us are presented to us every day. For me, those spaces were presented through things that triggered dark thoughts and feelings—feelings that only hindered moving forward, thoughts that were only counter-productive to experiencing the potential in every day. They were triggers that generated feelings of conflict and tension, rather than contentment and peacefulness; that generated despair, rather than hope.

When I looked into the darkest parts of me, it was a scary place—and I felt that if I even started to look into those places, it would be overwhelming. It was bad enough when negative thoughts and feelings were triggered by things around me, so the thought of intentionally opening that box of nightmares and jumping into it was terrifying.

Instead of discovering and confronting all that lay within, I had spent all of my time creating false realities to distract me from my *self*. I had spent all of my energy creating "safe places" around me, but I had never discovered the safe places within me.

Before my journey, I hadn't allowed my *self* the space to feel the company of spirits. I hadn't felt the unlimited potential of being part of the awe that surrounds us. I hadn't felt the powerful uplifting of the winds or the peaceful light of the full moon. I hadn't felt the hand of the North Star, or the guidance of the compass within. I hadn't been overcome with the power of scenes filled with grandeur. Instead, I had been constantly overwhelmed trying to keep my *self* and the "safe places" I had created together.

I reflected on how long I had been trying to keep a step ahead of the demons within, and how futile and exhausting that had become. Pema Chodron's words resonated with me, "Even if we run a hundred miles an hour to the other side of the continent, we find the very same problem awaiting us when we arrive. It keeps returning with new names, forms, and manifestations until we learn whatever it has to teach us."

I couldn't continue trying to keep one step ahead—it was too consuming. I needed to stop in my shoes, stand firmly, and then leap into the darkness.

Standing in the midst of this prehistoric cavern, I felt the darkness become more familiar. A peacefulness luminesced from the hundreds of glowing stalagmites and stalactites. The dozens of chambers nestled throughout the cavern called to be explored. I felt a sense of deep calmness rising from within me and resonating with the peacefulness of the vast cavern. With that calmness, I started to feel that the things that lay within the depths of me were things I could explore, and with which I could come to peace. The feelings of fear of the darkness that was within my depths started to fade.

At the Grand Canyon, I had sat on the edge of the clouds. Here, in the cavern, I was at the depths of darkness. If the outside world is a macrocosm of our inner worlds—a mirror to all that is within—then I felt the lesson was clear, and the voice of the universe was reassuring.

*"There is no fear to have at the depths or at the heights. There is only discovery, new mysteries, new perspectives, new truths, and new states of being in which one can calmly and peacefully abide. One must step bravely into the heights, and just as bravely into the depths. Then we will find the truths that light our way."*

Standing amidst the darkness and light of the caverns, I realized I had never felt brave enough to venture into the depths of my pain and my demons. I had never paused to fill my *self* with the gifts of the universe. Now, I felt filled with the touches and the company of the universe, and ready to step into the depths to confront all that was within.

The French novelist, Marcel Proust, wrote, "We must never be afraid to go too far, for truth lies beyond." Without venturing beyond, without plunging into the depths, I knew the heights to which I would be free to soar would always be limited.

Instead of being free to soar, I had spent all of my life trying to contain the box of nightmares that I felt within. I tried to keep it buried deep enough so that it wouldn't emerge. Yet despite my efforts, pieces of the nightmare were emerging every day in ways I couldn't control—disproportionate reactions to the smallest things, intense feelings triggered by inconsequential events. I could handle the "big" things, but the "little" things would trigger the worst feelings—intense anger, hate toward people, hate toward me. The feelings of hate and anger were the most frightening. Feeling those things inside was like feeling an untamed monster who could overpower and destroy every piece of my being in any moment. The thought of unleashing that monster from its cage, looking it in the eyes, and confronting it, seemed as though it would be more self-destructive than helpful.

The problem was, I was still only just surviving, and my being felt tired and heavy from trying to contain the monster within. I could either let the monster, and all of those self-defeating feelings and thoughts, keep eating away at me, and expend all of my energy trying to suppress them; or I could deal with them on my terms. I could dig into those depths, look the monster in the eyes, let all of those feelings rise, be present with them, and then let them fall.

Over the years, I did all that I could do to create a "safe" and "stable" reality in which to exist. I tried to keep away from the things that stirred memories, or that confronted me in a way that triggered those negative thoughts and feelings.

The steps I took to create a safe space around me were things I needed to do to gain some sense of control. Yet until I found those safe spaces within me, I was only building a fragile house of cards that could fall in any moment.

Moving out of home as soon as I could was a big step toward creating my new reality. It was an enormous relief, but at the same time, it was deeply sad because it meant, in particular, leaving my younger ten-year-old brother, with whom I was very close. My younger brother had been a bright light in the darkness. He helped me survive. I could give him all of my love and attention—he represented all that was good and pure. He was so little, so innocent. Leaving him was leaving the most precious thing in the world.

I stepped out of the life of my family, because I couldn't stay in it without being destroyed. If I visited, my father was always there, still seeming like a predator waiting to pounce. Neither my brothers, nor my mother, knew why I left and why I stayed away. To them, I think, I had abandoned, disregarded, and forgotten them. The pain of that isolation was always with me. My survival meant disconnecting, but disconnecting only made me feel more cold and isolated, more unworthy, more inconsequential, more as though my existence was a mistake.

I wish someone, anyone, would have asked, *"Why?"* Children and teenagers don't turn their back on love and family without a reason, and that reason isn't usually something created by the child—that is just not the way the human condition is "wired." Why are we so afraid to ask, *"Why?"* What is within our own depths, of which we are so afraid?

Changing my last name was another step toward a new "reality." The last thing I wanted was to carry my father's name. Every time I looked at my name, I was reminded of him, and that was a daily reminder I didn't want.

Soon after my twenty-first birthday, I started to look for a new last name. I didn't have any criteria except finding something that "felt" right. Given that my natural heritage included a mix of French and Scandinavian, I favored something that had a touch of either of those origins. More importantly, I just wanted something that I had chosen for me. I wanted to be reminded of a fresh start every time I saw my new name.

One day while I was in my college library with a friend, I came upon the name "Anderson" in the library catalogue while I was looking through possible names with a friend. My friend liked it. I liked it. It started with "A," which for me, represented the beginning. But I also wanted something a little unique, so I changed the last "o" for an "e," and "Andersen" became the name I chose.

Three days before my twenty-second birthday, my change of name became effective, and Kathy Andersen was born. I felt cleansed. I felt as though I had erased an ugly tattoo that had revolted me for so long. Leaving my father's name behind was an important step I needed to take for me in moving forward and leaving the past behind. The decision to change my name, however, also came with further isolation. To my mother and brothers, my change of name was further evidence that I didn't want or need to be a part of the family. Nothing could have been further from the truth.

Throughout that time, I continued to believe that it was better for my family to think the worst of me, rather than to know the reality of the man they called "father" and "husband." Knowing the truth, I thought, would have only destroyed the family and created so much pain, especially for my mother. I wasn't prepared to deal with that responsibility. I couldn't go through that. I thought I would be just fine without them knowing, so I decided it was better not to destroy anyone else's life. I hoped that over time, they might put my actions down to my experiencing "growing-up stuff," and that maybe in the future, our relationships would somehow heal themselves.

The problem with hiding the truth to protect the people we love, is that so much gets missed in maintaining a "false reality." Relationships and experiences between people become superficial. There is a limit to the depth of the relationship because there is a limit to the "relation" that a person can feel with another. The basis of a "relationship" is the ability to "relate." If we don't know the depths of a person, we can only relate to that person at a certain level. There is little revelation, little discovery. We help each other maintain a status-quo.

Within the false reality, the opportunity to help each other grow authentically through the frailties and realities of the human condition is lost. The opportunity to celebrate each other is lost, because we don't really know each other. We limit our ability to become fully aware, to become fully compassionate toward our *self* and others. We lose the opportunity to draw strength and to be inspired. We lose sight that we are part of a collective whole, each able to help one another—the whole greater than the sum of its parts. Instead, we become isolated, like "mites" in a dark cavern. The "protection" that we seek to provide only acts to create another prison. The truth, no matter how "ugly," is the only key that can unlock our soul and set us free.

Every day I had felt as though I was living in a prison of secrecy and silence. I was closed off from my family, and my friendships were never deep friendships. Keeping the truth a secret only served to keep me more isolated. Each day was consumed with maintaining the false reality—with faking a smile to cover screams, with pleasant conversation to try to conceal a rage of anger, with forced kindness to hide depths of resentment, and with a gesture of care when I didn't really care about anything. My entire being became fake—a "made-up" way of being just to get through each day.

The thing is, people can typically pick up on a fake smile, on superficial conversation, and on signals that indicate there isn't much authenticity behind the person in front of them. I was full of those signals because I felt fake and meaningless. I was often called "cold" and "aloof," and I went through life wearing those labels. There seemed no way to even begin to explain all that was behind the mask.

During the years after I left home, I think my family increasingly thought of me as "cold and aloof" because of the distance I kept, and the apparent lack of care I showed toward anything happening in the family. I didn't go to family events, I didn't call often, and I generally just stayed away.

In the eyes of my family, I'm sure my cold-heartedness culminated during the time when my father was dying of cancer. Several years after I left home, my father was diagnosed with terminal cancer. I had absolutely no compassion for him during that time. My family, of course, didn't understand why I wouldn't visit "my poor father" during a long year of deterioration.

To me, there was no point to seeing him. I had already killed him in my mind many years before, and I wasn't the least interested in allowing him to think he could leave this life with my forgiveness, or with any sense of resolution. I was working on resolving what I needed to resolve for me on my path. He would have to work out his resolutions in whatever afterlife to which he might be headed. I wasn't interested in being a part of that. I had no sense of feeling that I needed to be a part of that.

When he died, I remember standing over his body at the hospital after my mother had asked for me to come. I remember looking at him, feeling as though I was looking at a pathetic, useless lump of flesh. *"Bastard,"* I thought. *"I'm glad you suffered so much and knew you were dying."* Then, for a moment, I felt a thought come over me that I should tell him that I forgive him, that I should tell him to rest in peace—my Catholic upbringing was echoing that was the right thing to do. I also didn't want to be captured in negative thoughts. I was trying to escape those thoughts and move on. So I looked at him, and let the words come, "I forgive you. Rest in peace." I left the room, but rather than feeling resolved, I felt betrayed by the words I had spoken.

*"Are you kidding?"* I thought. I wasn't ready to forgive him. I was still so full of anger and hate toward him. I hadn't yet found a way to let that go. I was glad that he was dead. I was glad I would

never have to feel his stare again, or think about what I would do if I ever saw him again. I felt relieved. It wasn't in my heart to send him off to the afterlife with peaceful thoughts.

I went back into the room, walked up beside him in his death bed, and looked at him as though I was staring right into his soul. "I don't forgive you. You're an asshole. Rot in hell," and I walked away.

At his funeral, I was noticeably unaffected by his death. As I watched his coffin move along the belt into the furnace at the crematorium, I felt as though I was merely watching trash move into a burner. I felt that things were the way they should be. Trash removed.

I felt bad for my younger brother. He was only fifteen, and he saw his father as any fifteen-year-old would—as a wonderful dad. For my mother, I felt sad. She had done her best to be a wonderful mother and wife. Yet it seemed that she didn't receive much warmth or laughter from her husband, despite her being such a happy and vibrant person. Given his abuse of me, I wondered if he was a human being capable of giving her the love or relationship that she needed or deserved.

I couldn't help but start to think that maybe my mother and I shared a common abuser, just in a different way.

That thought was the start of my thinking that maybe one day there might be a point to telling my mother what happened. Maybe we shared a pain that had kept us apart, but that could be a bridge to each other, and to healing. Yet that thinking was much too hypothetical to risk all of the emotional upheaval and confrontation it could bring. So I cast the thought of telling my mother way back into a box, and locked it.

It is only now, twenty years later, that I feel there is a "greater good" to telling my mother, and that is to write this book in the hope of helping others. Through writing this book, I have also come to accept that if I want to have a truly authentic relationship with my mother, she needs to know my truths, and I need to know hers.

It is also through writing this book, that more than ever, I believe truth only comes from truth. If we can't be strong enough to hold and nurture each other's truths, then what is the purpose of a loving relationship? How can we possibly select which truths to share and which to hide? That is a choice already filled with predetermined judgments.

Surely, the unconditional love that we are each worthy of receiving, and each capable of giving, is about loving without selecting which pieces of someone's truth we accept or don't accept, and which parts of our truths we share or hide.

We each can be the light that shines on each other's hidden truths and brings them out of the darkness, so the power of secrecy is lost. We each can help each other walk through our darkness and emerge from it, simply by sharing and accepting our truths.

After a while, a secret becomes a lie, because it covers our truths. As long as we keep our secret, we can't *be* our truth. We can't act our truth. We can't speak our truth. We can't live our truth. We become a false persona to keep the truth safely buried, to protect the lie.

When I finally came to share my truth with my brothers and tell them of the abuse, I had reached a point where I was tired of maintaining the lie. I was tired of making excuses as to why I had cared so little about my father when I "should have been so grateful for all he did for me." It was as though his adopting me was constant evidence that he was such a wonderful, selfless person. I was tired of being judged. I wanted an opportunity to have a relationship with my brothers that included their understanding and accepting the truth of what happened to me. I needed to turn the darkness and guilt that I felt about the things I did for me, into a lightness that came from accepting that I did what I needed to do to take care of me.

More than anything, I needed to set my *self* free from the persona the lie had created. I needed my brothers to know that I wasn't the cold sister they must have thought I was. In absence of knowing the truth, they could only know me so well. They certainly couldn't understand me, or understand anything that had happened. They couldn't understand why I was so distant, or why I changed my name, or why I was so cold to my father—why I didn't visit him while he was dying, and why I didn't cry at his funeral.

I especially wanted my younger brother to understand, because I felt I had abandoned him when I left home, and that he must have thought I just forgot about him. He didn't know that one of the hardest parts of every day after I left home was feeling as though I had walked out of his life, even though it was to try to save my own. At the time, I just didn't know what else to do. He was only ten years old and idolized his father, like any ten-year-old boy. What was I supposed to tell him?

Six years after my father's death, my truth came out to my brothers. I hadn't planned it, but circumstances brought it to the surface at a family barbecue. It started with a simple conversation, and before long, the topic turned to my father. I finally felt that I just couldn't go through another of the same conversations about how wonderful he was, and how nice it would be if he were here.

In a few passing moments, a thousand thoughts went through my head, and a thousand feelings raced through my heart at the thought of telling what happened—at the thought of finally revealing my truth. I was terrified, but I was also numb. I had so many conflicting feelings—guilt, shame, embarrassment, fear, sadness, hope, pointlessness. What if they didn't believe me? Did I care anyway? Was it more important to tell my truth or keep silent and maintain the status quo? Was it worth it to risk the relationships I had with my brothers? Were those relationships real without the truth anyway?

In those moments, a thousand emotions collided. It was as if a switch were flicked inside me, and the words just came out.

"There was a reason that I never got along with him," the voice came as if it were someone else's, "He sexually abused me for all of my childhood."

Silence.

My older brother turned his head slightly, with a somewhat bewildered look on his face. His movements seemed to be in slow motion. I was expecting him to question me. I expected he wouldn't believe me. Instead, I felt an equally bewildered look upon my face, when he simply said, "Wow, now I understand why you were like you were." My younger brother nodded his head with affirmation.

I was struck by their acceptance.

*"Would it have been so simple to say those words so many years ago, and to have everything end?"* I thought. That was an impossible question. I think when you are living through the nightmare, you are so consumed by just surviving each moment, each day. More so, I think you live in the hope that the next day the nightmare will end, if you just hold on and keep quiet for long enough.

I spoke to my brothers about my wanting to tell our mother, and my fear that telling her would only cause her pain for no purpose. My brothers agreed that telling our mother would devastate her, and that there was no point to her knowing. They had seen that over the years my mother and I had developed a nice relationship. She had probably put my behavior down to my simply going through "things" that teenagers go through. At the time, I was content to accept that. Over the years, I continued to believe that compromise was justified.

Today, twenty years later, I'm not content to decide what truths I tell and which I don't.

The only way I can walk through the world and feel that I am honoring my *self*, and honoring those in my life, is to speak my truths fully. The only way I can step forward is to have faith that the strength of the love around me and within me, will outweigh the sometimes painful journey toward truth and authenticity that we must travel with our *self* and with the ones we love.

The Buddha said, "There are only two mistakes one can make along the road to truth; not going all the way, and not starting." It had taken a long time for me to start to discover and speak my truths. Now that I was on that journey, I felt compelled to keep going all the way. I knew that telling my mother would be a part of that journey. Writing this book has led me to that point on my journey. That revelation will take us both to places of darkness, but I believe that it will ultimately create light for both of us.

The movement and vibrancy of New Orleans, the next stop on our trek, was a vivid contrast to the caves and canyons of the desert. In less than a day, we were transported from the natural and easy solitude of Mother Nature to an over-the-top party town filled with twenty-four hour bars, party poppers, and endless chains of Mardi Gras beads. It seemed that everyone was celebrating something here—in this seemingly timeless "Carnival." There were clearly characters in this town—living and dead, it would seem—if you were to venture on one of the ghost tours.

Arriving on Bourbon Street in the heart of the infamous "French Quarter," one didn't quite know where to start. Every bar seemed to call to passers-by, with sounds of the south spilling into the streets, and with each establishment over-flowing with very merry patrons. There were sounds of classic jazz and blues, old style washboard jazz, piano bars that would play you any tune you wanted to hear, and karaoke bars that would give you a stage to sing any song you wanted to sing.

Walking along Bourbon Street, I felt as though the magical fortune-telling machine, "Zoltar Speaks," from the Tom Hanks movie *Big* would be tucked away around the next corner asking, "What is your wish?" and instantly transport its visitors to living that wish somewhere here in the French Quarter. It seemed to be a place of dreams—lost and found.

If you have seen the movie *Big*, you will remember the teenage character of Tom Hanks, twelve-year-old Josh, who yearns to be "big"—to be a "grown-up"—after he was told he was too short to enter a carnival park ride while he was trying to impress his teenage sweetheart. He finds "Zoltar," the fortune-telling machine, who grants Josh his wish to be "big" by instantly transporting Josh into the "big" world—as a thirty-year-old. Ironically, it is Josh's child-like, uninhibited, and intuitive personality that gets him a "dream" job, where he meets his "dream" girl. But soon enough, Josh longs to return to his reality, ultimately feeling lost in his new "dream" world, and chooses to leave it behind and return to live his childhood.

Looking around Bourbon Street, it seemed everyone here was seeking to become lost in this fantasy scene. The carnival atmosphere lent itself to escaping into the sounds and colors, into the carefree uninhibited playground of the streets. It was easy to blend into the movement, and enjoy the feeling of being immersed in a fantasy world, but it was far from feeling the soul-stirring immersion of the caves and canyons. The immersion here was fun and vibrant. It allowed anyone to be anyone in the carnival atmosphere—to wish a wish, and to dream a dream. Yet there was a very transient and temporary feel to this world of fantasy.

Sometimes we need to detach from our everyday environment to gain a new perspective on our desires, dreams, and wishes. We need to be immersed in a fantasy world, filled with color and sound, to spark the creative spirit that sometimes gets locked away in our daily routines and schedules. Amidst our busy schedules, there is little time to dream—we feel that dreaming is wasting time. We feel that dreaming is sometimes a guilty self-indulgence, taking us away from the "important" activities of the day.

The thing is, we can live a life full of activities, but empty of dreams. Yet our dreams are as essential as breathing. Our dreams breathe life into us.

Within our dreams, we can find purpose; and with purpose, we can find our dreams.

Without our dreams, we suffocate in a world of endless activity, and we depart feeling expended, rather than expanded.

The opportunity to expand our *self* through our dreams is constantly present, like a gift waiting to be unwrapped. So often, we busily pass by the beautifully wrapped box every day, waiting for that "right" moment. We forget that we are the ones who can create that "right" moment—by simply pausing and unwrapping the gift.

We can create the space for our dreams. We don't need to search for a place where "Zoltar" will appear—our dreams are not in the hands of others. We can tell our own fortunes. We don't need to go to a fantasy world. We have our own authentic world of magic, color, life, and creativity within us. We just need to step in and find our dreams, and then step out and make them happen.

Throughout the French Quarter, the carnival was set against the infamous underworld lurking around every corner. Advertisements of tours through haunted houses, bars, and cemeteries, with images of ghosts, witches, and demons were all around, tempting and teasing visitors. The "paranormal" seemed to be the "normal" in this place, and many came eager to experience both the brightness of the carnival and the darkness of the underworld.

I couldn't help but reflect on why we are drawn to experience some things that obviously set out to scare and haunt us, yet want to stay far away from parts of our *self* that scare and haunt us. In the French Quarter, one could easily move in and out of the scary places to "safe" places of festivals and celebrations. There was a huge safety net protecting the dive into the depths of this underworld that doesn't exist when we dive into the places within that scare us.

I realized that part of my fear of digging into the darkest parts of me was the fear that I would get stuck there, that I would lose my *self* in the darkness. I didn't know what the faces of the ghosts and the demons would look like, unlike the posters of ghosts and demons in the French Quarter; and I didn't have a quick exit, like the haunted houses of the tours here.

I also had only felt the presence of evil through my child-hood—the presence of angels felt far away. I only knew the dark side. I hadn't felt the "goosebumps," the awe, which in a moment can overwhelm everything else. That sense of magical awe that was now present was like a light that could illuminate everything in the darkness—a light that could overpower the darkness. I felt there was a power of good at work in the universe that was much more spectacular than the darkness. Feeling that light emanating from deep within, I trusted the darkness could be confronted and conquered, and the light would remain.

For so long, I had kept the light out, I had felt guilty and ashamed to let it in, and thought that I was meant to live in the darkness—me, the monster.

Once I felt "goosebumps" of awe, I felt another way of being that was so long forgotten. I felt like a giggling, playful little tod-dler—before the laughter and giggling were destroyed.

I felt the little girl inside, ready to step out into the sunshine.

Sometimes, simply understanding why we are fearful, helps us to take another step to confront our fears. For me, my fear of exploring the darkness within was that I might be caught in an ines-capable pit, where there would be no sunshine. Especially because the darkness had become such a familiar feeling. You forget that any other feelings are possible. They are so long lost.

Now, I came to see that where there was darkness within, the opposite would also exist, and it would be more powerful. I started to feel light illuminating all the gifts within that had been hidden in the darkness. I started to feel the enormity of the infinite potential of the light that exists within each of us.

I knew that for every haunting encounter, there would be a carnival. I knew that if I encountered a demon, there would be an angel. I knew if a door closed behind me, another would open before me. I knew that the highs and lows of the journey would be temporary and transient, and that after any storm, an inevitable calm would soon follow. I knew that within the deepest caverns, there existed beautiful and peaceful light.

I had to wholeheartedly believe in the laws of universal energy, of *yin* and *yang,* of balance and harmony. I needed to believe in the presence of spirits who would guide me, whether I was in the quiet solitude of Mother Nature, or in the midst of the color and movement of a carnival.

The opportunity for balance and harmony, for calm after the storm, for emerging from our darkest places and stepping into the sunshine, is there for each of us, wherever we are.

We simply need to give our *self* the space to step into those places of pause, to allow our *self* to experience the "goosebumps" and the feelings of awe. We need to step into the depths of the cavern and know that light will emerge. We need to be the bird that knows the dawn is coming through the darkness. We need to know and have faith that the forces of light that illuminate our truths, our dreams, and our soul, are so much more powerful than any of the forces of darkness.

## MOMENTS OF PAUSE

1. How honestly and without inhibition have you searched within your *self* to explore your greatest and most exhilarating desires, and your deepest and most hidden fears? What are they? Have you dug deep enough? Have you reached high enough?

2. What are the most limited, safe, and superficial aspects of your reality? What are the most unlimited, purposeful, and passionate aspects of your reality?

3. Where do you seek happiness in the "wrong places"? Where do you find "authentic" happiness in your life?

4. How well do you know the darkness within you? What does it look like? How often do you step into your darkness—to explore it, sit with it, let it rise and fall, and disempower it?

5. How well do you know the light within you? What does it look like? How readily can you call upon the light within you to outshine the darkness within?

6. What "false realities" are you maintaining in your life? What are the truths you are hiding—from your *self* and from others? How is hiding your truths limiting your growth and the growth of your most significant relationships? How is hiding your truth keeping you trapped?

7. What is the world of color, magic, life, and creativity within you? How often do you pause the busyness of endless activity to stop to unwrap the gift of your most creative dreams?

## MORE MOMENTS FOR YOU

# Eleven

# The World is Your Stage!

*"All the world's a stage ...
and one man in his time plays many parts."*

—WILLIAM SHAKESPEARE

THE WORLD IS FULL OF STAGES. Broadway, Times Square, New York City, is the epitome of stages. In this place filled with stages and performances, of acts and players, of applause and encores, Shakespeare's words resonated with as much intensity as the bright lights of Broadway, "All the world's a stage, and all the men and women merely players: they have their exits and their entrances; and one man in his time plays many parts."

Arriving in Times Square marked the end of the journey from Los Angeles, and more than ever, I was ready to embark upon new journeys traveling completely solo. I had finished my series of treks, and the rest of my travels were at my whim—I could go wherever I chose to go in the moment.

The journey from Los Angeles had taken me through many surreal places, each tapping into a part of my soul that had long been lost. Suddenly, the world seemed full of choices and possibilities that I had never been able to entertain in my world of darkness. The opportunity to step upon new stages, to leave negative thoughts and experiences behind, to let my spirit soar—free of shackles I had let hold me—was as uplifting as the towering buildings of Times Square were high.

The world is full of so many stages that we each have the choice to explore, to exit, and to enter. We have the ability to create the parts in which we feel whole, to write our own script, to compose our own music, to stand solo, to be part of a cast, to applaud, and to perform as many encores as we desire. The challenge lies in finding the authentic roles, the scripts that take us closer to our *self*, the music that resonates most deeply with our heartstrings, and encores we never tire of performing because they endlessly propel us to greater heights.

Amidst so many plays and performances, so many costumes, scripts, and scores, how do we find clarity to discover and expose our own uniqueness, our distinctive "I" that is purposeful, authentic, and meaningful, without becoming lost on an array of stages? How do we know when the costume we wear is a harmonious reflection of our inner being, rather than just another "suit" that others will momentarily applaud?

How do we know that when we change our shoes we will end up in a better place?

The thing is, we don't *know* anything in advance. If we did, there would be no journey—it would be like knowing the next page of a story before it unfolds, the next scene in a play before it is performed. By default, everything would be predetermined, the script already written, the characters already created, the events already crafted.

I don't believe in a predetermined life. I believe that with each moment our choices determine the next moment. Those choices either lead us closer to authentic happiness, or closer to feeling lost on an unfamiliar stage. We don't know what will unfold, but if we pause long enough, we can *feel* what feels right and what feels wrong. If we are honest about our motives, we can determine which are pure and which are contaminated. We can feel when our internal compass is resonating on its True North—if we pause to feel the vibrations it sends through us.

It is *our* feelings, in *our* life, on *our* journey that are *our* most reliable guide.

Whichever spirit, or god, or essence, or divine being resonates within each of us, that presence speaks to us. It moves us. We don't need to look beyond our *self* to make the right choices on our journey. We simply need to look and feel within our *self*.

We can close our eyes, feel the depths of our soul, and let our spirits start to soar.

We can empower our *self*.

The problem when you are abused, or in any state in which you feel disempowered, is that you doubt *your* ability to empower *your self*. When you have been constantly overpowered, physically and emotionally, you lose any sense of confidence that you can determine your own path. When you have been stripped down on the outside, and violated on the inside, you numb your senses so as not to feel anything, let alone your "inner voice."

You can get stuck in the role of being a victim, and feel at the mercy of all that is around, rather than feel that you have the strength to break free. Sometimes you are simply too exhausted to struggle free. You can't see the page turning or the script changing. Your entire being can become a self-fulfilling prophecy down a negative and hopeless path. You can feel as though your spirit has left you and you are an empty vessel.

Ironically, at the times when we might feel the most empty, we can start to see the greatest possibilities to fill our *self* with new things. When so much is stripped from us, there is so much space to refill.

Ultimately, I had to see the opportunity to fill that space with the things I chose, not with the things that had been imposed on me. I saw the opportunity to create. I saw a blank canvas. I saw an empty stage. With every step of my journey, I could see that I had the choice to paint the colors that I wanted to paint. I could fill the stage with anything I wanted. Once again, I had the thought, *"My life—in my hands."*

We are our own directors, our own artists, our own playwrights. *We* can create what *we* choose to create!

The larger-than-life billboards, flashing lights, and the orchestra of sounds of Broadway were a perfect reinforcement of the opportunity to create our own stage—to tap into our unique talents, our distinctiveness, and the passions that lie within. I thought of Trudy the bag lady, and those moments of awe that can give us goosebumps and lead us toward living like a no limit species. Broadway and New York City seemed to shout, "No Limits!"

That evening, as the universe would have it, I was walking down Broadway and looked down 45th Street as I began to cross. In shining lights on a luminescent white billboard outside the Booth Theater shone, "Lily Tomlin and Jane Wagner, The Search for Signs of Intelligent Life in the Universe." From Seattle to New York City, it seemed the "search" was ever-present.

This was one of those moments of strange "coincidence" when you look around to see if anyone else might be sharing your improbable moment, and of course, there is not. There is just the universe smiling at you, and letting you know that even in the middle of the busiest city in the world, there are moments of awe and moments of pause around every corner.

I couldn't let this "coincidence" pass without pursuit, so I wandered to the theater to see the show times. I thought at least I could share my moment of coincidence with Lily. As I approached the theater, I saw the crowd—there must have been 200 people lined up around the entrance and spilling along 45th Street. Reaching the theater, I was able to slip through the crowd and into the foyer, where there was at least some room between people. *"How am I going to get through this to see her?"* I wondered.

At that precise moment, Jane Wagner burst through the security door right next to me and rushed out the side door of the theater that led to the alleyway. Ignoring that she seemed to be quite preoccupied, I let my instincts take over and followed her through the door.

"Hello Jane!" I called after her.

She looked around, not slowing too much in her tracks, and then stopped, her eyes fixed on me with one of those perplexed looks of seeing someone completely out of context.

"Do you remember me from Seattle—I came to see Lily?" I asked.

After a moment of silent pause, she smiled, "Yes, yes! You were traveling from Australia."

"Yes, I still am—I was just wandering down Broadway and happened to see your billboard."

I felt as though I was seeing a long lost friend—when you travel and move through so many spaces, a familiar face becomes a treat. Jane must have noticed, or maybe she was just in a hurry and cold in the mid-November chill of New York City. "Come with me," she motioned me to follow her and, of course, I did without hesitation.

We went into another entrance to the theater, and I followed Jane up a narrow stairwell that echoed with each step. "We're about to start the second act," Jane whispered, "Stay here and you can hear all of what's going on." With that, we arrived at the door to Lily's dressing room, and Jane quickly opened the door for me and just as quickly disappeared to her nearby control room where she managed all of the sounds and prompts for the performance.

Soon enough, Lily's voice came bursting through the speakers in her dressing room from the stage. I smiled as I heard a familiar scene with Trudy the bag lady talking to her alien friends. In the background, from the control room, I could hear Jane's carefully crafted and absolutely precise countdown to prompts and sounds that followed Lily's every movement on stage. It was definitely a treat.

After about an hour, once again, as in Seattle, the closing sound effects filled the theater, and I imagined Lily disappearing off the set into the darkness with the stars of the universe surrounding her on the stage. What I didn't expect was almost as quickly, the door to the dressing room flying open with Lily bursting in with all of the energy of her solo stage presence, and Jane flying in behind her.

Lily's smile was as big and welcoming as it had been in Seattle. I think she was even more bemused at this Australian who was sitting in her dressing room smiling back at her.

"I couldn't help but stop by when I saw your billboard here!" I said still beaming at the coincidence.

"I'm glad you did!" Lily's warmth and friendliness leapt out of her. "I remember our talk in Seattle," she smiled.

As Lily changed her clothes and makeup, she asked me about my travels since Seattle and where I was heading after New York. My answer was as undefined as it was in Seattle, and Lily remembered what she wrote in my journal, *"When you get "there"—there will be a there there!"*

We chatted for a while longer until Lily and Jane were ready to head out for an after-show appointment. As Lily packed her final things, she reached into her bag and pulled out two small black pouches, and handed them to me. "Here, take these—you're going to need them!" As I looked curiously at the pouches, I realized they were ear warmers. I smiled a big smile. My red nose must have given away that this girl from Down Under wasn't quite used to the icy-cold New York City winter!

We once again set off on our ways, and despite the chilly wind whistling down 45th Street, I felt surprisingly warm with my ear warmers and another hug. Lily's saying had become a truth for me throughout my journey—in each moment, there is a "there" there.

New York City is full of journeys ending and beginning. The iconic Statue of Liberty, representing Libertas, the Roman goddess of freedom, rises dramatically out of New York Harbor. For many, the monumental statue symbolizes the inspirational journeys of millions of travelers and dreamers seeking their higher aspirations.

The description of the statue in the Statement of Significance by UNESCO upon the statue being designated a world heritage site in 1984, is a reflection of the quest for higher aspirations that we share, and that we can achieve. "A masterpiece of the human spirit ... She endures as a highly potent symbol—inspiring contemplation, debate and protest—of ideals such as liberty, peace, human rights, abolition of slavery, democracy and opportunity."

I headed to Battery Park, at the southern tip of Manhattan, to see the iconic statue, and to take the ten-mile round trip on the Staten Island Ferry. The ferry, according to my trusty *Lonely Planet USA*, gave a breathtaking view of Manhattan, and passed right by the Statue of Liberty. I boarded the ferry and we set off across New York Harbor with the statue in full view. Instantly, I was transported to the scene from the movie, *Yentl,* with Barbra Streisand standing on the deck of a New York Harbor ferry, after coming to the United States to seek a life of freedom.

The journey across New York Harbor of Streisand's character seemed representative of the tens of millions of journeys of people from all around the globe. Each has traveled the harbor, with the Statue of Liberty ever-present and symbolizing the quest for freedom and opportunity that is the common pursuit of those millions, and millions more who have yet to make that journey. Many made great sacrifices and endured horrific hardships in their journey to freedom. My journey, in comparison, seemed an extraordinarily simple and uncomplicated one, but I felt an overwhelming sense of the common pursuit of the human spirit to be free from our chains.

Whether it is taking the step to board a boat for a new land, or simply taking the step to pursue a new path in one's own land, as Lao Tzu the founder of Taoism famously said, "The longest journey begins with the first step." I had come to see that was true, no matter the circumstance.

Within that first step, there is always doubt and fear. When we let the sense of freedom and opportunity overcome the doubt and fear, all else will follow. So many have done it. So many have overcome tremendous obstacles to pursue their dreams. We each have it within us to do the same—it is in our nature—it is a part of the "masterpiece of the human spirit"—of *our* spirit. It simply takes a first step.

We each have the spirit within us to take that first step. We each have all we need within us to reach our highest aspirations, and to take an extraordinary journey to our greatest self. We each have it within us to "make it" our greatest life.

As Frank Sinatra and Liza Minnelli each sang, "I'm gonna make a brand new start of it in old New York … if I can make it there, I'm gonna make it anywhere … It's up to you, New York, New York!" Every stage upon which we stand provides us with opportunities to make it. On every stage, it's up to us to make the choice. To make it happen. To find the courage. To overcome the fear. To take the step.

Several days later, I was in the Barnes and Noble store in Greenwich Village. There was an exhibit at the store of a photographic essay book recently released by Chester Higgins, Jr., *Elder Grace: The Nobility of Aging.* I was captured by the expressive photographs of African-American men and women, each shining with the wisdom of their age; each seeming at peace with their journey.

In his introduction, Higgins wrote of an older relative who imparted the following to him.

*In my twenties, I was clueless as to who I was.*
*In my thirties, I began to understand who I was, but I didn't like myself.*
*In my forties, I accepted myself.*
*In my fifties, I began to celebrate myself.*
*In my sixties, I have blossomed. It can only get better.*

The journeys of our life are so much a product of how we think—about our *self*, about each other, about the world. Many "healthy living" books ascribe that "you are what you eat." I think, more than anything, we are what we think.

In his photographic exploration, Higgins included a quote from each of his subjects. With each photograph and each quote, came a moment of pause, each a gift of reflection of the most precious insight of each life presented. I pulled out my journal to capture some of those words of wisdom, and to create a moment of pause for each.

*"Once you put yourself down, you are in trouble. You must be good to yourself before you can be good to anyone else."*
Bernice Nona Staggers

*"I've learned to put the past behind me and move forward."*
Eleanor Jones

*"Everyone is a part of spiritual strength. All of us have the power to have a realistic spiritual force and the ability to call upon it."*
Zedfrederick Alston, Sr.

*"The most important thing anybody can do is to get rid of guilt. All guilt is self-destructive ... When we feel guilty we are punishing ourselves."*
Louise Meriwether

*"I know who I am. Being me is important to me."*
Maria Ortiz

*"Whatever you do, it's important that you make a mark on life, or else you could very well die undeclared."*
March Forth McGowan

For so long, I had thought there was more to gain by closing off from people. I was starting to experience that the only way to grow on our journeys is through people.

We have so much to learn from the journeys of each other. We just need to pause to hear. We have so much in common with each other. We just need to pause to see.

New York, this city of journeys beginning and ending, is a city among cities, among countries, among regions, on a single planet on which we all seek fulfilling journeys that take us to higher places. We are each other's teachers. We are each other's students.

My $30 to $40 a day budget was faring surprisingly well in New York City. Upon arriving in Manhattan, I checked into a hostel in the Chelsea area of the city and was very happy to be paying $20

a night for accommodation. My remaining $10 to $20 was enough to cover public transport, admission fees to galleries and exhibits, some simple souvenirs to send home, and some basic food. Of all the things I experienced in New York, the world-renowned restaurants were not one of them! However, the famous New York bagel (a saltier, fluffier, doughy bagel, with a more moist crust than other styles of bagels—so I was to find out), along with an apple from the corner fruit stands, became a staple daily diet. You could say I did the Big Apple on a little more than an apple a day!

Another part of the culinary experience of New York is the over-sized pretzel, freshly-baked from one of the many pretzel stands that mark most corners. Then, there is the distinct smell on every other corner of the always-busy hot dog stands. There seems to be an endless variety of "dogs" and sauces to put between those wonderfully soft and fluffy white buns.

I was looking forward to keeping things to the essential during the rest of my travels. I wanted to stretch my budget as far as I could so I could travel for as long as possible. I was happy to keep to the simple things—away from the fancy restaurants, shopping, and expensive hotels.

The New York subway system enabled me to explore the different areas of New York City—from Queens to The Bronx, to Greenwich Village, to Harlem, to Coney Island, to the West Side, and to the East Side. The journeys of so many people from so many places were evident in the mix of communities throughout Manhattan. What was also striking, was the mix of "poverty amidst plenty."

As I had traveled across the United States, I was struck by the extent of poverty and homelessness. From California to Seattle, through the South and up to New York City, a common element seemed to be that only a block away from the wealthiest areas, there was extreme poverty and homelessness. Coming from Australia, I hadn't seen that kind of contrast in such close quarters, and I wasn't expecting to see that in one of the "richest" countries in the world.

Late one evening, walking along the Upper East Side, I couldn't have been more struck by the contrast. I decided to wander through Bloomingdales, just to see what all the fuss about this famous store was about. As I walked through the store in my very casual traveling clothes, I was given a very unwelcoming look by a richly dressed woman. She was loaded up with Bloomingdales bags in one hand, and with the leash leading her white poodle (just as richly dressed), in the other hand. I smiled and decided I had seen all I needed to see, and proceeded out to the street.

Within a few blocks of Bloomingdales, homeless people of all ages and ethnicities emerged on the streets. It was a world apart from the nearby Bloomingdales store, and the richly dressed woman and poodle. The boutique-lined streets of Fifth Avenue and Park Avenue that were blocks away, also seemed to be a far-away land.

It was striking to see that in a world of so much, so many could be so obviously without. What was equally striking, was that the homeless seemed to be walked past with as little attention given to them as was given to the trash on the streets. It was as though they had become an invisible part of the sidewalks that people simply walked past every day, with disregard, without attention, without a care. It was as though with every passer-by, there was a statement issued, *"Poverty is your problem, not mine."*

I knew from my days of mergers and acquisitions that the problem was not a lack of money or resources in the world. The problem was one of distribution.

In a world of so much, there is no good reason why so many are without. That was strikingly clear in this financial and shopping capital of the world.

With Thanksgiving approaching—one of the most popular holidays in the United States—there was an obvious contrast to the way many would celebrate the holiday. Many would be sharing with family and friends, in front of fireplaces. They would share Thanksgiving turkeys the size of several American footballs. In contrast, many would be spending the holiday in shelters or on the streets. They would keep warm in the winter chill by whatever means they could find, and make do with whatever scraps could create a meal.

Ironically, the Thanksgiving holiday originated in giving thanks for bountiful crops for all. The stories of the origins of Thanksgiving told how the early American settlers were close to starvation in their first year, not knowing how to harvest the land. The Native American Indians not only provided the settlers with plentiful food and crops, but also showed them how to tend the land. With that help, the settlers were able to grow crops and sustain themselves. Thanksgiving became a time to share feasts among neighbors. That was in 1621.

Centuries later, the spirit of Thanksgiving remained stronger than ever, and larger than life. Every store was filled with an endless array of Thanksgiving turkeys and accompaniments, decorations, gift baskets, and pumpkin pies. What seemed to have not kept up with the *spirit* of Thanksgiving was the *sharing* of Thanksgiving. As I stood amidst the obvious disparity between those with so much, and those with so little, it seemed that the sense of sharing may have become lost in the holiday celebration.

On Thanksgiving Day, the Macy's Parade filled the streets of Manhattan with color, music, fantasy, and celebration. The parade balloons filled the crisp blue sky with everyone's favorite characters and American icons—from Snoopy, to Ronald McDonald, Scooby-Doo, Sponge Bob Square Pants, Mickey Mouse, Charlie Brown, Garfield, Spiderman, and every other shape and size of balloon character imaginable. It was a feast for the eyes. I had arrived on 34th Street, right across from Macy's, at 5:30AM in order to get a prime location to see the parade. By noon, as the parade was finishing, my feet were almost frozen, despite the double layer of socks I was wearing inside my Blundstones!

Walking from the parade, I heard the joyful sounds of bells. I turned to find the familiar red shield of the Salvation Army atop a swinging "red kettle" donation bucket. Staff were bundled up in thick navy Salvation Army coats ringing their bells, and calling for donations. The Salvation Army had been a familiar scene all around New York City, trying to help those who had little. Especially at Thanksgiving, the Salvation Army was helping everyone to maintain the sharing of the holiday.

As I approached, I saw a flyer asking for volunteers to help with Thanksgiving lunch for the homeless at various Salvation Army community centers throughout the city. With time left to help, I jumped on the subway and headed down to the West 14th Street center. Walking into the center, I saw every chair and table completely full of people who had come to enjoy a wonderful Thanksgiving meal.

The smells of roasting turkey and baked pumpkin pie filled the center. Every type of seasoning and accompaniment was laid out on what seemed to be an endless table. The afternoon went by in an instant as we served hundreds of homeless a Thanksgiving feast. By 4:00PM, every last pumpkin pie disappeared from shelf after shelf of pie racks. Every turkey was gone from every roasting pan, and all of the seasoning, green beans and gravy went from serving tray to dinner plate. It was as happy a scene as was the colorful Thanksgiving Parade outside Macy's on 34th Street. The difference was, as these people left, most returned to the chilly streets of the New York City winter.

The disparity was strikingly present. It wasn't anything I knew how to reconcile in that moment. I just had an overwhelming feeling that this shouldn't be—just as children shouldn't be abused, women shouldn't be beaten, and voices shouldn't go unheard. I had a sinking feeling that surely in the twenty-first century, there shouldn't be so many with so little, amidst so much.

The world should be everyone's stage.

## MOMENTS OF PAUSE

1. Upon which stages would you most like to be "playing"? Which stages are calling to you?

2. On which "stages" are you "stuck"? Which negative thoughts and experiences are keeping you trapped?

3. On which "stages" do you feel you are being propelled to your greatest heights? Which positive thoughts and experiences are giving you freedom?

4.  Which "roles" and "parts" that you play in your life feel most authentic to you, resonate most deeply with your "heartstrings," take you closer to your distinctive "I," and are most meaningful to you? Which "roles" and parts are least authentic, move you further from your distinctive "I," and are least meaningful to you?

5.  Which feelings in your life, on your journey, are your most reliable guide? What are those things within you that give you the greatest sense that you are making the right choices for you?

6.  How are you empowering your *self*? How are you giving your *self* the strength to follow your own path, to break free, to let your spirit soar? How are you taking your life, in your hands, and making it a life of "no limits"?

7.  As you think about the "longest journey ahead," and the path of your greatest and most purposeful aspirations, what is the first step that would take you on that journey? Into which shoes would you need to step?

8. How do you like your *self*? How do you accept your *self*? How do you celebrate your *self*? How do you help your *self* to blossom?

9. How do you like, accept, and celebrate others? How do you help others blossom?

10. In a world of plenty, which things strike you as the greatest inequalities that enable some to soar and others to remain lost? What is the positive change you would most like to create?

## MORE MOMENTS FOR YOU

---

---

---

---

---

---

---

---

---

---

---

# Twelve

# In the Groove!

*"You must live in the present,*
*launch yourself on every wave,*
*find your eternity in each moment."*

—Henry David Thoreau

I N SAILING, THERE IS A TERM, "In the groove." "In the groove"
is when your sailboat is so perfectly aligned with the wind, that
the boat glides effortlessly on course without even having to be
steered. You can let go of the helm and the wind will do the rest,
maintaining the boat in perfect balance on the course you have set.

My next "planned" destination after New York City was Oslo,
Norway. However, having spent more time exploring the United
States and Canada than expected, December was not a time to go
to Oslo. My backpack was not nearly large enough for the winter
coats I would need for a Scandinavian winter!

*"So where to now?"* I contemplated. My current plane ticket included stops in Oslo, Madrid, Bangkok, and then Sydney. *"I could go to Asia, now,"* I thought, *"and then head back to explore Scandinavia and Europe in the summer."*

Traveling to Asia meant a little research. First of all, I needed to find out which countries required a Visa and which required vaccinations. I listed some countries—Malaysia, Vietnam, Laos, Thailand, India, Cambodia, Nepal, Borneo. Then, I listed the vaccinations—Hepatitis A, Hepatitis B, Tetanus, Typhoid, Malaria. Quite a list! My STA travel agent just happened to be traveling through Asia, and was currently in Singapore.

"Come to Singapore!" Pia exclaimed in her email. "Spend New Year's Eve here—there's a bunch of us here and we'll have a great time!"

New Year's Eve in Singapore with Pia was sure to be fun—and meeting some new friends was appealing. I imagined traveling around Asia after New Years, heading to New Zealand, and then exploring Australia before heading back to travel through Europe in the summer (I had traveled to a few places in Australia for business, but I wanted to fully explore Australia as a dedicated traveler).

Amidst the anticipation of Asia-Pacific, there was the sound of a little voice. It was that little voice that gives you the feeling that something is just not right. That little voice, that little undercurrent moving within, had become my inner compass, and my most reliable guide. For reasons that were not at all apparent, that voice was telling me that it wasn't yet time to leave the United States. Everything made "sense" to leave, but that voice was making me *feel* otherwise. A year ago, I would have ignored the voice, and followed the rational plan that made "sense." Now, I had come to trust my inner compass, rather than what seemed to be a rational plan.

As I paused with the feeling that it wasn't the time to leave the United States, images of sailing in tropical blue waters emerged. I loved sailing, and I knew the Caribbean was an idyllic place to sail. *"Maybe I'll head to Florida and see if I can find a boat to sail around the Caribbean,"* the thought came. I smiled at the thought of tropical waters, palm trees, and sailing boats. Then, I smiled more at the *feeling*. My True North was pointing me south, and so I packed my backpack and headed for the Caribbean.

Little did I know then, that decision would change the rest of my travels in a way I could never have planned.

While I was in New York, I found out there were crew houses in Fort Lauderdale, Florida, where I could stay while I looked for a boat on which to crew. My *Lonely Planet USA* gave me my first contacts for crew houses. After calling a few options from New York, I managed to secure a room in a smaller crew house, and I was ready to book my Amtrak rail ticket and be on my way.

The Amtrak trip from New York to Fort Lauderdale felt very long. I left New York the day after Thanksgiving to arrive in Fort Lauderdale the following day. By the time the train pulled in to the station the following afternoon, I had completed my sailing resume that I was expecting to provide to a number of crew-finding agencies. I further contemplated life while reading more of Steve Zikman's, *The Power of Travel*, and the Dalai Lama's *Transforming the Mind*, and I managed to sleep just a few hours on the floor of the carriage—it turned out the floor was much more comfortable than the seats!

As I departed the train, my backpack felt a lot heavier on my somewhat bruised back. I think with every rail track the train passed over while I was "sleeping," my back received another bruise! The crew house was a short bus ride and walk from the Amtrak station, and I was looking forward to any kind of soft bed for the evening.

The crew house was a quaint assortment of small guest houses around a main house. I was one of about twelve who had found their way here on a quest to sail the Caribbean.

My first task was to make up some business cards at the local Kinko's to leave in the various establishments around Fort Lauderdale. My crew house companions had given me this tip as a way of finding a boat on which to crew. I purchased the cheapest cell phone I could find to receive calls in response to my business cards, and hoped that would be my ticket to sailing the Caribbean.

Almost a week passed, and I hadn't received even one call on my cell phone. Then, on the sixth day, I received the one and only call I would ever receive on that phone. It was that one call that would send me to a place for a day of sailing that would turn into a lifetime of change.

"Would you like to come down to Miami and help out on a race committee?" the voice asked.

Rick was head of the race committee for a sailing race that was to be held in Coconut Grove in Miami. He had seen my business card in one of the locations in Fort Lauderdale. I leapt at the opportunity to be on any kind of boat at this point, and to meet some fellow sailors out on the water.

"I would love to!" I jumped in without hesitation, "When do you need me?!"

The race was a two-day weekend event, starting the next day. The only thing I knew about Miami was what I had seen on the television series *Miami Vice* back in Australia—drugs, guns, and crime, crime, guns, and drugs! I remembered that one of my American friends had told me before I left Australia on my way to the United States, "Just don't go to Miami—of all the places to avoid, avoid Miami!" So much for that—by late afternoon, I was boarding my next Amtrak bound for Miami.

My bed for the evening was going to be in the Miami Beach International Traveler's Hostel on 9th and Washington Street. That didn't mean anything to me at the time, but after one night, I realized this was the hostel for anyone who wanted to live the South Beach night life. By the time I was ready for bed, everyone else was ready to go out to hit the hot spots, and as I was waking, everyone else was just stumbling back in the door. Needless to say, I didn't get much sleep that night—the streets outside sounded like an endless party. Welcome to South Beach!

As is the nature of things, it wasn't the sailing that proved to be the highlight of that weekend, it was one person I met, and what he introduced to me.

Shake-A-Leg Miami was a small non-profit organization in Coconut Grove that took children and adults sailing on Biscayne Bay. After the race on Saturday, I was chatting with one of the racers, and he told me all about this small non-profit with the enthusiasm of a child waiting to sit on Santa's lap.

"You have to come to Shake-A-Leg and meet the people there!" Arthur exclaimed. "It's such a special place, and they do wonderful things to change the lives of kids! You'll love it!"

Arthur was racing the next day, and offered to pick me up from the hostel. We could have an early breakfast before the race, and I would meet one of the people from Shake-A-Leg. I couldn't help but accept. Arthur's excitement was infectious, and I was curious to find out about a place that could stir someone with such enthusiasm.

The next morning, we went to Coral Bagels—a small bagel diner that was a local breakfast joint and somewhat of an institution in "The Grove." It was there Arthur introduced me to Meredith, one of the program staff at Shake-A-Leg. Meredith burst into conversation about the organization before I could even squish across the diner booth. *"What is this place?"* I was thinking. *"It sounds like Disneyland with magic dust!"*

Meredith and Arthur told stories of kids with disabilities sailing around Biscayne Bay on specially designed sailboats, of adults with disabilities racing against each other on the Bay, and of teenagers who had been caught up in drugs and gangs who came to this place as part of their conditional release from juvenile detention to try to give them a positive experience.

The stories were touching, and it was an easy decision to stay another night in Miami, and go to visit Shake-A-Leg the next day. It turned out that the next day, the organization needed another skipper to take some kids out sailing. My just happening to be there was maybe not simply a coincidence. The head program instructor, Ashley (who was filled with as much enthusiasm as Meredith and Arthur combined), took me through a "skipper check-out." Soon enough, I was sailing out on Biscayne Bay with kids in tow. The transformation of these "juvenile offenders" as they sailed out on the bay was as though magic dust *had* been sprinkled in the air.

That evening, when I called home to Australia, my mother was more than worried as I told her that the "kids" I had taken sailing on the bay were gang kids on release from juvenile detention. My mother had watched episodes of *Miami Vice*, too. My assuring her that everything was fine didn't help at all. "Don't worry, Mum," I reassured her, "a Miami police officer with a gun was on board to make sure there was no trouble!"

There was a special energy around Shake-A-Leg and Biscayne Bay. I felt my internal compass resonate peacefully sailing on the bay with these kids, and being in the company of people who were overwhelmingly purposeful in what they were doing.

As I watched these "delinquent" kids sailing on the beautiful, bright blue tropical waters of sunny Biscayne Bay, there was an obvious contrast to the dark world from which they came. These were kids with whom I related—they were lost, they were on their own, and in one way or another, they were abandoned. Their parents were absent, their teachers had given up hope, they were treated with disregard, and they were living on the wafer-thin fringes of life. They had been left to exist in whichever "system" could deal with them.

The education system couldn't cater for them, the social services system couldn't cope with them, and the family unit didn't exist to nurture them. The streets of Miami, however, had plenty of room for them. They were easy prey to the drug, solicitation, and crime rings that readily lured them. These kids were seen as the perpetrators of offenses—but they were much more clearly the innocent victims of professional offenders.

Sailing on Biscayne Bay, we were all literally in the same boat. We were from opposite sides of the planet, but here, we had much in common. As I gave the helm to each one of the kids, they each confidently steered the boat, as though they had been sailing forever. They found "the groove" without any trouble, and it was magical to be sailing with the arms of the wind firmly around us.

For these kids, you could see that simply being given the helm of the boat, and being able to steer "their" boat on "their" course, on the wide open bay, filled them with confidence and a sense of accomplishment—and it came so naturally—effortlessly. It took so little to give these kids so much.

These kids weren't asking for much—they had given up asking and hoping that someone would pay attention. I knew that feeling intimately. These were kids who could just as easily sink or swim—survive or drown. A little attention, a little empowerment, a little respect, was a life jacket for them.

On my way back to Fort Lauderdale that afternoon, Shake-A-Leg and Miami felt like a magnet to my compass. I was drawn to these kids and all they represented. I was drawn to this place that gave opportunity and hope to kids who might otherwise drown.

The next day, I packed my things, and headed to Miami.

A week after leaving Fort Lauderdale, I was starting to feel that Miami might become my home for the winter. The thought of spending the winter taking underprivileged kids sailing on Biscayne Bay felt right. My compass felt aligned, and my senses were telling me that this was the place to be. That's all I needed.

Meredith, Arthur, and Ashley had each offered me a place to stay at their respective houses. With the holidays upon us, they were traveling in and out of town, so I could house sit and pet sit while they were away, and share with them while they were here.

I had never experienced the authentic welcome, hospitality, and friendship that Meredith, Ashley, and Arthur offered so readily. We all clicked instantly, and were to become the best of friends trying to make Biscayne Bay the most magical place for kids who were in need of a lot of magic.

Over the following weeks, I would take children of all backgrounds and abilities sailing on the bay. I never felt as much "in the groove" as I felt at Shake-A-Leg. I never experienced so many people finding their groove, as the people who came to Shake-A-Leg.

Stories of inspiration were found in every face of every person.

Children whose lives were restricted to a wheelchair could be transported to a new world of freedom, as they found a new chair in the specially adapted sailboats that enabled them to sail all over the bay. Children who relied on ventilators to breathe, could breathe with the wind in their faces, sailing in their keelboats. Teenagers and adults who had been paralyzed in tragic accidents—some now quadriplegics, some paraplegics—could find new hope and self-esteem as they moved across the blue waters of the bay. Children with developmental disabilities—Down Syndrome, Epilepsy, Autism—who struggled to integrate in the day-to-day world, found new friends and best sailing buddies every day.

This was Disneyland—a world where anything was possible, where any dream could come true—and there was magic dust all around.

Walt Disney said, "It's kind of fun to do the impossible." At Shake-A-Leg, it seemed the impossible happened every day, amidst the fun, smiles, and laughter of children who needed the impossible to be possible.

After a few weeks, I had the opportunity to put my business skills to a much better use than I ever had the chance to do in the corporate world—to help make this Disneyland bigger. The organization was being considered for its biggest grant to date from one of the largest foundations in the country—the James L. and John S. Knight Foundation. The executive director needed some help preparing the proposal to the foundation, so Meredith and Ashely introduced me to Harry, the executive director, to help put the proposal together.

Harry Horgan was the Walt Disney of Shake-A-Leg—the biggest dreamer behind the dream. Harry was paralyzed at twenty-two in a car accident in Rhode Island, only weeks after graduating college. While rehab helped Harry's body, it didn't help his spirit. That's when Harry decided he needed to get into "the groove" that always made his spirit soar—sailing. With the help of friends and some boat designers, Harry designed a sailing boat into which he could be hoisted and sail beyond the confines of his wheelchair. Not only did Harry regain his spirit, he also captured the hearts of so many to help him in his quest to share this freedom with other adults and children with disabilities.

During his rehab, Harry's family tried to keep his spirits up. "Hey Harry, shake a leg! Get up and do something!" they would say. It was his grandfather who led the chant, and when Harry decided to start a non-profit to help spread his freedom through sailing, "Shake-A-Leg" the organization was born in Rhode Island.

"Shake-A-Leg is an attitude," Harry would say. "It means 'Get up and do something and don't wait for someone else to do it for you!'" Harry was living that every day, and trying to recruit as many helpers as possible.

The other dreamer behind Shake-A-Leg Miami was Dr. Barth Green—a top neurosurgeon in the country and the co-founder of the Miami Project to Cure Paralysis. Barth heard about Harry's program, and saw his own spinal cord patients who visited Harry's program come back to Miami transformed. They had a new thirst for life, and they were physically improved. It didn't take Barth long to convince Harry to move from Rhode Island to Miami, and run the program year-round on Biscayne Bay. Their dream was to serve thousands more people in Miami in partnership with Barth's Miami Project to Cure Paralysis, and other local organizations.

A few years later, when I happened upon Shake-A-Leg, helping Harry and Barth to get funds to grow this Disneyland was like filling Santa's sack with gifts for people in need.

Soon enough, that first proposal to the Knight Foundation turned into a $250,000 check, and Disneyland was growing.

At that time, the organization was run out of two beaten-up City of Miami trailers that were on their way to the junk yard. Harry made the trailers into work spaces, and they were conspicuously parked in a dreary run-down parking lot alongside a closed boat ramp on Biscayne Bay in Coconut Grove. In the Miami summer, with tropical storms an ordinary part of every day, you needed to be careful to avoid the leaks from the roof, while maneuvering the holes in the trailer floors. The $250,000 was going to help expand programs in a new facility. The expansion would allow the organization to serve thousands of disadvantaged children and adults every year, instead of hundreds.

Unbeknownst to me at the time, the $250,000 would be the start of getting millions more dollars to help the organization. Before I knew it, my weekend in Miami turned into a much longer stay. I ended up volunteering for the first year, then selling my apartment in Australia to give me funds to stay in Miami. We wrote grants and endless proposals to raise money that would fund new educational and recreational programs for kids in need. Instead of my business skills helping to provide "extraordinary profits" to shareholders, I was helping to turn extraordinary possibilities into reality for thousands of children. That was more wealth than any corporate balance sheet would ever realize.

Over the next four years, we transformed the two beaten-up trailers into a three-level state-of-the-art education and recreational center. With grants from foundations, corporations, and generous private philanthropists, we were able to fill the center with computer classrooms with adaptive technology for kids with disabilities, and multimedia centers that were far from the broken-down classrooms the kids were used to at their schools. Many of the kids didn't even have a classroom—the school system in one of the richest countries in the world was so poor that there were not enough classrooms, desks, or chairs. The kids would often sit in the gymnasium or in the cafeteria, or even on the floor.

At Shake-A-Leg, the wide open waters of Biscayne Bay became the biggest classroom for these kids. They could sail and kayak to explore math and science with a new sense of adventure and accomplishment. Their school grades soared like their boats through the water. They created colorful art out of the coconuts, palm fronds, shells, and other art supplies that Mother Nature had left all around the bay. With underwater cameras and microphones in hand, they expressed themselves through music and video. They came to life.

We were not only able to serve children with disabilities, but also the impoverished kids, and the "delinquent juveniles" in whom society had lost hope. Kids with disabilities sailed side by side with gang kids and street kids, and they became each others' mentors and best buddies.

Teachers cried seeing "troubled teenagers" on whom they had long ago given up, put their arms around a child in a wheelchair, lift them into their sailing boat, and sit beside them as they went off sailing on the bay together. Parents cried as their children who seldom had cause to smile in their wheelchairs, laughed uncontrollably as they left their wheelchairs behind on the dock and set sail with the helm in their hand. Children strapped and restricted to ventilators for oxygen were lifted, along with their oxygen bottles, into boats where they could breathe easy and move freely on their sailboat. Brothers and sisters who were left on the streets, prey to pimps and drug dealers, found safety and friendships on waters that could nurture them.

We always watched in awe as Anthony set sail solo on the bay. A young teenager with severe Cerebral Palsy since birth, Anthony lived his life in an electric wheelchair, which he steered by a joystick with awkward and abrupt hand movements. On the Shake-A-Leg dock, Anthony was lifted into a one-person specially adapted "Access" dinghy. A joystick was wrapped to his chest that reached up to touch his chin. He could move the joystick with his chin to control the movement of his boat. The "able-bodied" kids watched in disbelief as Anthony raced against them and went sailing past them with his head thrown back in the air, laughing high into the blue sky as he beat them all.

Every day there were many tears at Shake-A-Leg, but they were always tears of happiness. Tears that came from miracles. Tears that came from the simplicity of one person caring for another. Tears that came from dreams coming true, and the impossible becoming possible.

Without non-profit organizations like Shake-A-Leg in the community, many of the kids who came to Shake-A-Leg would most likely end up in jail, on the streets, and without any fair chance for a future. They would remain invisible, their voices unheard. Their dreams unrealized.

For me and many others, Shake-A-Leg was a place to help make a difference in the world. It was a place to give a voice to those who were unheard, and to bring life to those who had been made invisible. It was a Disneyland of hopes and dreams that became reality for those who dared to dream beyond horizons, and who wouldn't believe that anything or anyone could hold them back. For the grand opening of the new Shake-A-Leg facility, I was honored to write the invocation that was to be read by one of our kids. In the voice of a child, the invocation came to life.

*Let This Be A Place*

*Invocation*
*Shake-A-Leg Miami Grand Opening*

*When there are barriers that seem insurmountable,*
*Let this be a place that inspires the human spirit to rise above.*

*When those who are disadvantaged feel weakened*
*by their struggles,*
*Let this be a place of strength and encouragement.*

*When those who are lost seek belonging,*
*Let this be a place of healing and rejuvenation.*

*When there are troubled times,*
*Let this be a place of tranquility.*

*When a safe haven is sought,*
*Let this be a place of peacefulness and refuge.*

*When the community seeks to share kindness and compassion,*
*Let this be a place where the gift of giving brings fulfillment to all.*

*When there are those who seek to strive beyond their limitations,*
*Let this be a place that brings independence and opportunity.*

*When children and youth seek fun and laughter,*
*Let this be a place of new friendships and lifelong bonds.*

*When there are those who need nurturing and mentoring,*
*Let this be a place where new visions are born.*

*When children and adults from all backgrounds*
*and abilities wish to set sail for new horizons,*
*Let this be a place where dreams become reality:*
*A place where no dream will ever be too large.*

I looked out to the busloads of kids and teachers who had come to the grand opening, along with the city officials, the philanthropists, and the corporate and foundation representatives. We had all helped make this dream a reality. It was clear that it "takes a community to raise a child," and that together we can all help to make the impossible become possible.

The words I wrote in the invocation were inspired by the children, teenagers, and adults I had seen over the years come to Shake-A-Leg, find their "groove," come to life, and help the lives of others. It went beyond the individual to the next person, and the next person, and the next person. With each person whose life was touched, that person would invariably share that touch with another, and that person with another. I saw that a touch could cause extraordinary change to happen. When so many people would say, "It will never happen," we made it happen.

One of our favorite quotes among Ashley, Meredith and me was from Margaret Mead, "Never doubt that a small group of thoughtful, committed citizens can change the world. Indeed, it is the only thing that ever has." We all saw that happen at Shake-A-Leg.

In the eyes of children, we saw the impossible change to the possible. In the smiles of children, we saw hope for every person.

In my journal, I wrote a short verse, which I titled, "A Child."

> *The laughter of a child that sings innocence.*
> *The eyes of a child that is untouched ocean.*
> *The touch of a child that is a warm sunset.*
> *The child that is the reflection of a new day.*
> *The child that brings hope of restoration.*

The "groove" into which I had sailed at Shake-A-Leg set me on a different course for the rest of my journey. I had swapped my Blundstones for sailing shoes, and in that "groove," I found something unexpected. I found a connection to people that had long been lost. I felt a sense of being part of a community, a family, whose lives were about pausing to hear the voices that couldn't be heard; who in every moment, took the time to notice the child who was asking for help; who realized that children weren't inherently bad, and offered a hand to help them get back on track from abusive and hostile environments.

I had always believed that I could accomplish what I needed on my own, and that I had no option for life to be any other way. At Shake-A-Leg, among some of the most challenged people I ever met, I saw that there is nothing of significance we can accomplish on our own. Shake-A-Leg opened my heart, and showed me that compassion and care among people did exist. I had stopped believing in that a long time ago.

For the first time, I was in awe and felt goosebumps, not through the wonders of nature, but through the magic of people helping people.

Suddenly, I was in a groove where my compass felt rested. I felt aligned and centered in the realization that through our own experiences, we can connect to others. We see that this journey is bigger than each of us individually. We see that the help we give to others, helps us to grow. It's as though our collective humanity expands. We feel more complete by helping someone else become more complete. Our own challenges become surmountable as we help someone else overcome their challenges. Our dreams come within reach as we help others grasp their dreams. We launch our *self* toward our greatest heights, as we help others soar to their greatest heights.

## MOMENTS OF PAUSE

1.  What does being "in your groove" feel like to you? When do you feel most "in your groove"?

2.  Which people and places have most inspired you—have shown you that the impossible can happen, that the most challenging odds can be overcome, and that the most extraordinary dreams really can come true?

3.  What are you waiting for the universe to bring to you? How are *you* "getting up and making it happen"?

4.  How are you steering your *self* in the direction of your dreams? Are you taking charge of "where you will go," or are you allowing someone else to be at the helm of your boat?

5.  When have you felt that your path and your purpose has connected you to "something bigger than you"? What is that "something bigger"?

## MORE MOMENTS FOR YOU

_____

_____

_____

_____

_____

_____

_____

_____

_____

_____

_____

### Thirteen

# Moving Mountains

*"The man who removes a mountain*
*begins by carrying away small stones."*

—CHINESE PROVERB

WHEN WE BELIEVE we can move mountains, we can accomplish anything we choose to embark upon. With each stone we move, we create ripples of change that start with each of us, and extend far to reach many.

My trip to Miami not only introduced me to some of the neediest and most neglected populations in the United States, but also led me to some of the neediest people on our planet. Only an hour and a half away from the shores of Miami, in the poorest country in the Western Hemisphere, I would meet the people of Haiti.

"Dye mon, gen mon" is a Haitian proverb, "Beyond the Mountains, More Mountains."

In the mountains beyond mountains of Haiti, I was to discover a world of poverty beyond anything that documentaries or images could reflect.

"Bondye do ou: fe pa ou, M a fe pa M," is another Haitian proverb, "God says do your part and I'll do mine."

In Haiti, there was much to be done, and we all needed to play a part.

Dr. Barth Green, who had brought the magic of Shake-A-Leg to Miami, was also trying to cast his magic and move mountains of poverty in Haiti. Barth had first experienced Haiti on a rural medical mission with one of his medical school classmates and fell in love with the people and the country. He was compelled to help.

Barth was one of those truly special people who was a hero in life, not just in his profession. In addition to the magic Barth wove through Shake-A-Leg, he was renowned in his profession for creating miracles every day for spinal cord patients. He was one of the world's top neurosurgeons.

Barth was intent on creating miracles in Haiti. When I heard Barth speak about Haiti, it was like hearing a story from another planet. It seemed unbelievable that a little more than an hour away from one of the richest countries in the world was a country that had been seemingly abandoned by the world. I felt compelled to find out, and so when Barth and his team of doctors next went to Haiti, I changed my sailing shoes for outback shoes and went with them.

Arriving in Haiti *was* like landing on another planet. As the beautiful tropical aqua Caribbean waters disappeared behind the plane, and the coastal shores near the capital of Port au Prince came into focus, poverty could be seen even from the sky.

Instead of the lush tropical vegetation and white sandy beaches one would expect to see rising from a Caribbean island, there was only barren brown land and a murky coastline to be seen. Instead of endless glistening tropical streams flowing through the land, there was only the dull reflection from endless metal roofs packed haphazardly across stretches of shanty towns. It looked somewhat like masses of broken dominos. Not even ninety minutes had passed since we left Miami.

As we emerged from the small and simple airport, the eyes of hundreds of Haitians cramming the streets outside seemed to be upon our group of white visitors. United Nations peacekeeping trucks and tanks seemed to be permanent fixtures beyond the crowd, and the blue helmets and dark rifles were an obvious sign of deep unrest. Yet I sensed a gentleness in the air. I was to find out that gentleness was very much a part of the energy of the people of Haiti. In the poorest country in the Western Hemisphere, I would find a people rich in spirit.

Before I came to Haiti, I had read several books about the history of the country. This was not a country that became a "failed state" simply by itself. I was to learn that poverty often does not "start at home," but is often inflicted by others. The story of Haiti was very much a story of abuse and abandonment by the world around. When a country is strangled by trade policies, aid policies, and political interventions that do more to create dependence than freedom, a country and its people have little chance of survival.

In Haiti, that abuse and abandonment contributed to creating life in a country where starvation was a part of everyday living, where the death of a baby was an anticipated part of giving birth, where children lived without mothers who had been one of the many who died during childbirth, where a mother would typically lose a child before the age of five, where families struggled to earn even a dollar a day, and where every day thousands of infants, children, mothers, and fathers died needlessly as a result of preventable diseases.

When I had traveled through New York, I visited the United Nations headquarters, nobly rising from its wall of flags representing all of its member nations—Haiti being one of them. Inside the headquarters, I browsed an array of framed art that lined the foyer, each containing an article of the Universal Declaration of Human Rights. The first piece showed a person lifted into the sky on the wings of a dove, with the first and very simple article of the declaration printed below, "All human beings are born free and equal in dignity and rights ..." It seemed that while the peacekeepers of the United Nations had reached Haiti, the declaration had not.

As we walked along the outside of Port-au-Prince airport, there were no lines of taxis filled with gas waiting for passengers—that would be a luxury beyond most of the local community. Instead, beat-up cars and pick-ups that one would expect to find in a junkyard ready for the crusher, piled up with people, and then sputtered away.

Our ride from the airport would take us to the Central Plateau of Haiti—the poorest region in the country. We would spend a week in the plateau providing health clinics to various rural communities through the non-profit organization, Project Medishare, which Barth had established ten years before. The medical trip that had brought Barth to Haiti all of those years ago had shown Barth a world in which he was compelled to try to work his magic.

The road from Port-au-Prince to the Central Plateau was not like a road by any reasonable definition. It was more like a steep trail for mountain goats. Boulders protruded from the loosely packed trail every few car lengths, causing the driver to constantly zigzag along a path where there was barely room to maneuver. A maneuver too far to the right would result in the 4WD tumbling down the side of the mountain, where we could see many trucks had already been laid to rest. The trip to the plateau took almost eight hours of slow, rocky, bumpy riding. The distance was only eighty miles—in most countries that would take one hour.

As we traveled through the mountains of Haiti toward the Central Plateau, we passed through seemingly endless villages. Each was scattered with young, naked, bony bodies wandering along the roadside and popping out of tiny, thatched, ramshackle huts. The little bodies were disproportionate to the huge bellies that were swollen from infection. Instead of their bellies being filled with food, they were filled with worms and other intestinal parasites that infested them from drinking polluted water contaminated with human and animal waste, and other waterborne diseases and pathogens. Their hair, which should have been rich and dark, was orange and patchy—a sign of the severe malnutrition that had slowly depleted the nourishment from their small bodies.

It seemed that Haiti had become not a place to live, but to die.

Eleanor Roosevelt, during her time playing a key role in the creation of the Universal Declaration of Human Rights, said, "The destiny of human rights is in the hands of all our citizens in all our communities."

I looked out at these forgotten children and wondered, *"Where are all of the hands to help Haiti?"*

We arrived at the town of Thomonde in the Central Plateau shortly after dark. The smell of charcoal fires was abundant, and the faint voices of small children floated through the air. Ordinarily, the smoky aroma would be accompanied by images of warm fireplaces in cozy homes filled with children playing carefree. In this remote subsistence mountain community, there were no cozy fireplaces in such an imaginary setting. The flicker of the tiny fires was barely enough to cast a light.

The darkness was striking. Light didn't reach this community. The light ended where the power lines stopped much farther down the mountain.

At night, the "main street" of Thomonde seemed like a quaint neighborhood walkway with mostly younger people wandering along the streets. The apparent difference was the quiet. In absence of electrical power, there was barely a sound. It seemed that the wind didn't even reach this place. There was no rustle in the few trees, which even seemed lonely in the quiet darkness.

Soon enough, we pulled off the street and the familiar Project Medishare logo appeared before us as we entered the small compound from where the organization managed its community health program. Our 4WD bore the logo of Project Medishare, which possibly explained the friendly waves and smiles we received through the streets. The eyes of children and parents alike, welcomed us. I was to find out that they knew the presence of the 4WD with the Project Medishare logo meant the "white doctors" had come to provide additional health clinics in the community.

For expectant mothers, the 4WD carrying the Project Medishare logo meant an extra chance to survive childbirth. For other mothers, it meant their malnourished infant might beat the odds and live beyond the age of five. For the elderly in the community, it meant they might receive a simple aspirin to relieve the constant aches and pains of growing old in poverty—at least the physical aches. There was no pill to relieve the emotional aches of outliving children and grandchildren in a community that was dying with the passing of each year.

As we stepped out from the 4WD, the land beneath my feet felt wonderfully still. The eight-hour ride up the mountain felt as if we were on an amusement park ride, except there was a distinct lack of amusement. The reality of the people who lived along the tracks of this "ride," was beyond the imagination of any amusement park. At the end of the ride, they couldn't simply walk out of the gates. They were stuck somewhere between entering and leaving. As distinct from a missing car in an amusement park ride, here it was as if no one knew these people were missing. Our ride seemed to be an invisible ride to an invisible world. Where was the light at the end of the ride?

As we walked toward the small structure of the community health headquarters, we were greeted by the local staff and a generously prepared cooked meal of plantains, rice, and goat. I wondered how many hours had been spent preparing our meal, and how many it could feed in the community.

There is an unreconcilable disparity standing in the midst of such an impoverished community. We come to help, but we come in our 4WD that will stay for a while and then leave. The preparation of our food consumes the precious charcoal that continues to add to the deforestation that destroys the ecosystem. With every mouthful of food, the mouth of a malnourished infant could be fed.

There is no way to reconcile the difference, except to have hope and faith that we bring more help and resources than we consume. Still, it doesn't seem fair. In these "mountains beyond mountains" hope and faith are survival.

I knew, even after such a short glimpse of life here, that these lives would stay with me forever. You can't just switch the channel the way we can do so easily on our televisions; we can't turn the page as easily as we would turn the page of a news magazine. This is every day. This is life for most of the two-thirds of the world who live in poverty. This is a life that is a prison, without justification, but with a life sentence. In many cases, this unjust life is a death sentence.

As we finished our meal, we received a briefing on the following day. We would be spending every moment of light traveling to even more remote communities in the mountains surrounding Thomonde. To thousands of families whose descendants fled slavery hundreds of years ago, these isolated mountains beyond mountains represented their freedom. Yet now, it seemed that poverty was their enslaver.

Our beds for the night were the floors of the few small rooms of the house near the Project Medishare headquarters. Several volunteers chose the roof as a bedroom under the stars. We all had brought sleeping bags and mosquito nets, and more important than a soft bed, was the protection the nets offered from malaria. Our sleeping quarters were luxurious compared to the standard in the community.

We had a small amount of water with which to wash, although quite a few of us preferred to use sanitary body wipes in an effort to consume as little resources as possible during our stay. We brought bottled water for drinking and to brush our teeth. Just a mouthful of the local water was enough to cause stomach and intestinal illnesses, to which a few of the team fell prey, despite their care.

The local community had developed some resistance to the pathogens in the water and even to the mosquito bites carrying infectious disease. Often the feeling of sickness had become so much a part of every day that many of the children and adults were in a state of feeling perpetually sick. Diarrhea, headaches, stomach cramps, and itchiness from skin lesions were a part of waking, sleeping, and breathing.

We woke the next morning to the sound of roosters—Mother Nature's universal wake-up call. I looked to see if any mosquitos had infiltrated my net during the night, but it seemed not. I packed my essentials into my pack for the day—mosquito spray, muesli bars, water bottles, and camera.

That day, we were expected to arrive in five surrounding communities. We would split into groups to reach each of them. I had offered to take photographs throughout the trip—a hobby that I was looking forward to using to capture images that would help to generate funding and awareness when we returned.

Arriving at our first location, I saw immediately that my camera lens wasn't going to be enough. A camera could capture compelling images, but it couldn't adequately convey the feeling of the endless eyes of mothers and children looking at you as their hope between life and death. That sounds dramatic, but in the barren and forgotten mountains of Haiti, isolated from basic food, water, and medicine, help from the outside world was their only relief. Their own country simply didn't have enough to provide for them. The deforested mountains couldn't sustain them.

These communities needed the hands of the world to reach out to them—not to depend on, but to help them become self-sufficient. We needed their voices and faces to reach the outside world, so people more fortunate might feel an obligation to help—not out of sympathy, but out of an overwhelming sense that in a world of plenty, it is simply not right that others die every day from not having enough.

Why is it that the voices of the majority of the world living with so little remain so unheard every day? Why does it take a natural disaster to make headlines to compel people to help? Hundreds of people might die in a natural disaster that makes international headlines, but where is the headline that tens of thousands of people died today from poverty? Poverty is the world's most vicious killer, yet it is allowed to continue without even making headlines.

Is it because we feel that we don't have the power to make a difference? Is it because we feel that whatever we do to try to affect an enormous challenge will be a drop in the ocean, a ripple that won't be felt?

Don't we see that a ripple can turn into a tsunami? Don't we believe in the potential of our unlimited collective power that comes from the power of one?

Bishop Desmond Tutu said, "It means a great deal to those who are oppressed to know that they are not alone. And never let anyone tell you that what you are doing is insignificant."

We must believe we can move mountains, before the soil will start to shift. When we believe enough, we can cause a landslide. We can displace the earth. Mountains will move.

The more we practice moving mountains for others, the more mountains we will be able to move for our *self*. We will realize that our unlimited power only becomes greater when we extend it to others.

Imagine our lives if every day we woke believing that we had the power to move mountains. Mountains for others. Mountains for our *self*. Where would we start? Which mountains would we choose to move for our *self*? Which mountains would we move for others?

"The man who removes a mountain begins by carrying away small stones," teaches an ancient Chinese proverb.

Here, amidst the mountains beyond mountains of Haiti, among hundreds of faces, one could feel overwhelmed by the challenge of how to help. But with every smile that is returned to you, you realize that one person at a time, one smile at a time, one gesture of help at a time, we remove one stone after another. With each stone we remove, we lighten the load of a mother, of a child. With each stone we remove, the next feels lighter. With each stone we remove, the belief that we have the power to move mountains grows.

Belief is a choice, and with the choice to believe, we have all the power we need.

As a child, I didn't know I had that power, and so I became a victim. As an adult, I know I have the choice, and I choose to believe in that power.

As a child, I had an instinct to survive. As an adult, I can combine that instinct with belief and purpose.

As a child, I was waiting for someone to come to help me. As an adult, I choose to help my *self*.

As a young adult, I thought that helping *me* to get by was enough to live. Now, I know that I can live bigger by helping others.

We can all live bigger. We can move mountains for our *self*. We can move mountains for others.

By the end of the day, we had seen hundreds of people at our small health clinic outpost. The outpost was an old isolated abandoned concrete structure that seemed as if it were on the edge of its own mountain in the middle of these mountains beyond mountains. We drove for miles in our 4WD to get to the outpost, along what seemed to be more like dusty hiking trails than any type of road.

Small trees and shrubs emerged every now and then, but there seemed to be nothing more around. There was no sign of life.

As we were navigating the trail, our outpost appeared in the distance. The clue that it was our destination was the large group of people that gathered all around. In the middle of these seemingly empty mountains, such a large gathering of people was a landmark.

Through Project Medishare's network of local community health workers who walked miles each day to reach isolated families, word had traveled far that the doctors would be here. The people came from all over the mountains. Many came, despite the pain of walking for miles, hoping for some kind of relief. Mothers, children, the elderly—they all came.

As I looked around, there was no sign of a community. There were no houses, not even any of the thatched huts that we had seen in the villages along the drive from Port-au-Prince to Thomonde. Yet people kept arriving from trails leading off into the mountains. It seemed incredible that so many people could survive in such isolation. The reality was, they were only barely surviving.

In these rugged mountains, shoes were a necessity that were a luxury. These mothers and children would walk for hours each day in bare feet through jagged tracks that our feet would only survive in hiking boots. Instead of hats shading their faces from the sun, heavy containers of water upon their heads cast the only shadow.

Again, the disparity was striking. *"In a world of plenty, how can so many be without?"*

I found my own answer, *"Their voices are simply not heard beyond these mountains. Their faces are simply not seen beyond these mountains. Their experiences are certainly not lived beyond these mountains."*

I believe in a compassionate world. It has been said that we each have a cross to bear. Maybe we bear that cross so we know the struggles of another. I believe that ultimately we each want to help another, but finding the way can be difficult.

If we start with the simple question, "Who do I want to help?" and simply make the choice to help, then help begins. It need only start by moving the smallest stone.

If we keep asking, "Which mountains do I want to move?" I think we find common threads between the mountains we desire to move for our *self* and the mountains we feel compelled to move for others. When we discover that "one thing" that is the link between helping our *self* and helping others, I believe we find authentic purpose. Then, I believe our unlimited power is unleashed.

I started to realize that "one thing" for me was about not having a voice, about not being heard, about being vulnerable and with no one to help. It would take longer for me to realize all that "one thing" was about, but for now, I was feeling purposeful helping vulnerable and impoverished communities—whether in Miami, or in Haiti, or elsewhere.

I was so far away from the corporate world for which I had "trained," but I was so much closer to feeling as though I was playing a more purposeful part in life. With that sense of purpose in life growing, so too, was the feeling of being at home in life.

Over the next five days, we visited many communities scattered throughout the mountains. Despite the devastating poverty the communities shared, they also shared an incredible spirit and an enormous sense of pride.

Two years earlier, I experienced that same extreme pride in the impoverished border town of Acuna, Mexico. I traveled there with a non-profit organization, Every Child Is Ours, to give school supplies to some of the poorest schools in the area. I was struck as we drove through the most impoverished communities where metal sheets and mesh tarps were strung together to make shelter. Each shelter had been made into a home that was clearly the pride of the woman of the household. The homes were settled upon a ground of dirt and clay, and the image of a mother sweeping dirt off the harder clay below yelled pride and dignity. The healthy plant sapling in a small plastic planter next to the metal sheet of the entrance of many of the shelters, told a story of care and nurturing in a community where water was a luxury.

In the Central Plateau of Haiti—the poorest region of the poorest country in the Western Hemisphere—pride and dignity were immensely evident in every community. People wore their best clothes to come to see the doctors, and if they barely had clothes, the clothes they wore had been cleaned for hours in the nearby streams. The whites I saw in the clothes of the children were whiter than any clothes I had seen.

Every day, warm smiles greeted us. The gratitude was immense. The patience of mothers and children who walked hours to come, who would wait for hours, and then walk hours home was humbling. There was an unrelenting resilience among all who came. Their parents and grandparents had overcome slavery, and it seemed everyone was doing all they could to honor that history by not allowing poverty to enslave their communities now.

The sense of spirit, shared community, and collective responsibility among these communities made rich countries look poor in comparison. In poverty, there is an essential need to help one another. There is an essential need to care for each other. In contrast, living in an environment where everything material is available, the need for others, our sense of community, seems to become diminished.

The Dalai Lama, in his book, *Ethics for the New Millennium*, observes the loneliness often found in wealthy communities that seems to take the place of the sense of community often found in the poorest communities. "In place of the sense of community and belonging, which we find such a reassuring feature of less wealthy (and generally rural) societies, we find a high degree of loneliness and alienation [in wealthier communities]. Despite the fact that millions live in close proximity to one another, it seems that many people, especially among the old, have no one to talk to but their pets."

Instead of seeking community, we seek independence, as though the greater the independence we gain from each other, the greater is the sign of our individual advancement and achievement. The Dalai Lama comments that such "advancement" only leads to isolation, far from happiness and the realization of our dreams.

*They are so caught up with the idea of acquiring still more that they make no time for anything else in their lives. In their absorption, they actually lose the dream of happiness, which riches were to have provided. As a result, they are constantly tormented, torn between doubt about what might happen and the hope of gaining more, and plagued with mental and emotional suffering—even though outwardly they appear to be leading entirely successful and comfortable lives.*

In our quest for material gain and survival in "wealthier" nations, we often have no time to pursue what is most meaningful. We often don't even have time to pause to think about it. Until it is too late.

What wealth is there in our lives when we are poor inside? What is going to sustain us when the material things become an unmanageable burden? What difference can we make when our bellies are full, but our spirits are empty?

In the mountains beyond mountains of Haiti, one can't help but feel blessed with the opportunities we have in wealthier nations. We have food in our bellies, schools in which we can learn, and health and wellness centers where we can rejuvenate our minds and bodies. Most of all, we have the opportunity to be of so much help to others.

One can't help but feel that we have been given an enormous gift that we can give back to others. We can help to create communities that have enough to provide physical comfort. We can help to provide a sense of shared responsibility to provide inner comfort. Through small acts and large acts, we can show there is always help at hand.

When we come together to help, there is no end to what we can accomplish. When there is a mountain that needs to be moved, we can join with others to take away the stones. We can know that our efforts can be infinitely multiplied when we care enough to act for each other.

The images of Haiti have become a constant companion. It is a country and a people that stay with you once you visit and stand amidst communities full of spirit and hope. I left Haiti wanting to find solutions, believing that I must be able to help. I would end up returning many times.

Over the years, I worked with several non-profit organizations. We built schools, health clinics, maternity clinics, and helped farmers grow more crops. With each effort, we moved more stones, hand in hand with the local communities.

One of the organizations with which I helped build a school in Haiti was Step by Step Foundation, a Miami-based non-profit appropriately named to try to affect change in Haiti and elsewhere—step by step. When we walk with the local people, step by step, we are committed to a long journey, and we have their courage, resilience, and determination as our greatest inspiration.

There is so much to be done in Haiti and elsewhere in the world—step by step, stone by stone. If we can each play our part, mountains will move. The people of Haiti believe in moving mountains, even if, beyond mountains, there are more mountains. We can believe too, and we can keep helping until every mountain moves.

We will see that we can each move mountains, far from us, close to us, and within us.

## MOMENTS OF PAUSE

1.  When you pause to consider that which is most meaningful in your life, beyond that which is material, what emerges?

2.  What are the mountains that you wish to move in your life?

3.  What are the mountains you wish to move in the world? Who do you want to help in the world?

4.  Are the shoes in which you are standing adequate to help you move the mountains you wish to move?

5.  What are the first stones you need to move to start moving your mountains? What first steps do you need to take? What is helping you? What is hindering you?

## MORE MOMENTS FOR YOU

### Fourteen

# From Haiti to Harvard

*"Above all be of single aim; have a legitimate and useful purpose, and devote yourself unreservedly to it."*

—JAMES ALLEN

W HEN WE CHANGE OUR SHOES, we can discover worlds filled with purpose and significance. Throughout my journey, I was seeing how much we can change our life when we change our shoes. In Miami, in Mexico, and in Haiti, amidst the disadvantaged, the disabled, and the impoverished, I had seen that when we change our shoes and walk in the shoes of another, we can not only change our life, but we can also change the lives of those around us. We can start to change the world.

Sitting amidst the mountains beyond mountains of Haiti, I decided to change my shoes to try to create more change for Haiti and for other impoverished and disadvantaged communities. This time, I would change the outback boots I had needed for Haiti to the walking shoes I would need to get around Harvard campuses.

Over the past years, I had taken some executive education programs at Harvard Kennedy School. Those programs introduced me to a family of people who were compelled to make a difference in the world. When I decided that I wanted to further my studies in the area of global health and development, Harvard Kennedy School was the only place that I considered.

Haiti had compelled me to commit all of my energy to create change in the world. Sitting amidst the mountains of Haiti, I had one of those most precious "ah-ha" moments when you feel as though all of the experiences in your life converge to place you exactly where you are meant to be. You find that your journey has led you to a place where you can see a reason for all of the things that have happened in your life—like looking backward down a runway and seeing the lights lit up perfectly along a path to propel you forward.

Amidst those mountains, I knew I needed to dedicate all of my efforts to helping those whose voices couldn't be heard, who were vulnerable, invisible, and who were on the fringes without a thought from anyone. I was compelled to do so because it resonated so strongly with me. It took seeing my own reflection in the deep eyes of the people of Haiti, for that sense to connect to the deepest places in me. It moved all I had experienced into alignment. The mirror into my *self* had never been clearer.

I returned from Haiti, and set about applying for a Masters Degree at the Harvard Kennedy School. The Kennedy School was founded on the belief that each one of us has a unique opportunity and responsibility to advance the public interest, no better articulated than through the famous words of John F. Kennedy, "Ask not what your country can do for you, but what you can do for your country." In this era of globalization, when our world needs to be one community for all of us to thrive, it seemed that we also needed to "ask not what the world can do for you, but what you can do for the world."

I knew that doing a Masters at Harvard would enable me to explore that question. What I didn't know, was that the experience I would have at the Kennedy School would have an incredibly different impact on me than I ever expected. I would find that in order to "help the world," I still needed to do a lot of work on me. Harvard was the last place I expected to do that work, but it turned out to be the greatest learning I was to experience there.

It was another beautiful, sunny, "beach day" in Miami when I pulled out the *Official Guide to the GMAT* study book. This was the last thing I expected to be doing when I left Australia with my backpack four years earlier. There was no plan I could have created to bring me to this point. It seems that sometimes our plans can limit us because they are confined by our thinking at that time, and leave little room for unimagined possibilities to enter.

Michelangelo said, "The greater danger for most of us is not that our aim is too high and we miss it, but that it is too low and we hit it." I always thought my "plans" and goals had been ambitious, but the unimagined possibilities that the universe presented when I stopped the "rational" planning and allowed my spirit to be led in the direction that resonated with my "inner compass," took me beyond anything I could have ever planned.

The Kennedy School was all about believing that we have the power to make the changes toward which we aspire. There was an enormous sense of family around that belief. I sensed I wouldn't just be going to a school to do a Masters program, but that I would be joining a family of people all drawn together to try to create a better world.

The program would set me back financially, but following my dreams seemed more important than my bank account. I would need to use the remainder of the funds from selling my apartment in Australia to pay for my tuition. I wasn't a permanent resident or citizen of the United States, so I didn't qualify for the vast amount of scholarships available; and because I hadn't lived in Australia for several years, and didn't have a clear plan to return, I was ineligible for those scholarships. If I chose to do the Masters program, I would be putting all I had into the program. But sometimes, I knew, you need to be prepared to give something up to make the changes you want to make in your life.

When I left Australia, I put everything I had into leaving with my backpack, and it had taken me to extraordinary places. I had a sense that putting everything into Harvard would also take me to places I hadn't yet imagined. I didn't know quite where those places would be, but that, I had come to know, was the way of the universe.

In April, six months after submitting my application to Harvard, I received a creme-colored envelope in the mail bearing the familiar Harvard crimson crest. I had spoken to the program manager for the Masters degree the week before, and I knew the letter inside contained the answer to my application. With huge anxiety, I opened the envelope.

"Dear Katherine:

Congratulations! I am pleased to offer you admission to the John F. Kennedy School of Government's Lucius N. Littauer Master in Public Administration Program ..."

I had to read the letter a few times to believe it. This little girl from Down Under was going to Harvard.

My happiness for this new journey ahead came mostly from the feeling that the universe was giving me a check mark for the path that I was on. I felt so compelled to pursue this path, and my compass was resonating so strongly in this direction, that I had to believe in it with every part of me. Receiving the acceptance letter from Harvard was like the universe telling me, "We believe in you, too."

For me, having grown up in an environment that crushed every shred of my confidence, and left me feeling that my being in this world was truly a mistake—that in every sense of the word, I really was illegitimate—the feeling that something "bigger than me" believed in me, was like a lost child finding home. I flashed back to the image of sitting at my dining room table, my wrist bandaged from the cut I had made to try to end everything, my father glaring at me. I reflected on the time I had tried to take too much of the antibiotic medication I was on in the seventh grade, but failed to have any effect. I thought about the countless times I had contemplated suicide in other ways—being in a place of absolute hopelessness, and feeling that there was absolutely no point to anything, no point to living, and no point in trying.

Now, sitting with my letter of acceptance to Harvard, I was struck by how close I came to allowing someone else to take away the opportunities of life from me. I was so close to enabling someone else to cause me to give up on my *self*.

We are the only ones who can give up on our *self*, despite everything that may happen to us—no matter how many people will try to stop us in life. If we don't walk the next step, we will never know what is just around the corner.

Eleanor Roosevelt said, "You gain strength, courage and confidence by every experience in which you really stop to look fear in the face. You are able to say to yourself, 'I have lived through this horror. I can take the next thing that comes along.' You must do the thing you think you cannot do." Soon enough, with each step that we take, with every corner that we turn, with every choice we make to keep going, we move further away from what holds us back. Our fears fade, and we know that there is nothing we cannot do.

With each experience along my journey, I felt stronger, more courageous, more confident. I felt I could do anything that I chose to do, especially as I contemplated my acceptance letter to Harvard.

When I left home at seventeen, I didn't know what lay ahead, but I was determined to find freedom and take whatever control of my life that I could. Working as a check-out chick at a local grocery store made my family and friends question the path I was pursuing, but I didn't care. It gave me breathing space.

Over the years after leaving home, I was happy to work two jobs, day and night. That way, I could save enough money to gain some financial security, and go to college to create some choices for me. I worked through the days, and went to college at night. After night classes, I went to another job and packed grocery store shelves into the early hours of the morning. I kept going and going to try to create a hopeful future full of choices.

When I left Australia, searching for something more, I again didn't know what I would find. I just knew I needed something more to survive—more than the "false securities" that I had created around me.

My journey over the past five years since leaving Australia had taken me to extraordinary places, and now it was taking me to Harvard. Most importantly, my journey now felt more purposeful than ever.

With the possibility of going to Harvard now a reality, my thoughts shifted entirely to all that year could hold. The opportunity to be immersed in a Masters program at one of the best and most prestigious universities in the world was an enormous gift, and I didn't want to take an ounce of that for granted.

The particular program at the Kennedy School was the Mid-Career Masters in Public Administration. The flexibility and diversity of areas of study of the degree were immense, enabling cross-registration at any of the other graduate schools throughout Harvard—from the Business School, to the Law School, to the

School of Medicine, to the Divinity School. Now that I could look through the course options knowing that I was "in," I felt like a kid in a candy store. *"How do I possibly squeeze so many course options into one year?"* I contemplated.

As much as I was attracted to the opportunity to explore such an array of areas of study, I was equally attracted to discovering the extraordinarily diverse mix of fellow "Mid-Careers," as participants are known. The Mid-Career degree was renowned, among other things, for attracting distinguished leaders from around the world and from numerous areas including the military, government, private sector, the non-profit sector, international security, international development, and more. The alumni of the degree were a "who's who" of people setting out to "change the world." They included Nobel Laureates, Pulitzer Prize winners, Presidents, Prime Ministers, Secretaries of State, World Bank Presidents, and Secretary Generals of the United Nations.

The Kennedy School, of all places, was the place to devote oneself unreservedly to a legitimate and useful purpose, to be aspirational without limits. It was a place to dream big, and have the unshakeable confidence that we can move the mountains we seek to move in the world. It was a place where the motto "Never, Never, Never Give Up!" resounded without end.

Cambridge, Massachusetts, was the quintessential university town. Harvard seemed everywhere, and the crimson "H" appeared to be the most prominent symbol around, with every other person wearing the "H" somewhere.

The Masters program started with a one-month intensive summer program in June, which included an orientation for everyone. The greatest part of the summer program was meeting all of my classmates. Everyone came with extraordinary stories from extraordinary places. Many had lived through oppression and horrors of the greatest kinds—genocide, terrorism, war, poverty—and had been driven to act to do something about changing the future. The Kennedy School held that common dream for each of us.

None of us, however, really knew what the year ahead would bring. Everyone was already very successful in their fields, so the year was not about taking the next step "up the ladder." It was more about taking the next step toward that "legitimate and useful purpose." When it came down to it, amidst the somewhat intimidating hallways of Harvard, we were all just trying to find our way—to step into different shoes and explore new paths. There was a simple humility from that feeling that took away some of the intimidation of being amidst the hallways of the big crimson "H."

During the summer program, I would meet a professor, Ron Heifetz, whose courses would have the greatest impact of any of the courses I would take at Harvard. I would end up taking four of his courses over the year ahead.

Coincidentally, Ron Heifetz was the cousin of Dr. Barth Green from Miami. Ron was the founder of the Center for Public Leadership at the Kennedy School, and ran a series of leadership courses that were renowned for creating havoc amongst students. Stories circulated that participants would break down in tears, have torrential verbal exchanges with each other, that tempers would flare, the vulnerable would be exposed, and the strong would be broken down. Through all of that, it was intended that we might learn something about our *self* and about "leadership." It sounded like a military boot camp, but without the physical components.

Among other things, Ron Heifetz was a psychiatrist. One of the underlying premises of Ron's approach to leadership was that if you don't have your own "stuff" sorted out, you will be of little help to others. Ron's courses were more of an experimental laboratory in human behavior, than a typical "textbook" course on leadership—but then again, this was Harvard, and things didn't quite work the traditional way. As much as the economics and analytical courses were known to be intellectually rigorous, Ron's leadership courses were reputed to be personally grueling. We were warned that if we were under any emotional strain, we should think twice about Ron's classes. *"Hello!"* I thought, *"We are at Harvard, of course we are under emotional strain!"*

I had come across one of Ron's books while I was attending one of the executive education courses at the Kennedy School the year before. Ron's book, *Leadership On Line: Staying Alive through the Dangers of Leading,* had compelled me to take Ron's classes before I heard the stories of his classes. The book was the first I had read on leadership that boldly and fearlessly dealt with the inner world of the "leader" and, for that matter, of anyone trying to affect change.

Ron delved into the vulnerabilities that serve to defeat us, and the "triggers" from childhood and elsewhere that serve to "set us off" without warning. Ron probed all that is sitting in the depths of us that serve to cut us down, rather than help us to soar and achieve our dreams—those things that can stop us from helping our *self,* and from making a difference in the world.

"Every day brings you opportunities to raise important questions, speak to higher values, and surface unresolved conflicts. Every day you have the chance to make a difference in the lives of people around you. And every day you must decide whether to put your contribution out there, or keep it to yourself to avoid upsetting anyone, and get through another day." This was part of the introduction to Ron's book, and it struck at the core of what had been most personally confronting for me.

When the work that you do with most purpose strikes at the core of the things that have caused you the most trauma, how do you stay alive? How do we take care of our *self* when we pursue the things that are most purposeful to us and at the same time, are the most painful to us?

When we take up the cause to help the vulnerable, we put our vulnerability on the line. We feel the vulnerability all over again. When we take up the cause for children who have been abused, we see the pain of our abuse reflected in their eyes. We feel the pain again. When a mother creates a campaign to stop the suicide that took her child, she feels that loss each time she speaks to inspire others. We have already lived through our worst experiences once, when we take those up as a cause, we can risk being destructive to our *self* and to those we are trying to help unless we know how to survive.

Ron's courses were all about surviving though the most potentially destructive experiences along the path to creating the change we want to create in the world. If we don't prepare our *self* when we set off on a courageous path fueled by the injustices that we have experienced, our *self* can become our own worst offender.

Helping others can be traumatic because it can be a window into our own unresolved pain. Instead of becoming triumphant for our cause, we can become a victim to it once again.

My pain had always been my weakest link. I'm not sure that we ever really get rid of the pain. I think we develop ways to make the link stronger. Just like when we break an arm, the bone will heal, but the memory of the pain often stays. If we sense a threat to that arm, we might react much more aggressively and protectively than to another area. Most of the time our response happens before we can even think about it—it is instinctive. We don't have time to rationalize our response, let alone control and temper it.

I have spent a lot of time re-training my responses to things that tap into the pain from the past. The pain may never completely disappear, but now I am much better at stopping it from being destructive in the present moment. More than that, I can turn it into something purposeful. We all can. I came to realize that moving forward isn't about suppressing pain, it's about transforming pain. Buddhist philosophy and meditation had particularly helped me transform the negative energy of pain that traps us into the positive energy that moves us forward.

I came to see that losing pain is like losing weight—you need to stick with it every day. You need to know what is healthy for you and what is not. You need to create a "nutritional emotional diet." You need to fuel your *self* with things that will energize your *self*, and manage your cravings for things that you know are harmful. You need to make it part of your daily lifestyle. It is ongoing work, commitment, and perseverance, but few great accomplishments ever come any other way.

Maya Angelou's poem, "Still I Rise," is filled with the courage and triumph of rising from pain and oppression. These words had given me inspiration and determination along my journey. I could believe that I, like each of us, can rise.

> *...Did you want to see me broken?*
> *Bowed head and lowered eyes?*
> *Shoulders falling down like teardrops,*
> *Weakened by my soulful cries.*

> *...Out of the huts of history's shame*
> *I rise*
> *Up from a past that's rooted in pain*
> *I rise*
> *I'm a black ocean, leaping and wide,*
> *Welling and swelling I bear in the tide.*

> *Leaving behind nights of terror and fear*
> *I rise*
> *Into a daybreak that's wondrously clear*
> *I rise*

*Bringing the gifts that my ancestors gave,*
*I am the dream and the hope of the slave.*
*I rise*
*I rise*
*I rise.*

I had come to realize how much we are slaves to our pain unless we free our *self* from it. We can't rise above our pain if we are buried in it. When we rise from our pain, the shackles that have bound us fall away. The gates of our prison open. We can walk forward filled with light, rather than shrouded by darkness. We can feel the opportunity in each moment, rather than oppression. We can feel captivated by the magic in each moment, rather than feel captured by fear. We can feel our *self* come to life, and soar toward our greatest self. We can live our greatest life.

Oprah Winfrey has quoted Maya Angelou, her dear friend, many times as Oprah helped millions overcome pain and all that can keep us trapped. "When you know better, you do better." Once we know we can rise above our pain, what we can do becomes unlimited. We can do better for our *self*. We can do better for others. We can do better for the world. With each passing moment, as we rise above all that keeps us enslaved, as we come to know better, we come to live greater.

Throughout Ron's courses, it was striking how much pain was carried by so many in the room, still buried beneath the surface, still enslaving its host, still limiting all that we can be. I didn't expect in a class on leadership at Harvard, filled with leaders and aspiring leaders in their respective fields, for there to be so much pain, and so much tension and emotion erupting. For some reason, I thought everyone else had probably been better able than me to deal with all they had experienced in their lives. Instead, it seemed the playing field was fairly equal.

Over the years, I doubted my emotional strength because others had been seemingly able to "get over" their pain, whereas I could get stuck in pain that was still there. Yet in Ron's class, I saw so many people still holding their pain, and how much that pain was sparking destructive reactions, and causing chaos and conflict. Ron would refer to those "sparks" as "triggers"—those things that happen that "push our buttons" and send us out of control—sometimes only for moments, sometimes for much longer.

When those "triggers" occur, our weakest link is exposed. At the times when we most need to be strong—when we are most vehemently defending our causes, or pursuing our highest purposes—those weaknesses have the power to bring us to our knees.

Throughout the abuse of my childhood, I had constantly been brought to my knees. I had caved in emotionally to my father. I had caved in to my fear. I couldn't find a strong enough voice to stand up for me. As the years passed, I lost the confidence that I could stand up to an emotional exchange without caving in. I kept in the back of my mind that I would always be emotionally weaker than the next person. On the surface, I could put up a great debate, but on the inside a little girl was still trembling.

Intellectually, I could hold my own. Intellectually, I had laid solid footing. Emotionally, I was still fragile beneath a "competent" exterior, and each trigger would cause another fracture in my foundations. It was frustrating, because I understood what was happening, but there was something I was still missing that wasn't enabling me to overcome what was happening.

It took one of Ron's courses in the second semester, facilitated by one of Ron's colleagues, Dean Williams, for me to have one of my most significant realizations. I realized that what I was still missing was the voice I had never given to what I had experienced. I had never acknowledged my pain. I had never really given voice to my abuse. I had whispered it to a very few, but it was still a relative secret lurking beneath the surface. Sitting amidst the tension and tempers that had been provoked in each of the classes, the pain in the eyes of all of those around me was a mirror into my own pain.

While I was in New York four years earlier, looking at the Elder Grace exhibit, I noted a quote by Chester Higgins, Jr., "We all need a real mirror every now and then." Maybe this was the mirror into my *self* that I needed. Maybe the biggest thing I was missing was that my story and my pain were still buried, trying to escape, trying to be heard, trying to be acknowledged.

I didn't want to be continually provoked by triggers that would set off the pain. I didn't want to keep feeling that my father was still reaching into my life from his grave. I had to take that power away from him. I had to free my *self*. Through class after class watching people's pain play out in so many different ways, I kept wondering how it would feel if I shared the pain of my abuse.

In the class, it seemed that everyone was attacking another without any regard for all that might be happening inside that person. *"Are we so blinded by our own pain that we can't see that others are also in pain?"* I wondered. *"If we can only work to attack each other and not work to heal each other, how can we possibly make progress?"*

I contemplated telling my story to the class. I wondered whether telling my story could help me make a connection to others. Would it make any difference? Would it create a bridge to others in the class? Would it relieve me in any way? Would it help anyone else?

I reflected back over one of the earlier courses I took with Ron in the first semester that had been particularly confronting for me. I realized in that course that one of the pains that was most deeply rooted in me was that no one who should have cared, cared enough to help me. People who should have taken responsibility didn't, they simply turned their backs. It was easier for them, and less complicated, to walk away. That feeling was triggered in one of Ron's classes in a way that cracked every piece of me. Ironically, it was triggered by something seemingly so disconnected and so relatively trivial, but it plummeted me into a very dark place.

The seemingly disconnected event was related to one of the situations that I came to learn Ron often introduced at the beginning of his courses. Ron would invariably accept more people into his courses than space allowed and leave the class to deal with it.

In the first class of our course, people expressed varying degrees of frustration at the situation. Some people just didn't care, others felt the situation to be unfair because the extra people didn't pay for the class, while those who were officially enrolled had paid for admission to the class through a points system that meant they might miss out on another class. Others who had enrolled didn't want to sit on the floor while some of the additional people were able to sit in the limited chairs. Some were concerned about the fire hazard created by cramming so many people into the lecture theater. One person shared a story of how a family member was killed in one of the burning buildings in the September 11th terrorist attacks on the Twin Towers in New York City—for her the fire hazard created by the situation was particularly traumatic.

I was stunned as people in the class, one after the other, discounted the next person's concern. They just didn't seem to care. Even after the story of September 11th was told, people didn't even pause to consider the effect of the situation on that person. They wanted to move on to "more important" issues of leadership. I couldn't believe that in a class on leadership at the Harvard Kennedy School, the place where aspiring leaders supposedly came, that there was such disregard for others. Of all the places I expected there to be a sense of concern for the welfare of others, it was here.

In the final moments of the class, after considering how I could possibly express the sinking feeling inside me, all I could do was express the thought that was pounding in my head. "This isn't about an overcrowded room. It's about taking responsibility for the welfare of others. How can you sit in a class on leadership and not even care about the person next to you?"

The class ended with most people being offended at my suggestion, and others still not even seeming to care. I was left with an overwhelming sense of injustice, a sick feeling in my stomach that went far beyond the walls of the classroom. That was the start of my getting to the core of one of my biggest pains—the hopeless and angry feeling that ultimately no one cares, that no one will pause to acknowledge the pain of someone else, that it is a pointless endeavor to try to get others to care, and that you are ultimately alone.

I realized the connection I felt to the vulnerable and disadvantaged communities through which I had traveled, was seeded in what had happened to me. I felt the injustice from the wrong that had been done to me, by people who simply walked away without a second thought, who completely discarded their responsibilities. I realized that the depth of my drive to help others was seeded in the help that no one gave to me.

Yet the feelings that rose in me during the class, made me see that a big part of me still felt like a victim, and was still reacting from the space of a victim. *"Am I doing all that I am doing just to try to heal my self?"* I came to Harvard to see how I could better help "save the world." But now, my entire sense of why I was doing what I was doing felt thrown into chaos. *"Am I trying to 'save the world' just to save my self? Am I ultimately selfish, or really trying to unselfishly serve others?"* My sense of purpose was thrown upside down and inside out.

I questioned every aspect of what I was doing. I suddenly felt completely out of place, and questioned every part of my *self* all over again. *"Why am I here anyway? Is it a mistake to be here? Who do I think I am to be here? Inside I am still that worthless, discarded little girl."*

At that point, and during the rest of Ron's classes throughout the first semester, I felt the depth of my pain that came from people not caring for me through my childhood. I felt the pain of people walking away from their responsibilities—of a father who should have simply been a father, of the teachers who should have paid attention, of the doctor who should have intervened, of people I reached out to who couldn't be bothered to help. I felt an overwhelming sense of blame toward others—I had always directed that blame at me. Ron's classes opened a Pandora's box inside me that I thought was well and truly secure. The last thing I expected at Harvard, was to be thrown back into a darkness that I thought I had left behind.

It took one of my friends from the class, Mavis, to practically drag me to one of the course counselors for me to see that I needed help to work through all that was coming up. Mavis could see that I needed help long before I could see that. It seems that sometimes those around us can see more than we are able to see alone. Left to me, I would have done what I had always done, which was to deal with my feelings alone.

I realized in that moment, that dealing with my feelings alone kept me isolated, disconnected, and untrusting. It limited what I could do, because I could only do so much alone and isolated. In that space of isolation, the self-defeating thoughts and feelings were at home, and given the chance, they could emerge and take over.

The challenge for me was to take the step to change the way I dealt with those feelings. I needed to reach out to others to ask for help. That challenge, however, struck at the core of all of my survival instincts. It would cause me to go beyond who I had come to trust—me, to those I had come to not trust—others. All of my experiences in opening up to others had only resulted in more disregard and more abandonment. The thought of opening up to others now, rocked every part of me.

Yet in the present moment, I felt something more. There was something different that gave me confidence. My journey had shown me that there was so much more to me than the "little" part of me that I had always thought was *all* of me. My journey had made me less afraid of looking into the darkness and confronting it, no matter how painful it might be. I had come to trust in the light that would come through the darkness. Now, challenging my survival mechanisms, and stepping into unknown territory, seemed to be a necessary transition to something more, rather than something to keep me stuck, just surviving, in the same small space.

I had also come to be more able to separate the things that were the true source of my pain from those things that triggered that pain. When I felt intimidated, offended, minimized, or ignored, I came to see that I was reacting from a place that was full of pain from my childhood, rather than putting the present moment into its own perspective.

In Ron's class in the first semester, I realized the depth of what I was feeling was coming from my childhood, not from what was happening in the class. Once I was able to recognize and understand those "triggers," I could start to redirect that energy into something productive, rather than something destructive. I could more clearly consider what I needed to do in the present to move forward, rather than to be thrown backward. Those "triggers" became clues as to where I still needed to do work, to constantly tune-up, and keep nurturing the weakest parts of me so the whole of me could be strong.

I also knew that it would take ongoing work, exercise every day, to keep moving forward. There was no effortless path. There would probably be no end to the discoveries of those things that triggered the pain from my childhood, but as long as I saw those things as navigating points, they would serve to continually help me to stay on a path that was centered in the present, and not driven by the past.

As I sat in the class of Dean Williams in the second semester, contemplating giving voice to my abuse, I felt as though I had arrived at a major navigating point. As I saw the pain that was circulating throughout the class, my own pain and fear was triggered.

On one hand, the thought of finally giving voice to my biggest secret was terrifying, especially in such a hostile environment where everyone seemed to be shut down by the next person. I had long given up on telling my story when no one listened to me as a child. I had come to believe that my story didn't mean anything, and that telling it certainly wouldn't make any difference to anything or anyone.

On the other hand, the opportunity to give voice to something that held me prisoner for so long felt relieving. If I was ever going to be free, I needed to free the pain. I needed to speak the words. I needed to care enough for my *self* to find the courage to stand up and speak against the most wrongful thing that was done to me. How could I think I was going to stand for others, if I couldn't stand for my *self*? How could I be a voice for the causes I wanted to pursue, if I couldn't find a voice for me?

Coincidentally, over the past weeks, I had taken a self-defense course with some of my classmates through the Cambridge Police Department. The course was a "Rape Aggression Defense" program, specifically for women to defend against rape and attack. Police officers acted as attackers and we were shown how to defend against an attack. The course did something completely unexpected for me. For the first time, I was able to shout "No!!!" as loud as I could, and physically fight back. It was as though the scream I had been trying to unleash as a child was finally released. Those giant shouts of "No!" came from the deepest part of me. I felt more chains releasing and falling away inside me. As I shouted and knocked the officer to the ground, I felt as though I was standing for my *self* for the first time. Strong. Confident. Determined.

If we each want to stand for our *self*, to reach beyond the things that hold us back, to pursue the causes that are important to us, we each need to start by giving voice to the things that keep us silent. We may feel torn apart by the thoughts of what might or might not be when we give voice to the things that most terrify us, but we are already torn apart. Our voice can help bring us back together. Our voice can help us rise.

I had questioned and re-questioned what felt most purposeful to me in my life and in my work, and that remained to help others who had been made vulnerable, who had been cast aside, and who were struggling to find themselves amidst the pain of their experiences. I couldn't serve that purpose if I couldn't tell my story, and help others tell their story and be heard.

The Buddha said, "Your work is to discover your work, and then with all your heart give yourself to it." The only way I could completely give my heart to the work I wanted to do, was to open up, to speak, and to make sure I was heard. Until I accomplished the work I needed to do within me, I knew I wouldn't be able to accomplish the work I wanted to do in the world.

Suddenly, the thought of finally giving voice to my abuse felt energizing. It felt liberating—that there was a purpose to giving it voice. I felt the universe nudging me to tell my story, and that despite the terrifying feelings that were rising inside, the only way forward was to give voice to that of which I was most afraid.

As the class continued around me, all of these thoughts running through my head made the moments seem like hours. I felt torn between keeping the silence, and speaking out in the hope that maybe this time, things would be different. Maybe my voice would make a difference. In these moments, I felt my waypoints aligning—I had reached a point in my life when I needed to release my voice.

Yet now, I needed to speak in a way that could be heard. I decided that before the next class, I would share with some of my friends in the class, that I was going to tell my story. I would ask for their help to allow my story to be heard. In the hostile environment of the class, I knew I needed help to keep my voice alive. Otherwise, there would inevitably be someone who simply wouldn't care about my story and continue on to another topic of conversation without a second thought—my voice would be buried.

In our efforts to be heard, there is always someone waiting in the wings, ready to silence us. Unless we prepare to not be silenced by those who would continue to oppress us without a thought, our voices will continue to be conquered. For the sake of our *self*, and for the sake of others, our voices need to be heard, and our stories need to be told. Often enough, we need help to keep our stories alive.

The next class came, and I contemplated my words. Every ounce of fear that I ever had of my father was concentrated in that single moment. Every ounce of anxiety from hearing the door handle turn in the night filled that moment. Every feeling of sickness that ran through my body with each touch of my father filled me in that moment. I looked around the room to see if my father was somehow lurking there, glaring at me, as though he still had power to keep me silent, even from his grave.

*"How do I get these first words out?"* I thought. I had prepared what I wanted to say in the days before the class, but still, my heart was pounding out of my chest. My throat felt too swollen for words to come. My hands were wet with heat, and my entire body felt as though it was on fire, burning from the inside. It was as though my body was having a trained reaction to silence the voice—it was overwhelming, as it had been for so many years. But today, as overwhelming as it was, I needed to overpower it. I needed to draw on all that had filled me through my journey, so my voice could emerge.

Despite the terror that I felt bubbling inside, and that had kept me silent for more than thirty years, today things were different. I had so much now that I didn't have before. I felt the spirit guides from the Canadian Rockies flowing through me and around me. I felt the hand of the universe still holding mine. I felt the North Star, Polaris, shining brightly. I felt the support of my friends around me. All of a sudden, the pounding of my heart relaxed, the fire within cooled, my body relaxed, and I felt my voice rising to the surface.

Professor Williams motioned at me to speak, and so I began, "We spoke for an hour and a half in the last class about rape. I was sexually abused by my father all through my childhood—raped by my father over and over from the time I was four. I couldn't find a voice then. And I couldn't find a voice in the last class because I was terrified of being silenced again."

I could feel my confidence rise as I continued, "We're looking to go out into the world to create change, which will require all of us to work through so much of people's pain, anger, and conflict. Yet we can't even do that in this room. If we can't reach out to people through our pain, how will we ever create the change we want to see?"

I hadn't said that much, but to me, it felt as though a volcano had exploded in the room. The world seemed to stand still in my head. Sure enough, one of the people sitting not far from me started to go onto another discussion with hardly a pause after I spoke, completely unaffected by my words. Thankfully, one of my friends interrupted him, and asked the class to stop to consider what I had shared.

I was overwhelmed by the feeling of relief that went through me. Giving voice to my abuse was like closing the lid on my father's coffin for good. I felt free—as if every remaining shackle snapped open and fell away.

Those words were just a beginning, but in those moments, I felt as if I had walked through a door that opened onto many new paths. I felt my *self* rise.

With the help of my friends, the class stayed with the discussion of the pain that we each carry. Many people in the class shared their own stories of pain. After the class, and during the weeks to come, I was taken aback by how many people came up to me and shared their own story that they had never told.

It was so clear that we are not alone in our pain, yet so often we enable our pain to create the walls that separate and divide us, rather than allow it to bring us together. We each have our stories, each as significant as the next, each able to make a connection to another.

All of a sudden, I realized how much empowerment there is in sharing our stories. If we don't tell our stories, we will always be held prisoner by them. When we open the space for our *self* and others to tell our stories, and to give voice to the pains we each suffer, then we start to build bridges of compassion that can heal each of us, and set us free to pursue our higher purposes.

We can take charge of our story. We have the choice. We can keep it a secret, we can tell it with guilt and shame, or we can tell it with pride and resilience, having risen through it. Our own words can set us free. Our words can help others be free.

As a child, I didn't know how to use my words. I didn't know how to tell my story. Of all the things I expected to do at Harvard, the last was to learn to tell my story. That test was greater than any test of economics or quantitative analysis.

Our stories can help us step into the shoes of others, and better understand where we stand in our own shoes. We can build bridges to each other that we can then step across and know the humanity that is on each side. Bridge by bridge, step by step, we can cross oceans of divides.

We each have the strength of our stories to give us power on our journeys. Our stories can fill our shoes with the compassion, courage, and conviction we need to leap forward. In those shoes, we can chase our dreams, we can discover new paths, we can climb to our highest aspirations. We can rise, and rise, and rise to our greatest self. We can create for our *self* and for others, the change we want to see in the world, and commit to it, unreservedly, with all of our heart.

## MOMENTS OF PAUSE

1. When you pause to contemplate all of the experiences of your life, and look back along a runway to see all of those experiences aligning, what would be the purposeful journey ahead to which you are being propelled?

2. If you had to commit to "one single aim," one "legitimate and useful purpose," what would it be? If you asked, "Ask not what the world can do for you, but what you can do for the world," what would be your answer?

3. When you contemplate what you are aiming for, are you aiming too low? What would be the most unimaginable height toward which you could aim?

4. What are the worst things that have happened to you? What strength, courage and confidence have you drawn through those experiences to know there is nothing that you cannot do?

5.   What is the greatest pain that you hold within you that you must confront? How does it keep you a slave to it? How does it trigger you day by day? How does it reveal your greatest weaknesses and act to sabotage you?

6.   How do you reach out to others to help you move through your greatest pains?

7.   How do you re-train your responses to the things that trigger you? How do you transform the negative energy of pain that holds you back into the positive energy of pain that propels you forward?

8. What is your "nutritional emotional diet"? How do you fuel your *self* with things that energize you? How do you manage your cravings for the things that are harmful to you?

9. Have you told the stories of your greatest pain, your worst experiences? Have you given voice to the things that keep you captured in fear and silence? Have you been able to put words of pride and resilience to your worst experiences for having risen through them? How would you get those first words out? Who would you tell? Who could you help by telling your story?

10. When you pause to consider the strength of your story, what is the power of your story that helps you to chase your dreams, climb to your highest aspirations, create the change you want to see in the world, and live your greatest life?

## MORE MOMENTS FOR YOU

_____

_____

_____

_____

_____

_____

_____

_____

_____

_____

_____

_____

# Fifteen

# Take Flight to Your Greatest Masterpiece!

*"When once you have tasted flight,*
*you will forever walk the earth with your eyes turned skyward."*

—Leonardo da Vinci

ACH NEW STEP is an opportunity for us to leap higher, to fly further, and to create extraordinary masterpieces with our lives. The graduation ceremony at Harvard shouted this message as thousands of graduates across every school filled Harvard Yard. Surrounded by crimson and black gowns in every direction, I couldn't help but wonder the opportunities that would take flight from here.

For now, I had decided that the next flight for me would be aboard a plane. I wanted to jump back into my travel shoes, and finally leave the continental United States—at least for a little while.

The round-world ticket I purchased six years earlier had well and truly expired, but my desire to explore some of those unfamiliar places was still alive and well. It was time for me to take a "time-out" from my "time-out." I needed to push my pause button, relax and play for a while, and feel where my compass was pointing me.

It was somewhat surreal to me that six months in the United States had turned into six years, and here I was finally heading off to Europe with a new travel ticket, a new pair of shoes, and a new backpack (this time with wheels!). Sadly, my original Blundstones had worn through—between deserts, salt streams, beaches, and snow, they had come to lay to rest. Likewise, my Tevas had seen their last legs sailing on Biscayne Bay, and my backpack looked more like a relic than a functional travel companion.

After all that I experienced through Ron's courses at Harvard, and all that the universe had helped me to "let go" and "leave behind" over the past years, I felt as though I would be traveling much lighter on these next travels. Really, my entire being felt lighter.

I had left Australia feeling like I was running—running from a false world I created that no longer held any stability. Running loaded up with weights strapped around me, and with rusted chains binding me. Running from memories that tormented me in every moment, and made my head feel like a haunted house. Running from my *self*. Even though I knew that there was no place that I could run where my *self* wouldn't find me, it was all I could do. I ran with the hope that along the way "something" would emerge. I ran with the hope that the little girl whose hand I grabbed and pulled along with me, would find some rest. We were both so tired, surviving mostly on adrenalin, and by the time we left Australia our adrenalin was all but gone.

Six years later, I felt as if we had stopped running. Throughout our journey, we had ventured into the depths, and we had climbed to places higher than we knew existed. We had been able to play and to laugh with the innocence and adventure of children in the never-ending playground of Mother Nature. Most of all, we had been able to feel. Now, I felt the little girl beside me, peaceful and rested. I felt her hand softly touching mine, relaxed, and I knew her other hand was safely nestled in the hand of the universe. I knew that we were both going to be okay.

My plane ticket after Harvard took me to Europe and back. I was flying into Geneva from Miami, and flying back to Miami from Milan. I had no idea where I was going in between. It was June, and so the weather was fine north or south of Geneva. I boarded the plane with my trusty travel companion yet again—my *Lonely Planet* guide—to see which places most captivated me.

This time, I had more than one *Lonely Planet*, all of which weighed more than the rest of my luggage combined! Given that I had no idea where I was going after Geneva, I had brought along a collection of *Lonely Planet* guides—Europe, the Greek Islands, Switzerland, and Italy. I had no time to think about where I would travel before graduation amidst final papers, exams, and graduation celebrations, so I decided I would work that out on the plane.

When I first left Australia, Oslo was to be my next stop after New York City, from where I would travel around Scandinavia before heading to other countries. One option now, was to continue that path from Geneva. However, as I sat back in the plane and flipped through my various guides, the romantic descriptions of Paris, Rome, Venice, and the Greek Islands called to me. I loved art and architecture, and during my teenage years, the paintings of the Great Masters always captured me. Art had been a creative escape for me, a place where I felt transported into a world of color and possibility. A world where a blank canvas could be transformed into a life of its own, only limited by the imagination of the artist.

It seemed as though the Masters could see into a different world, and magically make that world become a reality. I think that was what drew me to escape into art—I wanted to paint a world on canvas and be able to make that my new reality—absent of darkness. Vincent van Gogh said, "I dream of painting and then I paint my dream." During my early high-school years, painting was a way for me not only to escape, but also to dream, and to feel in the company of other dreamers who had created their own art.

The thought of being amidst the energy of the Masters of Paris, the great philosophers and legends of Rome, and the ancient gods of Greece, suddenly sent those now familiar goosebumps charging through me, and my travels started to take shape. I felt my compass resonating softly, and I relaxed into my seat and read on. Soon enough, the plane touched down in Geneva, and my travels began.

I arrived in Paris a few days after flying into Geneva. The train arrived at the beautiful and enormous Gare De Lyon train station. This station was like a Notre Dame of train stations with hundreds of enormous metal struts reaching from one side of the vast ceiling to another.

My task at the train station was to buy a phone card, and find a phone booth to call some local hostels to find somewhere to stay. As usual, I hadn't done that in advance. Thanks again to my *Lonely Planet*, I was able to find a few hostels that sounded nice, and were close to the city. My first choice was the Hosteling International

D'Artagnan hostel—just fifteen minutes from the center of Paris, and seemingly a well-appointed hostel. The rate also met my budget of $20 a night!

I wanted to again keep this trip simple, staying in hostels and pensions that I would discover along the way. I found there was a quiet, simple, and relaxed ebb and flow in these quaint accommodations. The hostels and pensions were often located in tucked away little residential areas that always enabled wonderful local discoveries, which otherwise might have been missed.

I really didn't have much choice but to keep this trip simple. I had left Harvard with less cash than I had when I was a seventeen-year-old check-out chick at my local grocery store. I put almost all of my money into the Masters program, and so by the time I graduated, I needed to stay on a fairly tight budget. Thankfully, the credit card culture in the United States enabled me to get a few credit cards as back-up funding. I may not have been able to get a scholarship to help get me through Harvard, but at least I was able to get some credit cards if I needed a little help to get me through after graduation—I thought of it as a scholarship of sorts.

The budget I had set for the trip was $50 a day—almost double my budget when I first left Australia. I would travel mostly by Eurail from place to place, and then take whatever type of local transport would get me to where I wanted to go from there. That turned out to be everything from large ferry boats, to small sailing boats, to local buses, metro rail, cars, and of course, my new Blundstones and Tevas.

On the train to Paris, I was able to learn some essential French from the phrase section in my *Lonely Planet*. I was hoping to appear polite to the locals by having attempted to learn some of the language. I heard that if I at least attempted to speak some French, I would be much better received by the locals. Traveling alone to unfamiliar places, I was likely to need all the help I could get!

I was able to see if that theory worked as soon as I stepped off the train. There was hardly any English to be heard around me. But with my best smile, and a few friendly "Por Favors" and "Pardons," I was able to buy a phone card, make a phone call, and make my reservation at the hostel. Luckily, the D'Artagnan had a room available, and was just a metro ride away. So far, so good. I was on my way to my first night in Paris!

The Eiffel Tower was the first sight I wanted to see in Paris—a romantic icon that Gustave Eiffel brought to life, as he had the Statue of Liberty. The D'Artagnan was apparently an easy commute on the metro rail to the Trocadéro station—the stop nearest to the Eiffel Tower. That was about all I knew from the directions from the hostel staff. "Take the number three line to République, and then the number nine to Trocadéro." That sounded simple enough, and surprisingly, it was. Before I knew it, I was taking the steps up to the street level at Trocadéro, to be met by vendors selling freshly-cooked Nutella crepes. The rich chocolate-hazelnut aroma was my "Bienvenue à Paris!"

I didn't quite know where the Eiffel Tower was relative to Trocadéro station, and I was prepared for a walk of at least a few blocks. So with my water bottle in hand, I started out around the first corner and like walking into an enormous cinema screen, there was the Eiffel Tower rising right in front of me! The scene looked like a postcard, but the tower looked much more elegant and majestic than any photograph of the tower I had ever seen.

Before me, the tower shimmered like gold. It seemed to magically luminescence against the deep bluish-gray backdrop of the early evening sky. Fountains and large rectangular stepped pools, framed with lush green embankments led down, like a royal carpet, from the plaza of the Palais de Chaillot, where I stood. On either side of me, gold statues rose atop cascading fountains, and lined the plaza with sculptured reverence. The gentle vibration of goosebumps moved through me, and I opened and closed my eyes a few times to know that I wasn't in a dream. Really, I *was* in a dream—*living* a dream of simply roaming free!

The next morning I made an early start to the Louvre in order to miss the enormous lines that were known to form every day. As I entered the main courtyard of the Louvre, I was struck by the sight of the Cour Napoleon—the glass pyramid at the center of the courtyard that serves as the entrance to the Louvre.

The pyramid appeared somewhat juxtaposed—a child set down amidst the historical elders of a courtyard that aged back to the twelfth century. The scene seemed symbolic—that we are all simply children of the universe, set down in our time, with the past as our backdrop, and the future as our canvas.

Descending the stairs through the pyramid entrance was like traveling back through time. Each hallway of the Louvre was like an entrance to another world. In every direction, there were masterpieces from every time in history. There was an overwhelming sense of the extraordinary abilities that lie within us, waiting for us to tap into and express them. Greater than the scenes that were depicted in each painting, or the images that were sculptured into life, was the exhibition of the limitless ability we have within us to create.

The exhibit of our potential to create a masterpiece through the work of our lives was everywhere in the Louvre. From the eyes of Leonardo da Vinci's *Mona Lisa*, to the hands of Michelangelo's sculpture of *David*, to the embodiment of love and beauty of Alexandros of Antioch's sculpture of *Venus de Milo*, to the unknown sculptor's *Winged Victory of Samothrace* in honor of the goddess of victory, and to the ultimate expression of creation depicted in various representations of the *Creation of Man.*

Amidst such demonstration of the gifts that lie within each of us—as sentient, creative, imaginative beings, with the ability to create masterpieces from dust—who are we to not delve into our most overlooked abilities, and create masterpieces with our lives? Why would we waste such an extraordinary opportunity to create a life of magnificent artistic proportions? What masterpieces would we see within us, waiting to be transformed into reality, if we were to simply pause to uncover the creator within?

Claude Monet said, "It's on the strength of observation and reflection that one finds a way. So we must dig and delve unceasingly." Once we dig far, and tap into the vast ocean of our limitless potential, we find new paths and new ways of being that are of our own creation. We feel the hand of the universe, the resonance of the compass within us, the light of the North Star guiding us, and the freedom to choose to step into whichever shoes we desire. We start to transform our reality.

Picasso insisted, "Everything you can imagine is real." We have the power to imagine the greatest masterpiece we could wish to create with our life. So too, we have the power to make it real. We can reach out and touch the creator that lies within, we have the eyes to see it, the hands to touch it, and the love to nurture it. We have the victorious wings upon which to soar to our greatest heights.

"When once you have tasted flight, you will forever walk the earth with your eyes turned skyward, for there you have been, and there you will always long to return," said Leonardo da Vinci. Our ability to take flight is only limited by how far we wish to soar toward the sky.

Paris is filled with masterpieces of architecture along every street and around every corner. It is a city of immense grandeur and intricate details. It seemed that the evidence of the greatness of our capabilities was all around—in its grandeur and in its detail.

Over the next week, I walked all over the city, absolutely content to soak up every ounce of energy that filled each scene. If I reached out through the air, I felt as though my fingers would be wet with the paint of the scene, and softened by the smooth curves of the sculptures. With every goosebump, I felt inspired by the greatness and dared to feel a part of that greatness within—a connection to the greatness that timelessly flows through each of us.

As I walked along the River Seine, across sculpture-lined bridges, aside prestigious monuments, along the Avenue des Champs-Élysées—also known as La Plus Belle Avenue du Monde ("the most beautiful avenue in the world"), and past picture-perfect ornate buildings trimmed with gold-leaf and elegant decoration, I felt as if I were walking through a live canvas, and a moving sculpture garden all at once. From a distance, each scene looked to be a beautiful and abundant landscape painting, and as each scene drew nearer, each element became its own masterpiece. Each element distinctively unique.

The quest for the expression of uniqueness and distinctiveness was apparent in every scene. Picasso reflected, "To copy oneself is more dangerous than to copy others. It leads to sterility." The quest to constantly renew oneself in order to evolve and to not stagnate seemed at the heart of all of the creative endeavors of every artist, sculptor, and architect throughout the history of the city.

Our ability to create intricate masterpieces of our lives is at our fingertips. We can be constantly inspired by new influences that set us flying to greater heights, that continually challenge our creativity, and that make us more distinctive and unique with each brush stroke. Our lives can be an abundance of extraordinary creations, with one leading to another, and another, as we evolve with each piece of work. Each new day brings a new canvas upon which we can create a more distinctive and authentic scene.

With each piece of work, with each day, we have the ability to come closer to our *self*, to tap into our soul and to come to know, feel, smell, and touch our inner being. Vincent van Gogh said, "Art, although produced by man's hands, is something not created by hands alone, but something which wells up from a deeper source out of our soul." When we tap into the depths of our soul, there is no limit to the great masterpieces we can create.

"Unless you try to do something beyond what you have already mastered, you will never grow," said poet Ralph Waldo Emerson. Imagine if the Great Masters had stopped with their first great work. We each have the opportunity to grow with every brush stroke. Why then, would we stop our quests in life as soon as we felt content with where we were? With each great work, we have the choice to become more inspired or more content. Which do we choose?

If we choose a path where we find inspiration in each moment, we become bound to something much greater that keeps filling us with momentum and keeps us aspiring to greater heights. "He turns not back who is bound to a star," said Leonardo da Vinci. As we keep reaching toward the star to which we are bound, we are compelled to fly higher, and to create the life that is our greatest and most timeless masterpiece!

## MOMENTS OF PAUSE

1. Where are the places within you from which you run? Into which worlds do you escape to seek refuge? In which spaces do you feel as though you can "roam free"?

2. What masterpieces exist within you, waiting for you to touch them, to feel them, and to transform them into reality?

3. Digging unceasingly into your *self*, what new paths and new ways of being of your own creation would you craft into your current reality?

4.  What abundance of extraordinary creations would you like to craft in your life? What could be your greatest creation?

5.  How do you constantly renew your *self* in order to evolve and not stagnate?

6.  How do you approach the new canvas that is presented to you in every new day? With each brush stroke, with each step, how do you draw inspiration to keep aspiring to create greater masterpieces, to be bound to higher stars?

## MORE MOMENTS FOR YOU

### Sixteen

# Live ~ Laugh ~ Love

*"Happiness is the meaning and the purpose of life,*
*the whole aim and end of human existence."*

—ARISTOTLE

WE EACH HAVE THE OPPORTUNITY to be filled with life, laughter, and love. As a child, my quest was simply to live through one day to the next in a world full of hostility, humiliation, violation, and disregard. As an adult, throughout my journey, I started to see there was something more. For the first time, the hurt and angry little girl felt peacefulness in the hands of the universe. She started to live without caution in the arms of Mother Nature. She started to laugh at the simplest amusements. She started to feel love from the universe in unexpected places along the way. There was hope of happiness.

The next stops on my trip would further unlock doors to my senses that had long been locked. When you are stuck in survival mode, you don't live in every moment, you just keep pieces of your *self* from dying in each moment. When the only feelings that you have arise from acts of abuse, you want to shut down any feelings because they only act to betray you. When you look around, and all you see are places that scare you, you want to close your eyes and stop seeing anything. You don't dare laugh, because those fleeting moments only serve to remind you of the despair that fills you. When you come across opportunities for friendship and love, you shut them down because you know you can't hold together any more pieces that will be broken.

The chance to live, to laugh, and to love seemed only to exist in fairytale books—words and characters on pages, nothing real.

As I left Paris and headed to Venice, with images of the Greek Islands and Rome beyond there, I felt like I was traveling through a fairytale. The pages had started to turn when I left Australia. The more I stepped into unfamiliar places that allowed me to feel goosebumps and moments of awe, the fairytale became more and more real.

With each page that turned, I was seeing that there were places within me and around me in which I could live, laugh, and love. I could uncover my eyes and see endless masterpieces. I could smile and laugh and feel only more smiles and laughter. I could live one day to look forward to the next. I could allow my heart to open to all that was around and feel like a welcome child who had a place in this one big "home." I had started to love the things within me, and with that, I was able to start to love the things around me.

I began to see what Hans Christian Andersen proclaimed, "Life itself is the most wonderful fairy tale." He also said, "Just living is not enough ... One must have sunshine, freedom, and a little flower." My journey had exposed me to sunshine, given me freedom to roam, and enabled me to see many flowers along my path. As a child, "just living" was all that I could do. Now, with all I saw within, around, and before me, I felt so much more to life than "just living."

When we pause to feel the sunshine, to step into spaces of freedom, to see the colors of the flowers that we pass by every day, then we start to do more than just live. We let life enter us, flow through us, and fill us with color and movement. The pages of our life become filled with magic that takes us to places beyond our imagination.

I arrived just outside of Venice on the train from Paris. This time, I had called ahead to book a room in a small pension outside the city. Staying in Venice was not an option on my budget, and, as always, I was ready for the adventure of staying in a slightly out-of-the-way establishment.

As I approached the location of my accommodation on the local bus, I disembarked somewhat bemused. There was only a small pizzeria near the bus stop. Nothing much to the right. Nothing much to the left. Cars were passing by on the main road behind me. Venice was across the river in the distance. As I watched the bus pull away, I tried to look as though I was exactly where I was supposed to be—for what purpose, I had no idea. I think it was just a little positive self-reinforcement that all would be well!

"*I suppose the people in the pizzeria will be able to point me in the right direction,*" I thought. I pulled my backpack behind me and walked toward the pizzeria.

"Buon Giorno," I said as I entered, again with the friendliest smile I could conjure.

"Hello," the woman behind the counter replied, clearly realizing my Italian didn't extend far beyond my welcome. It seemed that I wasn't fooling anyone with my Australian-Italian accent!

"I'm looking for the pension. I booked a room." I didn't have much hope of a positive reply.

"Si, Si. You are here," said the woman.

As I looked around the pizzeria confused and curious, I couldn't see any beds. *"Did she think I asked for a pizza?"* I wondered.

"You are Kathy?" the woman asked, smiling, already seeming to know the answer to her question. I guess she was expecting only one Australian that day!

"Benvenuta. I am Maria, please follow me," she said with a warm smile.

I followed Maria out through the back of the pizzeria, across a yard that had old broken down and beaten-up pieces of cars lying around, through a fence, and beyond some trees and shrubs to find a quaint little guest house. *"Hmmm,"* I contemplated, *"I certainly found 'local' this time!"*

My visit into the city of Venice was a short fifteen-minute bus ride from the pizzeria. Crossing the bridge that connected Venice to the mainland over the water that surrounded the city was like entering a portal that transported you to another time.

Venice was like a city in a bubble that time had preserved from centuries past. Stepping foot in Venice, I could almost feel the city breathing as it inhaled and exhaled with the rising and falling of the tides. The labyrinth of canals that flowed through this floating "City of Water" took visitors on a different journey with every turn—past gothic cathedrals, grand old opera houses, ornate basilicas, and sculpture-lined facades. The constant flow of gondolas and antique water taxis created a rhythmic ebb and flow of life through the watery arteries of the city.

Crossing each bridge across each canal, you had the sense that you were traveling from one portal to another.

"To us, bridges are transitions," explained a local Venetian to author John Berendt, as he recalled in his book, *The City of Falling*

*Angels.* "We go over them very slowly … We cross from one reality … to another reality. From one street … to another street. From one setting … to another setting."

Meandering along the Grand Canal, I was met by endless canals, with endless bridges, each as alluring as the next, each as mysterious as the next. Bridge after bridge presented an opportunity to explore. Each bridge held the opportunity for discovery, if one took the step onto the next bridge to make the transition to unknown paths that disappeared along narrow waterways.

The only way to discover Venice was to cross the bridges and walk into the unknown labyrinths. As in life, in order to transition we must step across the bridges. If not, we simply remain, wondering what might lie beyond, and then turn to retrace known paths. On the steps of discovery, if we stand dormant, we miss the beauty and magic of all that lies beyond.

What do we see of the world that stands before us—steps upon which we can climb to discover magic and mystery, or obstacles that cause us to remain stuck in the same shoes, in the same place? On the steps of opportunity, we can wait, or we can make the step to transition to the other side.

As I wandered along the canals, and cascaded over one bridge to the next, I wondered where I would be if I hadn't changed my heels for hiking boots. I had no idea what I was stepping into when I first stepped onto that plane from Australia with my backpack. I just knew I didn't want to stay stuck. I didn't want to stand dormant. I didn't want to feel like I was "just living."

The simple choice to step out from a world where I felt no life, transported me to worlds that were flowing with life. If I had stayed in the same shoes, I would never have discovered the magic that flows around us. I would never have discovered life.

The magic and mystery that flowed beside me through the canals of Venice was like a comforting reassurance that the key to transitioning through the portals of life is often not found along the paths of certainty, but amidst the currents of uncertainty, toward unknown destinations. The only way to move forward, is to keep moving with the currents, exploring new canals, crossing bridges as they emerge, and feeling at home in the mystery and uncertainty that is an essential part of discovery.

Venice was full of life along every canal. Each canal seemed to lead to a different world full of color and movement. Music, art, and theater flowed through the canals giving life to the city, as if oxygen. Venice is known to be one of the most beautiful cities of art. Flowing with the canals, you feel the art seeping into you, and filling you with every step. You start to breathe in sync with the ebb and flow of the currents that move through you, if you allow the flow to enter.

The more I breathed in the color and movement around me, the more I became aware of how many sensations I had blocked from entering me since my childhood. To breathe in was to feel pain and ugliness. It became better to breathe cautiously. It was better to live with caution, laugh with caution, and love with caution. There was no calm ebb and flow within, only vicious currents that swirled into dark and dirty places. There were so many walls within that there was no easy flow, only blockages that created turmoil.

The currents that had flowed within me seemed to leak out into the space around me and fill that space. Until I transformed the currents within me, the world around continued to be a dark place, full of raging currents—a mirror to everything that was in turmoil inside. The currents that filled me were the currents that surrounded me. The only way to create a peaceful ebb and flow was to calm the waters within.

Now, amidst this city of currents, the peaceful flow of waters resonated gently with the currents within and flowed with ease. I felt the contrast to the many years of turmoil. The difference now was that I allowed the color and music to enter and flow without fear.

Throughout my journey since leaving Australia, day by day, I started to allow good feelings to enter and came to see that those feelings were not always followed by a greater darkness. I started to trust something greater than me, and I started to trust me. With trust, I could surrender. Once I surrendered to allow the currents of the universe to flow through me, the flow of good feelings started to wash away the pain, the ugliness, and the dirtiness. I felt cleansed. I felt new life.

I contemplated what had filled my being for so long. If I had taken a gondola through the canals within me, what would I have seen along the way? If we were to take a journey through the canals of our inner world, what would we find? Would we find a smooth and calm ebb and flow full of color and life, with bridges effortlessly connecting and transitioning, or would we find rapid torrential currents, broken bridges, and turmoil?

The canals that had flowed through me had become septic through my childhood. They had become toxic. As they ran through me, they slowly poisoned every part of me with each new day. With every violation by my father, the poison became more potent. The antidote I had found through my journey was to let waters filled with life, laughter, and love flow through me, and for those currents to be the source that cleansed the toxins, fed my soul, and renewed my spirit.

Throughout my journey, the universe had captured me in its currents and filled me with life that I had not felt before. From the currents that flowed along the coastline of Big Sur, down the waterfalls of Yoko, across the glaciers of the Rocky Mountains, along the hiking trails of Yosemite, through the canyons of the

Grand Canyon, the caves of Carlsbad Caverns, the monuments of Monument Valley, the mountains of Haiti, through the timeless masterpieces of the Louvre, and now to the canals in Venice, these currents of the universe had become my constant companion. These are the currents that are the constant stream of our life force.

The life force that flows through us enables us to live, to laugh, and to love. It is our fuel of life. It is the source that flows to create oceans of happiness. It is the force that can spread light through dark waters. It can transform us.

When our canals are septic, when the streams that flow through us are contaminated with toxins, we can't fully live. We are sick from poisons that prevent us from thriving. We expend so much of our energy fighting toxins, when we could be creating endless oceans. We start to spend more time keeping our *self* from dying, rather than creating extraordinary possibilities for living.

The opportunities to allow healing and rejuvenating currents flow through us are all around. Every day, we don't need to journey far to feel the life force that constantly flows around us. If we pause for long enough in the moment to allow the "sunshine, freedom, and a little flower" flow through us, we can feel the force of life. We can let the cleansing waters fill our soul. The pages of our fairytale can start to turn and come to life.

Our happiness can grow with each page that turns, with every current that we allow to flow through us. As we surrender and allow those currents to transform us, and the life force to fill us, we flow through the world with a different energy. We move in sync with the rhythms of the universe. Our life becomes so much more than "just living." Our life becomes a force for happiness, for our *self* and for others. We are free to live, to laugh, and to love with infinite capacity.

## MOMENTS OF PAUSE

1.  What are the places within and around you that propel you to live, to laugh, and to love?

2.  What are the things within and around you that block you from living, laughing, and loving?

3.  With which things within your *self* have you fallen in love? How do those things bring you happiness?

4.  What are the transitions you need to make in your life? Which bridges do you need to cross? What are you waiting for to take the next step—to discover the magic, and not stand dormant?

5.  If you were to take a journey through the canals of your inner world, what currents would you find flowing through you?

6.  How do the currents that flow within you, seep into the world around you? How do the currents around you act as a mirror to the currents within?

7.  What are the walls and barriers that stop the calm and peaceful ebb and flow within? What are the toxins that keep you from living fully?

8.  What do you need to do to transform the currents within you and create calm and peaceful waters that enable you to live fully?

9.  How do you pause in each day to allow the "sunshine, freedom, and a little flower" to flow through you?

10. How do you open and surrender to the life force that enables you to live, to laugh, and to love with infinite capacity?

## MORE MOMENTS FOR YOU

# Seventeen

# Conquer Your Self

*"The first and greatest victory is to conquer yourself."*

—PLATO

WHEN WE CONQUER OUR *SELF*, the most monumental and timeless pieces of our greatest self can be revealed. Our most purposeful and powerful life starts to emerge. As I left the magic and mystery of the floating city of Venice, the timeless myths and monumental legends of Greece and the Greek Islands were calling to me.

The train from Venice would take me as far as Ancona, on the northeastern coast of Italy. From there, I would catch a Superfast Ferry to Patras in Greece, and then a local train to Athens. I had called ahead from Venice to the Hotel Diethnes in Athens, which I managed to find while browsing the Internet in a quaint cafe by one of the canals in Venice. It seemed to be a perfect choice for my brief stay in Athens—close to the train station where I would arrive and with "… easy and quick access to all the major sites of Athens and Greece." It also met my 25 Euro per night budget! That was as much as I needed to work out before I left Venice. I would have plenty of time during three days of travel to Athens to browse the pages of the Greek Islands, and decide where to venture.

My approach to traveling through Europe was to find the most obscure and remote references to places on the Internet and in my *Lonely Planet*, arrive in those places, and then talk to locals about places that were even more obscure and remote. Those would be the places to where I would venture. I wanted to get as far into the unknown as I could. It seemed that often it was in the most remote places where the most interesting and unexpected discoveries and experiences were to be found.

From the maps of the Greek Islands, the Dodecanese appeared to be the most distant set of islands. They were the southernmost islands, and ran along the western coast of Turkey. Patmos was the northernmost island in the Dodecanese, followed by a trail of islands, the tiny size of which was instantly appealing. "Strung out along the coast of western Turkey, like jewels upon the aquamarine sea," was the description of the Dodecanese in my *Lonely Planet*. These jewels seemed to be the perfect destination.

The journey between Venice and Athens was a scenic expedition all of its own—much more than simply a transit between destinations. The train trip from Venice through France to Milan, then through central Italy to the coast of Ancona flowed with an intimate charm and an alluring romance. From Ancona, the voyage on the super-fast ferry was a beautiful oceanic passage through the Adriatic Sea along the northern coast of Italy, and then across the Ionian Sea to Patras in Greece. The ferry was more like a modest cruise ship than the simple passenger ferry I envisioned, with small eateries, spacious viewing decks, friendly bars, and an Internet room to catch up with friends by email along the way. The gentle rise and fall of the ocean was soothing and welcoming.

Arriving in the late evening at the Hotel Diethnes in Athens, I wasn't too sure if my room would still be available. It was almost 10:00PM, and the trip from the coastal port of Patras had taken longer than expected, with a series of trains and buses needed to travel the more than 100 miles to Athens. Thankfully, I was greeted by the very friendly Panos and Costas at the reception desk, as I entered and wearily leaned against the counter. I was looking forward to my bed for the night!

Athens was to be just a short overnight stop on my way to Patmos. The Diethnes was perfect for my short stay before having to wake at 5:00AM the next morning to get to the port and take the boat to Patmos. I hadn't been able to find a timetable for the boats to Patmos, but was told that most of the boats leave very early in the morning, around 6:30AM. Well, as things would go, that advice was just a little off (or maybe it was my understanding that was not quite right!). The boat to Patmos—so I found out in the darkness of the early morning dawn, with my bags packed on the dock and ready to go—didn't leave until 6:30PM that evening. All I could think about were the extra hours of sleep I could be having in that oh so comfortable bed at the hotel.

Arriving back at the Diethnes, Panos and Costas were still at the front desk and gave me a puzzled look as I returned. Smiling at my story, they offered me breakfast, and suggested a day in Athens (actually, they suggested much longer, but my travel shoes were calling me to Patmos!). I must say the rich Greek coffee alone was worth the trip back to the hotel, and gave me the wake-up buzz I needed. With the Acropolis looming over the city, I decided it would be remiss to pass through the city and not visit one of the most significant sites of ancient times. So leaving my bags at the hotel, I headed to the metro for my day trip.

Standing at the base of the Acropolis, with the Parthenon rising powerfully into the sky on its walls of pillars more than 150 meters above, I felt the intense energy of the site even from a distance. Then, after a steep ascent, I was awestruck as I climbed the final thick limestone steps leading up to Propylaea, the gateway to the Acropolis. The pillars that formed the gateway before me were gigantic. I felt as though I was standing too close to an enormous 3-D cinema screen, not able to fully capture the scene without pivoting my head through the most strained 360 degree rotation. It took a minute to stop the dizziness, and to keep my balance to avoid falling backward down the steps below!

Every step through the Acropolis had a similar effect. The extraordinary, seemingly super-human size of the pillars and the temples throughout the site were beyond what could be comprehended from a photograph. Here, in every sense, one felt amidst a place built for the gods.

The remnants of sculptures adorning the temples hinted of a luxurious oasis in the clouds. I recalled my visit to the Louvre in Paris, and the stunningly beautiful sculpture garden. The marble statues glistened like white pearl under the magnificent skylight at the Louvre. Many of the statues had been saved from the Acropolis over the centuries and restored to their original splendor. With the image of the sculpture garden at the Louvre vivid in my mind, the vision of what the Acropolis must have been, with those statues shimmering upon grand temples in the golden light of the sun atop the highest point in Athens, was breathtaking even to imagine.

Standing on the enormous rock plateau of the Acropolis, surrounded by towering temples and sculptures, I felt as though I was standing on the pages of a huge mythological book of ancient Greece. The poets and philosophers of Greece were the storytellers of their time. The artists, sculptors, and architects created the color, majesty, and beauty that leapt off the pages, larger than life.

The gods and goddesses of the Greeks were the first to be carved in the image of man. The greatness of man, in all of its beauty and splendor, with all of its wondrous attributes, was embodied in the Greek gods. The gods and goddesses of previous civilizations were made in the image of creatures imagined in nature or elsewhere in the universe, and possessed some type of alien or animal detail. The mythology of Greece was seen as an awakening to the immensity of the human condition as its own power, not dependent on the powers and influence of unfamiliar and alien gods.

To the early Greeks, man was the center of the universe, and thus was made the center of all art, sculpture, and thought. The love of the human condition, of its forms and its attributes, was reflected in the richness and beauty of the literature, poetry, art, sculpture, and architecture of ancient Greece. Standing amidst the Acropolis, one was also standing amidst the awe of the human condition, its splendor, its greatness, its capacity, and all that it had the potential to embody.

The battles depicted in Greek mythology were also testament to the destructive powers of man. Surrounded by the ruins of the Acropolis, one was caught in the duality of the creative and destructive capabilities of the human condition.

Reflecting on the duality that surrounded me, it seemed that the values we choose to embody in our lifetime determine whether we act as a creative or destructive force in the universe. We have, as part of our innate human condition, virtues and values that we can call upon to create or to destroy.

What do we choose to embody? Upon which pillars do we choose to build? The virtues of the universe are there for us to reach out and assimilate into our world—virtues of love and beauty represented by Aphrodite; the light and purity, music, poetry, and prophecy of Apollo; the healing of Asclepius; the wisdom of Athena;

the strength of Hercules; the courage of Odysseus; the justice and protection of Zeus.

In each moment, we have access to qualities that help us to create balance and harmony, or to create chaos and disruption. We can act to empower our *self* and those around us, or act to disempower our *self* and those around us. We have the capacities to build timeless cities upon pillars of the greatest attributes of a shared humanity, or to tear down peoples and cities based on fear and the need for domination for only part of humanity.

With our conscious choices, we can create timeless monuments of beauty or lifeless ruins of rubble.

"The measure of man is what he does with power," said Pittacus, one of the Seven Sages of Greece. Greek mythology is full of battles between Olympian gods and Titans, of immortals, demigods, monsters, mythical creatures, and legendary heroes who battled between forces of good and evil.

What do we choose to do with the powers that lie within us? What do we choose to conquer? The virtues that we choose to embody can be our greatest weapon to conquer that which we need to overcome within us and in the world around us.

As a child, I wasn't conscious of how much I had to draw upon in the universe. Maybe our unconscious summons those virtues that are hidden within us when we are on the edge of life, needing something to emerge that enables us to conquer those things that would otherwise destroy us. Maybe as a child, I unconsciously tapped into those things. Maybe that is when the pure essence of our being emerges, when our soul awakens to find us.

As purposeful adults, we have everything we need to conquer our demons. We have within us all of the virtues to be great for our *self* and for others. Whichever gods and spirits we believe reside within us and around us, we have the conscious ability to tap into those powers that can connect and propel us as individuals, and as one extraordinary humanity. We can consciously seek the essence of our being and awaken our soul.

In Greek mythology, the "beginning" of all things was a time of chaos. From the chaos, elements arose that brought order through one means or another. Much of the order was brought about through battles between the elements of nature, and among those who represented good and evil.

Chaos is a part of the fabric and nature of the universe. It exists around us, and within us. However, we have the means to conquer the chaos, and enable the good to prevail. We have within us the soul that is a seed of the soul of the universe. We have the elements of nature residing within us that have battled chaos since the beginning of time. We have the forces of good standing ready to overcome the forces of evil. We have our defenders and our heroes waiting to be summoned who can form an army to conquer the greatest challenges that confront us.

We need to visualize those elements and forces. We need to bring those forces to life in order to overcome the darkness. We need to call upon the extraordinary power that lies within us in order to be the greatest power we can be. We need to conquer and master our *self* if we are to be free. The Greek philosopher, Epictetus, said, "No man is free who is not a master of himself."

The chaos that had existed in my world became the master of me. I had been fueled by torment and evil that only continued to produce more chaos. The elements that existed in me became forces that started to overcome every part of my being. The thoughts of hate, anger, violence, and resentment, overpowered any good nature that existed. While those negative feelings at least provided fuel to keep me going, they were also destroying me, eating away from the inside. It was only a matter of time before I imploded.

My worst enemy was my *self*, but that *self* was also keeping me alive. When you are living on self-preservation, you lose judgement as to what is helpful to preserve and what is not. When it seems you are surviving on so little inside, you don't want to chance leaving any piece of you behind—it might collapse what is left of the fragmented puzzle of your being.

I didn't know how to conquer the parts of my *self* that were keeping me from living without destroying the "whole" of me. Those were the times when I would think most about ending it all. If I couldn't separate the pieces, it seemed that it was easier to kill off everything. The endless struggle every day was consuming and exhausting.

When I left Australia, I was tired of constantly struggling between thoughts of ending my life or trying to stay alive. There had to be more than continually struggling to survive each day to live another day only to battle the same demons. I needed to find the good beyond the external and material things on which I had come to rely to feel good about my *self*. I needed to truly transform my *self* and to finally conquer my demons. If I didn't conquer those parts of my *self*, my *self* was going to conquer me.

I needed to abandon the pieces of my *self* that were not part of the essence of my being, that were not part of the soul within that resonated with the universe and pointed me to my True North. These were pieces that I had constructed and captured since my childhood as weapons to defend me. These were pieces that now distracted me and drew me away from the power of my soul.

I believe our *self* is made up of pieces that are born of our soul, and of other pieces that we acquire throughout our life based on the circumstances that confront us. As we open our *self* to the universe, more pieces of our soul emerge, and we step closer to our True North. Our *self* becomes full of the pieces of our soul that have been waiting for us to awaken them. They fill us with the infinite and timeless truth and wisdom of the universe. We begin to see more clearly the pieces of our *self* that are not of our soul, that we have captured and constructed, yet that only serve to distract us.

As we conquer those parts of our *self* that don't serve us, that don't take us closer to our True North, we create more space for pieces of our *self* that are born of our soul to emerge. We continue to discover more forces of good that continue to enable us to conquer our demons and become our greatest self.

We each have the power of good within us, but our demons will overcome our goodness, unless we can summon that power to conquer the parts of our *self* that are destroying us. The Greek philosopher, Epictetus said, "Seek not good from without: seek it from within yourselves, or you will never find it."

My journey had allowed me to feel the good parts of my *self* with every moment of awe. I needed to find the good within my *self* before I could be good in the world. In order to find those good pieces within me, I needed to be good to me.

We need to treat our *self* as our greatest gift. We need to be kind to our *self* in order to conquer our *self*. We need to be good to our *self* in order for good to emerge.

Before I left Australia, I had never really been kind to my *self*. I didn't like my *self* enough to be kind to my *self*. I thought of my *self* as a coward for allowing my abuse to happen, for not standing up to my father. I was disgusted by my *self* for the acts in which I had participated. I saw my *self* as weak for not being able to say "no." I had read enough to know that what happened was not my fault. I understood that I was only a child. But "knowing" wasn't enough to shift those deeply embedded feelings, it wasn't enough to stop me from being negative to my *self* and about my *self*. Those feelings had become my demons. They had overcome all that was inside.

I blamed my *self* for what happened to me. I couldn't forgive my *self* as long as I couldn't let go of my demons. To forgive, in one of its original meanings, is to give up the desire or power to punish. In many ways, by not being kind to my *self*, I was punishing my *self* for the wrong I believed I allowed to be done to me. Being kind to my *self* was forgiving my *self*. I could start to feel compassion for my *self* and stop punishing my *self*.

"The more you know yourself, the more you forgive yourself," said Confucius. Maybe that is because when we discover the roots of our demons, we see that they grow from wounds within our *self* for which we have never shown our *self* compassion—from the places we haven't yet healed. We find we are punishing our *self* for things that will only be healed when we are kind to our *self*.

When I started to be kind to my *self*, when I started to show my *self* compassion, the demons started to fade away. The Dalai Lama said, "Compassion, forgiveness, these are the real, ultimate sources of power for peace and success in life." I took back the power my demons had taken from me with each act of kindness and compassion I did for my *self*.

The kindest thing I did for my *self* was to pack my backpack and step into the unknown. I gave my *self* a break from constantly pushing my *self* to prove that I was "something," when I didn't even know what that "something" was. I let go of the things around me that I had grown to rely on to make me feel good, and allowed my *self* to be drawn to things that made me feel good from within. I let go of the negative feelings. I let go of the pieces I had captured and constructed that no longer served me. I paused each day to let my *self* have new experiences that made the little girl within feel peaceful and happy.

It turned out that my demons were strongest when I nurtured them in the darkness that they knew. The more I stepped into new spaces of light, the more they became like scavengers retreating into the night. They couldn't survive. I stopped feeding them. I killed them with kindness.

"Your own soul is nourished when you are kind," said King Solomon. The more I fed my *self* with simple acts of kindness every day, the more the good feelings grew within me. I started to want to take care of my *self*, because I started to care for my *self*. I allowed my soul to be nourished.

Once I started to care for my *self*, I could see the pieces of my *self* that I needed to conquer were those things that kept me from being kind and good to me. They kept me from living the way I wanted to live now. I was able to see the past as the past, and that was the place where my demons needed to remain. I no longer needed them. There was no point to holding on to them. There was no fear of letting them go now that I could feel so many good things with which to replace them. They lost their power. I trusted that the gods, goddesses, and heroes within would fill those empty spaces. I trusted that the seed of my soul would continue to grow with each touch of the universe.

As I looked around the Acropolis, at the temples adorned by the beautiful sculptures displaying the magnificence of the human condition, there seemed to be a reassurance that we can be as magnificent as we choose. To the ancient Greeks, the human condition was extraordinary in its form, its intellect, and its psyche. I needed to care for all of those parts of my *self*—for my body, my mind, and my spirit—in order to conquer my demons, in order for my soul to fill my being.

I started to want to uncover and cast aside all of the demons to create more spaces for the new. I wanted to excavate all of the broken pieces, and in their place build pillars that I could stand high upon. With the pillars of the Acropolis towering around me, I could envision those pillars emerging within me.

The deeper we excavate into our *self*, the more room we create to pour the pillars that will hold us high.

In order to dig deep and excavate the pieces of our *self* that no longer serve us, in order to conquer the parts of our *self* that risk destroying us, we need to know those deepest and most hidden parts of our *self*. "Know thyself," said the Greek philosopher Socrates. "The unexamined life is not worth living," he insisted.

Standing on one of the greatest archaeological sites in the world, the discovery and insight that comes with excavation was all around. The careful examination of each uncovered artifact was a further clue, another piece of the puzzle that revealed secrets of mysterious worlds. They revealed how life was lived and why.

As we excavate our *self*, we uncover the pieces that are clues to how we live and why. We begin to know our deeper self. We can uncover our demons. We can reveal the gods, goddesses, and heroes within. We can name our demons and conquer them. We can name our gods, goddesses, and heroes and bring them into our being. We can deconstruct our parts to understand them, and we can reconstruct them to create the self we want to be now. We can reconstruct the pieces that are born of our soul and that help us to live fully, and put aside those pieces that weaken our being.

With the infinite power of our soul, we can not only conquer our *self*, but also all that is important to us in the world. The pillars upon which we rebuild our *self* are as monumental as are our dreams and desires. The self we can reconstruct is not determined by what existed in the past, but by what we envision for our greatest self. It grows abundantly from the seed of our soul—the seed that is full of the unlimited power of the universe.

## MOMENTS OF PAUSE

1.  Which virtues do you embody that act to empower you in all
    you want to accomplish in your life? If you were to name your
    gods, goddesses, and heroes within in, what would they be?

2.  Which pieces within you are born from the essence of your
    being, from the seed of your soul that is connected to the soul
    of the universe, and that connect you to your True North?

3.  If you were to name your "demons" within, what would they
    be? If you deconstructed your *self*, which are the pieces of your
    *self* that you need to conquer?

4.  What are the pieces of your *self* that you have captured and
    constructed over time that no longer serve you, and that now
    distract you from pursuing your True North?

5. What is stopping you from conquering your demons, of letting go of the pieces of your *self* that you no longer need?

6. What are the roots of your demons? What are the parts of your *self* that haven't been healed, that are waiting for your care and compassion?

7. What is the care that you need to give to your *self* in order to forgive your *self*? Are you punishing your *self*, instead of caring for your *self*?

8. How are you kind to your *self* every day? How do you care for your mind, your body, and your spirit in each day? How do you nurture your soul?

9. What are the next steps you need to take to conquer your demons; to care for your mind, your body, and your spirit; to nurture your soul?

10. If you were to reconstruct your *self*, which pieces would create the self you want to be—the self that grows from the seeds of your soul, the self that is as monumental as your dreams and desires? What are your first steps toward putting those pieces together?

## MORE MOMENTS FOR YOU

# Eighteen

# Reveal the Life Born of Your Soul

*"I've led such a little life.*
*I have allowed myself to lead this little life,*
*when inside me there was so much more.*
*Why do we get all this life if we don't ever use it?*
*Why do we get all these feelings and dreams and*
*hopes if we don't ever use them?*
*That's where Shirley Valentine disappeared to.*
*She got lost in all this unused life."*

—"SHIRLEY VALENTINE"
FROM *SHIRLEY VALENTINE*, THE MOVIE

W E EACH HAVE THE OPPORTUNITY to step into our greatest life. We can each embrace our most extraordinary feelings, hopes, and dreams, and bring them to life. We can each discover and reveal all that lies within that is born of something greater than our *self*.

*Shirley Valentine* is one of my favorite movies of a woman and her adventures in the Greek Islands. This is the story of a middle-aged housewife who leaves her "little life" to re-discover the pieces of her *self* that she has lost somewhere along her way. In Shirley's London home, her unappreciative and demanding husband and family keep her at their beck and call every day. The most pleasurable company Shirley enjoys is talking to the wall. "I'd like to drink a glass of wine, sitting by the sea, watching the sunset," Shirley tells her wall, and then decides to go on a two-week vacation in the Greek Islands.

On the island of Mykonos, Shirley not only drinks her glass of wine by the sea at sunset, but also finds how to live, laugh, and love again. "I've fallen in love with the idea of living," Shirley exclaims, as she becomes free to reveal those parts of her self that she had lost, "I'm Shirley the Brave. Shirley the Marvelous. Shirley Valentine!"

As the ferry from Athens to Patmos pulled into its first stop at Mykonos, I smiled at the images of Shirley Valentine and the thoughts of my own adventures in the Greek Islands. My home for a week on Patmos would be the Pension Avgerinos. The pension was described in my *Lonely Planet* as "slightly quieter ... affording good views over the bay, this homey choice is run by a welcoming Greek Australian couple ..." This is one of the things I loved about my *Lonely Planet* guides—they were always filled with little pieces of seemingly trivial information that enabled you to find the most homey places in even the most remote places. Staying with a Greek Australian couple would be the perfect home on Patmos!

We pulled into the small cove of Skala in Patmos in the darkness of the very early morning. The cove shimmered with small lights forming a welcoming smile along the curved shoreline. The light of the moon cast itself upon the quaint white rectangular houses, and the lights of small boats moved ever so slightly with the ocean in the foreground. It was a tranquil postcard setting, even in the darkness. Already, Patmos seemed the perfect first stop on my Greek Island adventure.

I hadn't anticipated arriving in Patmos quite so early, although I hadn't looked at the timetable to check. As long as I boarded and was on my way, arrival times became less and less important. I would arrive when I arrived and let the rest sort itself out. I smiled as I walked down the ramp of the boat to the small dock—there were only a handful of people who had remained after Mykonos, and most had rides ready and waiting (it seemed they had checked the arrival time!).

Patmos was a tiny island, and in early July, just before the peak travel season, it seemed that mainly locals and just a few visitors reached the island. Absolutely perfect for me.

I sat on the dock for about an hour, content to look out at the glistening ocean and watch the orange and red hues of the dawn awaken. When the faint light of dawn reached the cove, I decided it was a somewhat reasonable time to call the pension to find directions. That's right—not only had I not checked the arrival time, I had no idea of the location of the pension. The description in the *Lonely Planet* that it overlooked the bay didn't narrow anything down, as I looked at the many houses lining the rolling hills above the sandy cove. At this point, it was clear that I had completely surrendered to the moment by moment ebb and flow of things—and I loved it.

The owner of the pension seemed to be wide awake when he answered my call, and soon enough Michael's car was pulling in to the small parking area by the dock.

"We don't get many Australians visiting here," Michael said, "and at this time of the year, it's still early in the season, so you will have most of the island to yourself." I couldn't have heard anything better. All I wanted to do was lay on a quiet white sandy beach in the sun. Psili Ammos was the beach Michael suggested. The beach was relatively secluded in a small cove on the other side of the island. Even my *Lonely Planet* made only a tiny reference to it—perfect.

We arrived at the pension after a very short drive around the cove and up and around a winding hill. Small blue and white houses lined the curves of the narrow streets and one couldn't help but know this was a little Greek Island. The pension was nestled on a hill, and was just as homey as the *Lonely Planet* described. The typical Greek-island style pension was like a small inn—two levels, with white-washed walls and wood framed doors that led out to balconies on each room overlooking the cozy sandy bay of Skala. Bliss!

My vision for my stay was meandering around the island on a motorcycle, with my hair blowing in the wind and the sun upon my face, discovering remote beaches and happening upon tucked away local spots along the way. My first stop after breakfast would be the motorcycle rental outlets that were scattered along the cove.

"What do you mean a motorcycle license?" I queried at the first rental outlet. The thought in my head was confounded. *"Why on earth would you need a license to ride around a tiny little island—especially when there is almost nothing that you can seemingly run into?!"*

Three outlets later, it was apparent that no one wanted me riding a motorcycle around the island. *"Since when did little Greek Islands have rules and regulations?"* I thought with a slight huff and puff. Maybe they thought I would eventually cave in, and accept their offer of a small car—at a higher rental rate, of course. *"Maybe I'm just meant to be on four wheels,"* I thought. Inevitably, I accepted the will of the universe, somewhat reluctantly, like a small child who had just been told they couldn't have any more candy. Off I went in my little car, the wheels of which were not much larger than those on a small motorcycle, and I was on my way to discover the island.

The directions to Psili Ammos beach were very straightforward. There was only one main road around the island—and when I say "main" road, I mean "main" relative to the scale of a tiny Greek island. Two small cars passing each other created anxious moments!

"Park at the end of the road and from there just take the walking path to the beach," were the simple instructions from the rental outlet. As it turned out, the "end of the road" was an isolated patch of dirt at the end of a small, dusty track off the main road. At this point, I was appreciating the four wheels of the car. Trying to navigate the loose dirt around winding hills on two little wheels could have brought an early end to my Greek Island adventure.

Looking around the hills as I closed the door of the car, I could have been in the middle of a vast wilderness. In every direction, hills stretched off into the distance, with only the promise of a coastline somewhere beyond view. *"A walking path?"* I contemplated as I looked down and along a hiking trail that disappeared over the horizon. *"Okay, I guess I just start walking."* Two hours later, passing paddock after paddock full of goats, I finally saw water.

One more stretch of winding trail led me down the hillside to Psili Ammos. Coming to a stop as I stepped foot on the beach, at the sight of the beautiful white sand, and the aqua waters, the trek was instantly more than worth the hike. However, as I looked around the beach something was definitely missing. Clothing! I soon discovered why the beach was so far from the town—this was a Greek nirvana full of naked bodies. I was over-dressed!

There was nothing to do but act as if this were a perfectly ordinary part of my every day. So throwing off my clothes, and packing them into my day bag, I tried to look my most confident as I strutted along the beach, stark naked, to find the perfect spot to bask in the sun. I also tried very hard not to laugh at my predicament along the way, but gave into that very quickly as I smiled a big smile and made friendly gestures to locals as I passed by. They smiled back, but it was possibly more than anything else, at the sight of my white Australian body that had not been naked in the sun for as long as I could remember. My white body stood out like a sore thumb amidst the bronze beauties of this Greek island.

The cool Mediterranean waters felt delicious against my naked skin. *"I need to do this more often,"* I thought, floating atop the waters, my nipples popping through the surface. The feeling of complete inhibition was one of the most wonderful feelings. Free to absorb the moment, I smiled at the perfectly blue sky, and the sun smiled back. I decided every day in Patmos would be a day to find a new beach and swim naked in the ocean. I found many beaches!

In the past, being naked was accompanied by shame. Now, being naked felt like freedom. With my demons fading with each passing day, the fear of exposing my *self* also faded. I had a newfound sense of comfort within me, and with that comfort, I felt a renewed sense of expression. I could uncover the parts of my *self* that had been trapped for so long. I could bring them out into the sunshine and let the warm light expose them and bring them to life.

I came to love lying on the beach and swimming naked in the ocean. With every ray of sun that I allowed to soak into my skin, and every flow of water I allowed to immerse my body, I felt more and more at home in my own skin. With every touch of the sun and flow of the water, I felt the presence of the universe that had come to life throughout my journey. Each touch of the universe revealed something that had been lost—something that had been waiting for me to allow the light to shine upon it.

It was somewhat ironic that here, on the island of Patmos, where it is believed that St. John wrote the "Book of Revelations," the significance of revelation should be so striking. Unless we dare to reveal our *self* fully, how can we live fully? When we step into new shoes and onto new paths that help us to reveal all that lies within, then we can be free to expose our greatest self in the world around. We can align the self we reveal in the world with the essence of our being—our soul. We can live a life born of our soul.

Once we allow the spirits to flow through us, the hand of the universe to hold ours, the awe and goosebumps in the moments of each day to fill us; once we conquer our demons, allow the gods and goddesses to rise within; when we live, laugh, and love each day, then we can step out into the world and exclaim, "I am here! This is me! I am an extraordinary child of the universe!"

We can reveal our *self* without reservation, without inhibition. As Mark Twain said:

> *Sing like no one's listening,*
> *love like you've never been hurt,*
> *dance like nobody's watching,*
> *and live like it's heaven on earth.*

If we proclaim the most compelling and uninhibited parts of our *self*, as Shirley Valentine did of those pieces of herself that had been lost, what would we proclaim? I grew up believing there was nothing worth proclaiming about my *self*. My journey had shown me that all of our being resides in what we reveal and what we proclaim. Otherwise, the most precious parts of our *self* sit idle, wasted, and unused. Now, I can feel worth and happiness when I proclaim, *"I'm Kathy who is meant to be. I'm Kathy the gift. I'm Kathy the worthy. I'm Kathy who can reach the stars!"*

"Music in the soul can be heard by the universe," said Lao Tzu. Once we reveal the pieces of our *self* that are born of our soul, that resonate with the soul of the universe, our being becomes in tune with the universe. When we reveal the music of our soul to the universe, we allow our being to be conducted by the universe. We come to know that our music has a place in the orchestra of the universe. We allow our being to be an instrument of the universe. Our life becomes aligned to something greater.

The feelings we have within us are our best sensors as to whether we are living in the company of the self that is born of our soul in each moment, or in the company of the self that defeats us. We feel a flow of energy that enlivens us and keeps guiding us toward living our fullest life. "When you do things from your soul you feel a river moving in you, a joy. When action comes from another section, the feeling disappears," wrote the poet Rumi. The more we act from our soul, from the pieces of our *self* that help us to live fully and purposefully, the more we feel the flow of happiness in each moment.

We must choose to allow that flow of happiness to run through us. We must choose to shine in our light. We must choose to overcome the worst that happens to us and look beyond to where the sun shines on the horizon. We must choose to pause and hear the music of our soul rising through the thunderstorms of our shattered pieces.

"The shape of the experiences of your life is determined nonetheless by the choices that you make ... Give yourself permission to choose the most positive behavior in each moment ... release your fears and choose to heal ... align your personality with your soul and move toward becoming a being of the Light, fully whole and empowered and inwardly secure," urges Gary Zukov in his book, *The Seat of the Soul.*

We each will have experiences that threaten to defeat the light of our being. Our soul gives us the power to be our most empowered warrior on the path to our greatest self. We must reach deep within to touch our soul, and ignite the universal energy that flows within us.

Zukov continues, "Rather than a soul in a body, become a body in a soul. Reach for your soul. Reach even further. The impulse of creation and authentic power—the hourglass between energy and matter: that is the seat of the soul. What does it mean to touch that place?"

To touch our soul is to ignite our most powerful presence—our greatest self.

Propelled by our most powerful presence, we can move through the most turbulent waters, we can catapult to our greatest heights, we can capture our most purposeful pursuits, we can reach further than what appears before us today and boldly venture into the wondrous mystery of tomorrow. We can touch our soul, claim it, and proclaim it!

If we don't dare stand high on pillars and proclaim our *self*, who will hear us? The French philosopher Voltaire insisted, "Stand upright, speak thy thoughts, declare the truth thou hast, that all may share; Be bold, proclaim it everywhere: They only live who dare."

What can we accomplish in our lives if we are silent? How much impact can our lives have if we keep the self born of our soul invisible and hidden away? If we get lost in an unused life, how can we find our dreams?

We need to be bold and daring to reveal the greatest parts of our *self* that are born of our soul. With each revelation, we become more bold, more daring, more brave, and more confident. Our life becomes enlivened.

Since my childhood, I always felt insecure about revealing parts of my *self*. I wanted to stay small and unnoticed for fear of exposing that horrible, dirty little girl. I was filled with guilt and shame. If I did step out, I was always shut down. When people make us feel small, we can start to live small. Soon enough, we stop stepping out. We accept feeling small, and spend every day trying to compensate.

No matter how "big" I tried to feel on the outside—through my job, or my car, or how I dressed—I still felt small on the inside. There was nothing inside that felt good to reveal. The car, the job title, the clothes were easy, but they weren't nurturing my soul. They painted an artificial picture that was safe and that I could control. I could limit how much I revealed through the carefully constructed things I put around me. The only problem was that I knew the truth. We can sometimes fool others with the masks we wear, but we can never really fool our *self*. We know our own truths, no matter how much we try to cover them.

When we have conquered our *self*, when we have explored the darkness within, when we have seen our truths, and when we allow the universe to fill us from within, when we nurture the seed of our soul, then we stop struggling to reveal our "constructed self." We are free to put all of our energy into revealing the gifts within us, when we pause to unwrap our greatest and most purposeful self that is born of our soul.

We can only feel complete and at home when we discover and reveal the parts of our *self* that are born of our soul. "Then you will know the truth and the truth will set you free," said Jesus according to the gospel of the Apostle John.

As long as we maintain the false parts of our *self*, it's like having a foreign object within us that we are holding onto but that our being is trying to reject because it knows that piece does not serve us. Our being knows those pieces are not part of our highest self, that they are not born of our soul. Once we conquer those parts of our *self* that keep us prisoner, we are free to uncover all of the magical places within us, and walk with them each day, fully exposed.

We can throw our clothes into the wind, we can lay naked in the sun, we can expose every atom of our being in the world around. We can be free to *be* all that we are, and in each moment of being, we discover something more authentic that creates an even greater being. We can soar to our greatest self on the wings of our soul.

With each revelation, we discover a greater truth. We discover the uniqueness of our being. We connect to the energy of the universe, we feel our compass resonating, we feel the North Star guiding us to places we never imagined. As we reveal our greatest self to the universe, the universe reveals its most powerful presence to us. We begin to experience the infinite potential of our greatest self in every moment.

"There is just one life for each of us: our own," said the Greek playwright, Euripides. We need to grab our life, and take hold of all of the wonderful pieces. We need to shape our *self* in the likeness of our greatest dreams and aspirations, so we can live our greatest life.

Each part of our inner being is a purposeful piece of an extraordinary whole, just waiting for us to discover and reveal its completeness. With each moment, and with each experience, we have the opportunity to allow the authentic pieces of our *self* to fill our being. We can choose which pieces to put into place, and which pieces to discard. Each day and each new experience present an opportunity to reveal the pieces of our *self* that bring us to life, propel us toward our dreams, and enable us to live our most purposeful life.

Our revelations become our greatest self-fulfilling prophecy. The British philosopher, James Allen, said, "Dream lofty dreams, and as you dream, so you shall become. Your vision is the promise of what you shall one day be; your ideal is the prophecy of what you shall at last unveil." Each moment and each experience is an opportunity to unveil the pieces of the prophecies that can transform our lives. These are the pieces of our *self* that enable us to live our greatest life born from the depths of our soul.

My regular spot for breakfast was Irene's, a small and casual cafe on the sandy beach of Skala cove. Irene's was the first to open for breakfast, and to set out their wooden chairs and straw umbrellas on the sand. The smell of Greek coffee and freshly cooking sweet banana and praline crepes greeted me every morning as I walked along the beach and nestled into my spot by the ocean.

As I walked along the far end of the cove one morning after breakfast, I noticed a small sign in front of one of the boats tied to the sea wall. The sign was advertising day trips to the nearby island of Lipsi. The image of the island was enough for me to want to jump aboard and see what the waters beyond Patmos held. The boat left at 10:30AM and returned at 3:30PM the same afternoon. There being no time like the present, I decided to jump on board for the day.

Lipsi turned out to be a place that not only introduced me to beautiful tiny islands, but also to new friends who would set me off on another adventure beyond the Greek Islands. As our small boat pulled into the dock, the tiny cove of Lipsi was more quaint and picturesque than I imagined. Small white fishing boats with colorful stripes of orange, blue, red, and yellow were still sleeping, closely nestled in the arm of the waterfront like little ducklings huddled together in their mother's wings.

As I wandered alongside the boats, I noticed two beautiful navy-hulled rustic sailing boats. A large white canopy floated above the timber deck, and flags of all colors ran from the top of the mast down to the pulpit at the front of the boat. The twin boats were a picture to be taken, and I focused my zoom lens upon them. "Daily Tours" were the words that took focus in my lens. Was my wishful thinking having its way with me? As I strained to look closer, I noticed activity on board, and was excited to think that I could hop aboard one of these dream boats and hop around the islands.

As I approached, I noticed an older bearded gentleman on the deck wearing a sailor's cap. I presumed he was the captain. A few people were boarding the boat, and I smiled to the gentleman as I came to the small boat ramp. "Hello, are you doing a trip around the islands today?"

It turned out that the boat was going out for a tour of five remote islands around Lipsi, and included a picnic lunch with wine, cheese, and sandwiches—all for 25 Euros. The only problem was that the boat didn't arrive back at the dock until 4:30PM—one hour after the last boat back to Patmos departed.

"You no worry," said the captain. "My wife, she has a place for you to stay here on the island when we come back. You come with us."

What is a girl from Down Under to say?

"We leave now," the captain continued, as if having made my decision for me.

So with those wonderful feelings of living in the moment jumping inside me, I jumped on board.

With wine already being passed around, the brochure on the boat set the scene for the day, "Visit the islands of Makronissi, aboard our traditional caique, The Rena. First stop is Makronissi, where you can swim through the caves and admire the rock formations, then it's on to the dazzling white islands of Aspronissi, followed by a swimming stop in the turquoise waters of Tiganakia. Then we stop at beautiful Marathi for a swim and lunch, where you can eat at one of the tavernas, or bring your own picnic. Our last stop is the little island of Arki (population 50!) where you will have time for a short visit."

Alice was once again in Wonderland! The islands were as beautiful and enchanting as the brochure described, each surrounded by water that was a brighter turquoise than I thought possible. Best of all, we were completely alone. It was as though our boat had been picked up and transported, set down in solitude amidst a sparkling aqua oasis that stretched to the horizon in every direction.

As we dove through the waters, the almost iridescent turquoise transformed into clear liquid crystal beneath the surface. The white sand below sparkled like a blanket of fine diamonds illuminated by the golden rays of sun that reached through and polished each one. There was nothing to do but allow the sun to sprinkle itself upon us and soak up every ounce of magic dust.

Once again, I was reminded of the treasures that we each have beneath our surfaces, waiting to be revealed. The great Zen master, Hui Hai, said, "Your treasure house is within; it contains all you'll ever need." When we reveal our treasures, and allow them to shine through the surface, we cast our magic dust into the world. We can transform every grain of sand into beautiful diamonds. We can illuminate our life. We can create light for others. We can't get lost in an unused life as long as we uncover the treasure of our soul to illuminate the path ahead.

When we pause for long enough to look into our house of treasures, when we dive beneath our surface, when we change our shoes to step outside the self we have become accustomed to, then we allow our soul to unfold. "The soul walks not upon a line, neither does it grow like a reed. The soul unfolds itself, like a lotus of countless petals," said the poet and philosopher, Kahlil Gibran.

The journeys that we set upon to uncover our soul do not need to be journeys to far away places. Our soul is closer to us than any place to which we can travel. We simply need to give our *self* the space each day to reveal the truth of who we are. We need to pause to feel our soul that is present in each moment. We need to be aware when we feel the flows of happiness through us, or when we feel something else. We need to pause in those feelings to see what they hold.

The source of our soul might be a mystery—differing based upon our beliefs. Maybe our soul is a gift from God, maybe it is the culmination of lifetimes of reincarnations, or the echoes of past lives. Maybe it is psychic energy, or of astrological origins. Maybe it is a consciousness from another state of being, or vibrations from the physical energy in the universe.

Even if the source of our soul is a mystery, the presence of our soul need not be a mystery. It is waiting for us to reveal it and allow it to form the pieces of our *self* that can make us whole.

When we continually reveal those pieces of our *self* that are born of our soul, we will be abundantly filled with waters of sparkling treasures. Then we can allow those treasures to flow effortlessly into the world around us. We can bask in the richness of a purposeful life that is born of our soul.

We ventured from island to island under the perfect blue sky, sharing red wine, cheeses, and picnic sandwiches, like a group of long-time friends who had planned this island adventure for years. Yet part of the magic of the day, was that no planning could have brought me here. My new friends were a small mix of relaxed and casual travelers from the region—Italy, Belgium, and France. In broken English, we laughed about travel adventures and places of magic we had each discovered.

"You must go to Ischia when you travel to Italy," said Jo, my new friend from Milan. Jo and her boyfriend, Lupo, laughed at me earlier when I was the first to adventurously leap off the boat and into the water around the caves we were exploring. "Crazy Australian!" they called after me.

"There is a beautiful place called Negombo on the Island of Ischia, just off the coast of Naples." Jo spoke with an entranced reminiscence, "There is no place like it." The island, Jo explained, was a volcanic island, and an entire hillside had been transformed into a thermal park and spa, filled with natural saunas and hot springs. "You can stay at the spa, or stay elsewhere on the island. A day pass to the thermal springs is only 20 Euros." With every word Jo spoke, I was more drawn to experience the allure of Ischia. Jo must have heard my thoughts, "Just go across to Naples, and then take a boat to Ischia." They were the only directions I needed, and in that moment, I decided the island of Ischia would be my next stop after Patmos.

Arriving back at the dock, Captain John's wife, Rena, was waiting for our return, smiling, with dock lines in hand, ready to gently guide her namesake into its place. During the day, Captain John told us that his boats were his dream, along with his beautiful wife, Rena. After restoring the two twin boats to beauty, there was no other name to give them, but Rena, and so *Rena I* and *Rena II* were christened, and all remained the love of his life.

Rena gave me a welcoming smile as John introduced me as the Australian girl who needed a room for the night. "Welcome," Rena's smile grew as she motioned me to follow. Jo, Lupo, and I decided we would meet later at a local cafe to have dinner with some of their friends and watch the final of the Soccer World Cup. So off I went with Rena to settle into my new home for the evening before meeting for dinner.

The World Cup had been constant entertainment throughout my trip, and was culminating in the final that night. During my travels, I passed briefly through the Black Forest in Germany, and young children in the streets celebrated when Germany won its game. In Paris, as I sat in front of the Eiffel Tower, horns sounded everywhere when France won its game. In Venice, I went to a quaint bar by one of the canals, and was amidst screaming Germans and Italians throwing underwear in the air when Italy won. Now, on Lipsi, I would be in neutral territory when Italy played France in the final. Although, with my new Italian friends, it would hardly be a neutral evening!

Arriving at Rena's Rooms, I couldn't have contemplated a more idyllic setting. Rena's Rooms was a quaint white-washed, blue-rimmed terrace house set on the edge of a tiny sandy beach that flowed into endless ocean. By the time we arrived, the orange hues of the early sunset were casting a golden light across the waters that reflected back onto the white-washed terraces. I couldn't have described a more enchanting home for the evening. The golden waters splashing onto the sandy beach called to me, and soon enough I was once again submerged in the waters of the island.

Calyptso was the name of the small family-run cafe-restaurant where I met up with Jo, Lupo, and their two friends to watch the World Cup, and to spend my unexpected evening in Lipsi. I had tried to call back to the Avgerinos Pension to let Michael know that I hadn't been abducted, but the call wouldn't connect. I hoped he assumed I had found another rendezvous for the evening, and that he wasn't at all worried. As it turned out, he didn't even notice I was gone for the evening. *"Oh, to be unaccounted for!"* I delighted.

Our table of five was a raucous table of four Italians and one Australian. The special for the evening, handwritten on a chalk-board outside the open-air cafe, was "Local Goat Stuffed in the Oven with stuffed tomato and vine leaves." Goat seemed to be the local delicacy. I suddenly realized where all of those goats I had passed on the way to Psili Ammos beach were destined. With goat and wine flowing, and after several hours of hysteria among the thirty or so people at the restaurant (which was a large crowd in Lipsi), Italy won and the cheers roared across the tables.

We ended the evening over tall dessert glasses filled high with Greek yogurt infused with swirls of honey. I had never before tasted yogurt as rich and creamy. Every spoonful left us in a state of divine bliss. To this day, that dessert remains my very favorite, and I'm transported back to the cafe in Lipsi with every taste.

The next morning, I headed back to Patmos after a croissant and espresso at a cafe by the small cove, which was still filled with colorful fishing boats gently swaying with the tide. As I enjoyed the delicious aroma of my espresso before each sip, I reflected on the wonderful day before—it seemed like a week of discovery. I was reluctant to leave, yet thoughts of being immersed in the natural thermal springs on the island of Ischia captured me. With those thoughts guiding me, I smiled as the magical, sparkling, turquoise waters carried me back to Patmos, where I would pack my bags, and head to Italy.

Leaving Patmos on the ferry, the quote of Socrates floated across the waters, "It is not living that matters, but living rightly." We can each choose to live a life that matters built upon pillars that reach high and take us to greater places. Why would we waste that opportunity?

We can live our greatest and most purposeful life, rather than disappearing in a "little life" when there is so much more. We can embrace all of this in every moment, with every step, on every path, in every direction. We simply need to choose to make it so. We each can use every moment to uncover the pieces of our greatest self, to discover the treasures that lie within, to boldly proclaim our *self*, and to reveal the life that is born of our soul.

## MOMENTS OF PAUSE

1.   When you stand naked, what do you see? What do you feel? What are the parts of your *self* that you love to reveal?

2.   What are the completely uninhibited things you do in your life? What are the things you do each day that make you feel as though you are standing naked in the sunshine, free to reveal everything within you, and to absorb everything around you?

3.   What are the parts of your *self* that you are afraid to reveal, that make you feel insecure and uncomfortable? What are those pieces that you keep most concealed? Why?

4.   What are the parts of your *self* that have been lost, and become unused in your life?

5. What are the magical pieces of your *self* that are waiting for you to pause and unwrap them? What are the wonderful pieces within your *self* that you can shape in the likeness of your greatest dreams and aspirations?

6. If you stood on your highest pillar and proclaimed the most precious parts of your *self*, what would you proclaim?

7. Which experiences in your life have caused you to cover up parts of your *self*, and to lose pieces of your *self*?

8. How can you allow the sunshine to warm your lost, concealed, and unrevealed pieces of your *self*, and gently bring them back into the light of your life?

9. To what extent do you feel the essence of your being—your soul—is aligned to the self you reveal in the world?

10. What are the things you create around you to make your life "appear big"? What are the things you nurture within you to enable your *self* to "be big"—to reveal and live your most true, purposeful, and greatest life?

## MORE MOMENTS FOR YOU

## Nineteen

# Choose to Love

*"Love conquers all, and let us yield to it."*
—Publius Vergilius Maro Virgil

W HEN WE CHOOSE TO LOVE, we choose to live. We dive into the abundant waters of our *self*. We yield to all of the treasures that lie within, and allow them to flow into the world. We succumb to all that is waiting around us that can rejuvenate us in each moment, and allow those magical forces to enter and transform us.

The boat from Patmos took me to the port of Bari on the south-east coast of Italy, and from there I would travel by train to Naples, and from there to Ischia. The soothing and calming energy I was looking forward to experiencing amidst the thermal springs of Negombo, unfortunately, did not extend to the train trip to Naples.

"The two things you can count on in Naples are great pizza and getting mugged," a young couple sitting nearby in the train carriage warned me. I looked across at them, and whichever look I gave must have falsely indicated that I wanted them to tell me more.

"Especially traveling alone, you better be careful," they continued. "We were gassed on a train a few days ago, you know. It hit us before we knew it. We were in a compartment with sliding glass doors. One minute we were talking to a guy who came in, the next minute we were knocked out with gas, and all of our things were gone when we woke up."

I was grateful for the warning, but there comes a point when too much information only causes needless anxiety.

"Just make sure you hold onto everything really tight when you get off the train, and don't let anyone stop you. Just go straight to your ride!" they continued to warn. I think the book that I raised in front of my face finally gave the right message.

My *Lonely Planet* didn't afford me any greater comfort than did my train companions as I read the "Dangers & Annoyances" passage on the Naples page. "Travelers should be careful about walking alone in the streets late at night, particularly near Stazione Centrale ..." Yes, of course, that was my arrival station.

Needless to say, arriving in Naples in the thick blackness of the late evening had now become an intimidating experience. The train finally arrived at Stazione Centrale at 10:30PM after a five-hour delay due to worker strikes.

Walking across the barely-lit parking lot outside the terminal was far from a welcoming experience. The terminal from where I needed to catch my bus to the hostel was far across the other side of the lot. I was on full alert as I crossed the parking lot, feeling eyes peering at me from various corners. As I boarded the only bus at the station, the universe seemed to be taking care of me, as the driver knew exactly where I needed to go.

Getting off the bus where the driver instructed me, however, wasn't very reassuring. I contemplated the further words of my *Lonely Planet* as I stared down the dark alley where my hostel was supposed to be, "Never venture into dark side streets at night unless in a group." The barbed-wire fences and construction scaffolding that protruded down the alley were far from welcoming. "Breathe deeply. Just walk," I said encouragingly, as though the sound of my voice would make me feel like I had company.

After finally finding the door to the hostel hidden amongst construction scaffolding deep in the alley, I checked in at the front desk to find that the only room left at that time was one with three boys. Brilliant. At least I made it to the hostel. With nothing to do but make the best of the situation, I headed to my room, knocked on the door, and found the three young men happily drinking beer on the beds with no sign of sleeping any time soon. *"I think my days of hosteling are close to over,"* I considered with a sigh. *"One night only!"* I kept repeating like a consoling mantra as I covered my head with my blanket and prayed for sleep.

The next morning I arrived early at the port, and the night before seemed far away as the ocean breeze from the Gulf of Naples swept all around. As I searched the long stretch of ticket windows, I finally saw the sign for Ischia standing out with its flashing red departure light, showing there were only three minutes until departure. Running along the dock with my ticket in hand, the wheels of my backpack crashing along the concrete, I just made it in time for the gangplank to be taken up and the gate to be closed. I was on my way yet again!

The waters of the Gulf of Naples were a rich deep blue as we crossed to Ischia on a beautiful sunny morning. The trip was just over an hour, and before I could spend too much time imagining my day at Negombo amidst the natural spas and saunas, we were pulling into the dock. Time seemed to stand still here, even on the ferry.

The people at the hostel in Naples suggested I stay at a hostel in the community of Forio on Ischia for a night or so and then decide something more from there. That sounded like a reasonable start (the only one I had!), so I called ahead and booked a room.

Arriving at the hostel, I felt as though I was arriving at a small fraternity house that had somehow been mistakenly transported onto this beautifully quaint island. Given the source of the recommendation, I shouldn't have expected anything else, but I like to stay forever an optimist. I couldn't do anything at this point except check into my room (which turned out to have eight beds in the one room) and explore the island for a more tranquil setting.

As I wandered around that day, and explored the island looking for other places to stay, I decided to climb aboard a local bus to see where it would take me. To my delight, the bus ride was a spectacular sight seeing trip around the island. It traversed and zigzagged up and around the loop road, and climbed to the peaks of the island. The stunningly picturesque waters of the Mediterranean mesmerized me the entire way. The bus route ended at a viewing area that gave another incredibly spectacular view of the deep blue Mediterranean. To the left, Ischia's own little island, Sant'Angelo, rose dramatically out of the sea, connected to the mainland by a wide sandbar covered with orange, yellow, and blue beach umbrellas.

Nothing on wheels was allowed to pass into Sant'Angelo, and I was immediately drawn to this colorful and secluded place. Walking down the hill, and leaving the bus behind, I soon reached the end of the road. Before me, the gated entrance to Sant'Angelo enabled only those without wheels to pass. Beyond the entrance, the cliffs of the island sharply dropped into the Mediterranean. The cobbled walking path cascaded steeply around the white and pastel colored houses to finally meet the sandbar. Sant'Angelo was colorful eye-candy at every turn. Meandering paths led down through the village like a flowing ribbon, filled with stores of eclectic art, rustic cafes, cozy restaurants, and quaint white-washed homes.

With sunset approaching, and the sky starting to fill with an orange and pink hue, I decided to follow a particular path that seemed to wind up to the top of the mountainside. My hope was to see a wonderful sunset over the Mediterranean. As I reached the highest point of the path, and then wandered even farther up on a somewhat hidden path, I found Villa Sirena—a panoramic cafe sitting like a mirage. Its small tables for two were set out at the farthest edge of the path, capturing the most breathtaking view of the sun setting over the ocean. With no one in sight, I wandered over and sat at one of the tables, mesmerized by the sunset.

"Red wine for you?" came a deep Italian-accented voice from behind. "Or maybe champagne to watch the sunset?"

I turned to see a beaming dark-haired man with a wonderfully full mustache that only an Italian man could wear, striding toward me from the cafe.

"I am Giovanni and I am going to take care of you!"

"Hello Giovanni," I smiled, "I'm Kathy."

"Katy?" he queried and paused, looking out to the ocean with a slight, but peaceful frown. "Katy?" he queried and paused again as though something was certainly wrong.

"No, no!" he exclaimed, seeming to have solved the puzzle he was contemplating. "In Sant'Angelo, you are Katerina! Yes, Katerina—that is a much more beautiful name for you."

I laughed, and his warm smile and deep brown eyes were a perfect complement to the sunset. "And now, you will have champagne, Katerina!"

What is a girl to say? Champagne is the other perfect complement to any sunset! Moments later, Giovanni returned and delicately placed a glass of champagne on a linen napkin in front of me as though he was gently placing down a flower. That's how the Italians do things.

"Salute!" Giovanni smiled, and gracefully left me to my solitude. I looked out across Mother Nature's masterpiece in front of me. Through my champagne glass, the orange and pink hues of the sunset mixed with the rich blue of the Mediterranean and created a colorful effervescent pallet as the sparkling bubbles rose into the sky. *"Maybe it's time to celebrate me,"* I thought peacefully.

I realized in that moment that I had never celebrated "me" before. I had never paused to celebrate my *self*.

I had celebrated my accomplishments, but my accomplishments had often served only to cover up my inadequacies. I readily celebrated things around me, but never felt worthy of celebrating things within me. The things within me had always been things of which I was ashamed, and which only filled me with negative thoughts. Within me was the monster. Within me was the dirty little girl. Within me was the troublemaker, the ungrateful daughter, the one who was never meant to be here anyway. The mistake.

In this moment, the sum of all that was within me was greater than those negative thoughts and feelings. In the shoes I filled now, I felt a much greater presence than the tiny insignificant creature my father had tried to make of me.

The "me" that filled these shoes now was a child of the universe, with feet and toes shaped by the universe, fingers and hands carved by the universe, heart and soul filled by the universe. Through my journey, the universe had filled these shoes with all of its gifts, and one by one helped me to unwrap them.

With my little girl now sitting peacefully and happily within, it was time to celebrate me.

*"Salute,"* we both smiled out to the universe.

The evening that had started with a simple glass of champagne watching the sunset, turned into a night overflowing with red wine and pizza at Villa Sirena.

"Katerina," called Giovanni excitedly, as he came back to my table after I finished my champagne. "You must stay and join us for dinner tonight! My brother is making pizza in the restaurant for all of the guests of our villa. You will please be my guest, yes?" Giovanni smiled.

As it happened, Villa Sirena was owned by Giovanni's sister, Maria, and her husband, Michael. After Giovanni insisted several times that I stay, and Maria came out to welcome me, I couldn't help but accept the invitation.

The courtyard of the villa was beautiful. It was a haven of lush green vines, and pink and red bougainvillea. Fairy lights cascaded through a wooden trellis above candlelit dining tables. Soon enough, the smell of pizza drifting out from the large wood-fired stone oven in the corner of the courtyard, enticed everyone to the tables. This was like a big casual family dinner, with everyone seeming to know each other. It turned out that Maria and Michael had their very loyal travelers who visited and stayed with them each year, as if relatives coming for the holidays. It was easy to see why.

Endless authentic Napoli-style pizza was passed from the oven and around the tables for what seemed to be hours. Italian music filled the air, and red wine flowed. After several of Giovanni's marriage proposals that had the approval of Maria and Michael, it seemed as though I could have a permanent home on Sant'Angelo. But for now, this Cinderella needed to get the last midnight bus back to the hostel in Forio!

"Katerina," Giovanni said as he walked me along the path that led out of Sant'Angelo and to the buses, "You must come here to stay in Sant'Angelo. This is the only place for you. I will show you the island, and you don't have to marry me." I smiled and sensed that Giovanni was genuinely happy to simply show me the island that he loved and very proudly called home. This was his paradise that he wanted to share. "You can stay here at my sister's villa— she will have a room for you, and we will all have dinner together every evening."

The magic and charm of the evening had its way with me. *"Why not?"* I thought, *"Go with the flow of the universe and follow your senses."*

"Giovanni, thank you, I would love to," I said, "That would be wonderful!"

The next morning, I packed my bags and headed to Sant'Angelo. It was about 10:30AM by the time I made my way up the path to the entrance of Villa Sirena. Giovanni was at the front of the cafe.

"Giovanni!" I smiled and waved.

"Katerina!" Giovanni jumped up and looked completely surprised to see me. I wondered if he hadn't remembered his offer through the red wine from the night before, or if he just didn't think I was serious when I accepted his offer. Nonetheless, he strode toward me with a big smile and took my bags. "You came! I'm so glad! Please, sit, I will bring you water."

As I sat at my same table on the edge of the path overlooking the Mediterranean, I was still filled with the smile from the sunset of the evening before. It was another beautiful day in Sant'Angelo.

Giovanni returned to the table with a glass of water for me and sat beside me. "Katerina," he said seriously, "There is a problem." It turned out that Giovanni hadn't quite mentioned his offer of a room for me to his sister, and the villa was full. I smiled. "But no worry," Giovanni looked like a child who had been caught out by his mother. He was so embarrassed. "My sister has friends who have pensions nearby and we will find you somewhere to stay very close."

I felt perfectly relaxed in the hands of Giovanni and his family and friends. Soon enough, I was making home in an absolutely beautifully located pension a little farther around the mountain path from Villa Sirena. The view from the terrace was breathtaking. I looked out over the long beach that ran along the other side of Sant'Angelo and across the sailboats that were scattered throughout the ocean beyond. I couldn't have found a more idyllic spot.

The beautiful sunrises and sunsets kept me company every day in Sant'Angelo. At sunrise each day, I wandered to the small beach in the cove below. Sergio, the local barista, would be making rich, fresh Italian coffee in his cafe by the beach, and each morning, he would bring fresh coffee to me on the beach chairs on the sand outside the cafe. After my coffee, I would swim in the ocean with the early morning warmth of the sun upon me, and that would be my welcome to each day.

Day by day, Giovanni showed me different areas of the islands. Ischia was abundant with hidden thermal springs and spas, with more than one hundred thermal springs throughout the island. In the early morning, steam rose from all over the rich green mountains. Driving along the small winding roads to hidden parts of the island with Giovanni, the steam seemed like a thick white fog floating alongside the road. The entire island was alive with color and movement—a magical child of nature all of its own.

Negombo was a short bus ride and a walk from Sant'Angelo. I set off with only my 20 Euros for the entrance fee to the spa, and a few Euros for the bus ride to make sure I kept to my budget for the day—something that was proving to be surprisingly easy. Arriving at Negombo was like arriving in a luxurious natural oasis. The lush green mountain filled with natural hot springs rose high above the white sandy Mediterranean cove of San Montano Beach. In the morning light, the steam from the springs formed a golden aura around the mountain as though the sun was rising from its thermal depths. All I wanted was to be immersed in the warm waters of the earth, and to soak my body in the golden auras of the mountain.

The trail that led from the cove to the mountain was filled with natural springs, saunas, and thermal pools that were beautifully landscaped with colorful fauna, ferns, bougainvillea, sculptures, and rock formations. As I stepped deep into the first thermal pool, the warm waters engulfed me. The wonderful feeling of rejuvenating warmth traveled through every part of me, and my thoughts drifted into nothingness as I let the aura of the mountain consume me. *"This is being kind to me,"* I smiled as I watched the steamy water flow over the edge of the pool against the backdrop of the blue horizon, framed by ferns and rockeries to either side.

Around each curve of the path leading up into the mountain were new springs, thermal pools, and grottos of every shape and size—more than thirty were hidden all over the mountainside. As I nestled into one of the grottos that burrowed deep inside the mountain, the feeling of the steam engulfing me in this cavernous sauna was like being cradled in the womb of Mother Nature. I had come to love the feeling of loving the feelings within me. I had come to love indulging my senses, rather than starving them.

"You can search throughout the entire universe for someone who is more deserving of your love and affection than you are yourself, and that person is not to be found anywhere. You yourself, as much as anybody in the entire universe deserve your love and affection," said the Buddha. During my journey, I had come to give my *self* the love and affection that I had shut down from fear and from feeling unworthy.

The Dalai Lama said, "Love and compassion are necessities, not luxuries. Without them humanity cannot survive." I came to know that in order for me to survive, I needed to allow love into my being. I needed to choose to allow love to enter. I needed to inhale it with every breath and let it travel through me like the warmth of the thermal saunas.

The week in Ischia turned into a perfect romance, and I surrendered to every moment. I surrendered my body to the thermal springs and saunas of Negombo. I let the waters of the Mediterranean caress every part of me. I let the sand rest close against me. I let the sunshine penetrate me. I let the air fill me. It was an orgasm that I allowed every sense within me to feel, and to keep wanting more. I felt an insatiable desire for the touches of life.

*"Fall in love with your self, fall in love with life, then fall in love with another,"* the thought drifted to me.

I realized that I had never loved life. More than that, I had been completely closed to the love of life. I kept my *self* isolated from the love of others, and kept my *self* from feeling love for my *self*. There was no inspiration for love, no desire. My feelings of love were mixed up with feelings of violation, and I could never separate the two. For most of my life, whatever I allowed my *self* to feel, I kept very close to the surface, never allowing anything to enter very far. Whatever I gave, I gave from that same place close to the surface. To feel "love" entering any deeper was like feeling my father violating and penetrating me. To give it back, felt like reciprocating to him. It was a feeling from which all I wanted to do was run.

My ability to live, to laugh, and to love was stolen as a child. It wasn't just missing, it was something of which I became terrified. Every moment of living was filled with an endless death. Every burst of laughter was pierced by the torment that would follow. Every ounce of love was poison.

The romance of my journey since I left Australia had laid to rest my fear of allowing feelings of love to enter. Time after time, the universe filled every moment with anticipation of another wonderful moment, rather than with fear of another terrifying moment. Life had become a place to love to live, rather than a place to wish to die.

Before I could heal, I needed to feel that there was something worth healing for. When you only know darkness, and have not felt light, there is no point to healing only to exist in the same dark world. It is as pointless as continuing to drink water, so you can keep walking across an endless desert. For what purpose? If you have never touched the "greener grass," there is no other side.

My journey had shown me another side. It had shown me greener grass. It gave me back the ability to live, to laugh, and to love. There was a point to existing. There was a life worth living. More so, there was a life worth loving.

Love was certainly in the air in Sant'Angelo—but for me, it was the pure love of life. If Giovanni were a Giovanna, maybe there would have been an intimate love in the air. My choice to love, and to be loved, was in the arms of a woman, rather than a man.

Of all the things I needed in life, I needed to love without compromise. I had only ever found that love in a woman. Maybe that was influenced by what I went through with my father—I certainly didn't like the touch of a man. Maybe it was simply that the emotional, physical, and spiritual connection that resonated within me, and that I wanted to experience in a love relationship, was much stronger with women. Maybe it was a combination of both. Either way, that was the intimate love that felt right for me. The only thing I could do to be true to my *self* was to follow that. With all the love that my father had taken away in my life, I was the only one who could choose the love I needed to fill the rest of my life.

Opening my *self* to love was a conscious choice. I had always known that the love I felt was with women, but to pursue that love, and to open to it, was a very conscious and challenging choice. I allowed my *self* that choice during my twenties when I found someone with whom I was willing to trust and be open. It would have been an easier path to choose to stay away from relationships, or to pretend to find contentment with a man. With everything I was still dealing with in my life, I didn't know if trying to survive the rejection and judgments that were bound to come with my choice was worth the struggle.

All I knew was that I couldn't make a choice that wasn't true to me. That would be like betraying and abusing my *self*. It would have been as self-defeating as letting the type of oppression that my father imposed on me as a child, dictate my life as an adult. Fear would have kept me locked in the prison that I was trying so hard to escape.

The only way I could live free, was to love true.

The Persian poet, Rumi, wrote, "Your task is not to seek for love, but merely to seek and find all the barriers within yourself that you have built against it." I had built so many barriers to love throughout my life. Once I finally started to allow love in, I couldn't live with love that was a compromise.

I think when we compromise the love we give and accept, our life becomes like a faded piece of art. The color and vibrancy that was once there starts to look lifeless. The canvas becomes worn and fragile. There is no inspiration. The value is lost.

We are the painters of the canvas of our life. Why would we choose to settle for anything less than creating the most wonderful, vibrant, inspiring masterpiece?

The Italian Poet, Ovid, said, "Fortune and love favor the brave." How brave are we willing to be for the sake of our own life, for the sake of the love we desire, for the sake of our freedom in this one short and precious life? If we are not willing to be brave for the sake of our *self*, who else will be brave for us? How will we be able to be brave for others—our children, our parents, our spouses, our significant others, our friends?

It is our choice—to be brave enough to live and to love without compromise.

The French poet, Arsène Houssaye, wrote, "Tell me whom you love and I will tell you who you are." I think who we love and how we love tell us how true and how brave we are being to our *self*. We can tell, if we are honest with our *self*, if we are loving without compromise, and if we are allowing our *self* to be loved without compromise. We can tell if the love we live with creates a vibrant masterpiece, or a faded, shallow, and uninspiring image.

"Where there is love there is life," said Mohandas Gandhi. When we choose to love fully, we choose to live fully. We delight in every moment of our *self*. We allow our *self* to relax, and to be filled with the rejuvenating waters of our abundant self. We no longer yield to our demons and our fears, for we have smothered them with kindness. Instead, we allow our *self* to yield fully to love by our own conscious choice, secure in the knowledge that we are worthy of the uncompromising love that sets us free.

## MOMENTS OF PAUSE

1.  What are the things within your *self* that you celebrate? How do you find moments to celebrate your *self*?

2.  What do you do to indulge your senses, to immerse your *self* in the warm and rejuvenating waters of Mother Nature, and to allow the feelings that you love within you to emerge?

3.  How do you treat your *self* as the most deserving person in the universe of your love and affection?

4.  How do you allow love into your life? How do you surrender to it? How do you romance your *self*? How do you allow life to romance you?

5.  What are the things in life with which you have fallen in love? When are the moments you have felt the insatiable desire for the touches of life?

6.  What are the experiences where love has been stolen from you? What are the things that have caused you to be terrified of letting love in, and giving love out?

7.  In what ways are you compromising the love you want to live with? In what ways are you settling for less love in your life than you desire?

8.  What are the barriers to love that you have within you and around you?

9.  When you pause to look at the love you have in your life, what does that tell you about who you are?

10. What choices do you need to make to fill your life with the uncompromising love you desire, and of which you are worthy?

## MORE MOMENTS FOR YOU

# Twenty

# The Power of Our Presence

*"Creating is the essence of Life."*

—JULIUS CAESAR

ONCE WE HAVE WITHIN US, the insatiable desire for life, the laughter, the love, the spirit; when we have allowed the universe to fill us with its gifts, and unwrapped each one of them; when we leave our demons in the past, and see the future as infinite opportunity to be our greatest self; when we know that each moment is filled with choices to change our shoes, and to step onto new paths; then we see that our presence in the present is the source of our greatest power. With that presence, we each hold the power to transform our lives, to make our dreams a reality, to create the change we want to see in the world, and to live our greatest life.

When we stand firmly in the present, conscious of all the choices we have in that precise moment, we allow our *self* the opportunity to choose exactly what we need and all that our soul desires. In this single present moment, we are the sum of all that we choose to be. We breathe in and ignite the light within us, we feel the infinite possibilities of the universe fill our consciousness, we hold that breath in anticipation of unlimited realizations, and we release our illuminated being into the world as we exhale. With each breath, we are filled with the power to create our greatest presence.

The train from Ischia left in the early morning, and I felt as though I was leaving yet another "home." Along my journey, I more and more easily slipped into that feeling of "home" wherever I was. Each stop along the way, and each path between each stop, was filled with the simple contentment of feeling happily at home in life in each moment.

The farther I traveled, the further behind I left darkness and fear. With each step, I felt a greater presence in each moment, and a greater potential in each moment just waiting to be discovered. My journey was revealing the depth of power that lies in each moment, waiting for us to fearlessly embrace it, and become our most powerful presence.

The path from Ischia took me to Rome, and as always, more emerged than I expected. On the final stops of my trip, I would stand in places filled with rich and timeless energy. Amidst the Old City of Rome, the tombs and monumental statues of ancient Egypt, and in front of the Shroud of Turin, I would yet again feel goosebumps of awe at the magnificence, magic, and mystery of life. I would feel the presence of life in the moment, and the presence of life from beyond.

"All roads indeed lead to Rome, but theirs also is a more mystical destination, some bourne of which no traveler knows the name, some city, they all seem to hint, even more eternal," wrote the English poet and author, Richard Le Gallienne. The mystical destinations, those "more eternal cities" to which our paths lead can be illuminated with each step we consciously choose to take, or remain shrouded in mystery with each step we take without presence. These are our destinations of aspiration and purpose that we seek to discover on our journeys—places that we "know" not of, for which we have no name, yet which we pursue in anticipation of reaching a more "eternal" destination. As our presence in each moment grows, each step toward our eternal destination becomes more illuminated. Our power to transform our life and our world, grows with each step toward that destination.

Walking toward the entrance to the Roman Forum, in the heart of the Old City of Rome, the power of the presence of this eternal city was as enduring as the centuries-old temples and arches that stood like gods still watching over the city. Standing amidst the Forum, it was easy to imagine the marbled grandeur of the city, full of temples, basilicas, sculptures, monuments, royal baths, and pristine gardens. The mysticism of the city floated with the air—one could breathe it in standing on the cobblestones and by the towering pillars of the Forum that was once the center of life in the Old City.

Surrounded by the temples and shrines of legendary heroes and kings, one was consumed by the presence of the past and from beyond emanating from these monumental relics. The resting place of Julius Caesar in the center of the Forum held a magnetic presence all of its own. I was drawn to the energy without knowing its source until I was so close that the inscribed plaque on the wall in front of the resting place became clear. The small pile of dirt and stone where the body of Julius Caesar was cremated, was peacefully nestled into a modest semi-circular wall, and covered by a simple tin roof. Despite its small size, the pile of dirt and stone emitted a majestic presence beyond its simplicity.

We are all born from the same dust, with the potential to create majestic lives that extend far beyond our physical being in the small space that we fill. The extent to which our presence is projected beyond us is only limited by how much we limit our *self*.

"Creating is the essence of life," said Julius Caesar. When we choose to create our most powerful presence in each moment, we allow our *self* to soar beyond our limits.

When we continually choose to take each step in the direction of a more eternal destination, on a path to becoming our unlimited self, our life can be as legendary and heroic as the greatest of those who have come before us, and be timeless in the legacy we create for all of those who will come after us.

We are all children of the universe, and if we are not here for each other, then one wonders why there are so many of us sharing this one space.

"If I am not for myself, then who will be for me? And if I am only for myself, then what am I?" asked Rabbi Hillel, one of the most influential scholars in Jewish history. When we simultaneously do for others, what we need to do for our *self* to rise to be our greatest self, and to heal the inevitable wounds we each suffer, then our presence in the present becomes supremely powerful. We start to affect monumental change for our *self* and for others that leaves a legacy long after our dust has settled on the ground.

As I looked up and around at the towering arches and pillars of the Forum, the enduring remains created a vision of a timeless place, the scale and grandeur of which was as epic as the stories that were held within its walls.

*"How epic do we make our lives?"* I wondered. How powerful is the presence we create? What monumental endeavors do we undertake that last throughout the ages? With what heroic courage and conviction do we pursue that "eternal city," that destination that is beyond what is seen?

William Shakespeare famously wrote, "What a piece of work is a man, how noble in reason, how infinite in faculties, in form and moving how express and admirable, in action how like an angel, in apprehension how like a god."

All that we need to create an epic and enduring life is with us now, in this present moment. We simply need to call upon and activate the faculties within and around us. The power of our presence, our faculties, our form, our being, can be as angelic and god-like as we imagine our *self* to be. If we believe we are created in the image of whichever god or higher presence we believe in, then we have the power within and around us to be that extraordinary presence in each moment. We have the opportunity to be a presence far greater than the space that we fill.

"Each morning we are born again. What we do today is what matters most," said the Buddha. The more we pause to feel our presence in each moment, to be mindful of all that lies within us, to know that each new moment and each new day is an opportunity to be the presence we want to be, the more each moment becomes a step into infinite possibilities.

The English poet and novelist, D.H. Lawrence, wrote, "The living moment is everything." The more we live each moment, present in the *everything* of that moment, the more we tap into an unlimited power, a concentrated stream of energy. That stream fills us with a heroic courage and conviction. With that unlimited power, we can embark upon our most monumental endeavors, and create timeless legacies of epic scale and grandeur.

Throughout the Old City of Rome, beyond the Roman Forum, to the Colosseum, the Pantheon, the great arches, the grand basilicas, and the endless monuments, each timeless landmark projected a presence far greater than the enormous size of its remains. The entire city seemed to resonate with infinite potential, with endless possibilities, with the power and the strength that lies around every corner awaiting our discovery. Day to day, moment to moment, we simply need to pause to create the space to discover, and then choose to start building the landmarks of our life that are testament to our most purposeful presence.

Michelangelo, whose presence fills the city of Rome through his sculptures and architecture, said, "Every block of stone has a statue inside it and it is the task of the sculptor to discover it." We are each the sculptors of the block of our being, and we each hold the tools to carve the most enduring statue with the presence we create. When we carve our authentic presence, we set our *self* free to soar to our greatest heights. "I saw the angel in the marble and carved until I set him free," said Michelangelo.

I started to see the angel within me when I opened my *self* to genuinely care and have compassion for others, and when I started to feel care and compassion for my *self*. Throughout my journey since leaving Australia I had felt the touches of the universe with each experience of touching the life of someone else. I felt it when we set kids with disabilities sailing in Miami, when we built clinics and schools for impoverished families in Haiti, and when we gave school books to children in Mexico. I felt the power of our presence to move our *self*, and move the world around us.

I felt as though I had started to chip away at the block of stone of my being that had hardened so much through my childhood, to reveal a presence that could be purposeful in the world. I started to feel a presence that could have meaning and significance, and that could take all of what I had experienced to help others create the change they needed in their lives. I knew how easy it was to step onto the edge of life, ready to give it all up. I had been down so many dark paths with no light, content to dwell there until the darkness became permanent. I had given up so many times on serving any purpose, or of being meaningful or significant.

Now, instead of feeling that all I had experienced would be a constant burden, I could see my journey through those experiences as a source of strength, empowerment, and determination. I could see the power of all that existed within, and that when challenged, that source would only become a stronger presence—a presence that could continue to help me grow, and to help others.

I began to see that the greatest purpose that I could serve, was to continue to reveal the presence that would allow me to be of most help to others. By giving voice to my story, I could help others tell their story. By sharing my journey, I could help others journey onward. By extending a hand, I could help others to not walk alone through some of the worst that happens to us.

Through our collective stories, we can rebuild our lives around new narratives that are founded in resilience, determination, solidarity, compassion, and purpose. Collectively, we can make a difference to those things that are most important to us. Instead of sitting silent, knowing others are still isolated prisoners in their pain, we can rise together, until every person is flying free.

Ironically, it seemed that all I had been running from, once I was able to confront it, was what could enable me to live my most purposeful life. Living openly in the truth of my life, I could stand proudly and thankfully that I was still living. In that space, there is nothing more authentic or purposeful that I can do than dedicate my being to helping others rise through their struggles and live their most empowered and purposeful life.

Through my journey, angels had prevailed. I felt filled with light that made the darkness seem insignificant. The pieces of my *self* that were born of my soul had emerged, the compass within me resonated with my True North, and I felt the hand of the universe holding mine in every moment. I had seen that the core of everything around us is what lies within each of us.

The Roman poet Lucretius wrote, "We are each of us angels with only one wing, and we can only fly by embracing one another." When we unveil our angels, we can reveal our most powerful presence in the world around. We can help our *self* and one another soar to our greatest heights.

To affect change in the world, we need to affect change in our *self*. The power of our presence in the world is only as strong as the presence we have within us. We each have the tools to reveal that presence. We just need to pause to see the angel in the marble, and choose to be the sculptor to set our being free to soar.

The following day, walking across St. Peter's Square in Vatican City, with Michelangelo's grandiose silver-blue dome of St. Peters Basilica rising far into the sky, the presence from the past and from beyond collided with a divine and exalted intensity. The 140 statues of saints that stood high upon the two great semi-circular colonnades around the square, and upon the facade of the imposing basilica, seemed to cast a thousand eyes from the heavens.

Inside the basilica, Michelangelo's dome seemed to reach just as high into the heavens as it created its own enormous sky above the tomb of St. Peter. The canopy of the massive and majestic baldacchino that rose on grand gold and dark bronze columns over the sunken tomb, formed a reverent shrine and sanctuary that had the presence of a protector dwelling infinitely in the sky within the dome.

There was no escaping the divine presence of the epicenter that marked the beginning, the present, and the future of the faith, belief, dreams, hopes, and aspirations of more than a billion people of one of the largest religions of the world. Irrespective of one's own religious or spiritual beliefs, the power of the presence of a shared humanity built on the foundations of desires for a greater mankind, crosses boundaries of religions and peoples.

In that present moment, one collective presence transcended any individual presence.

Beyond the walls of the basilica, in the present moments of each of our lives, we have unlimited opportunity to extend our individual presence to form a greater collective presence. With that collective presence, we can create a greater mankind. We can harness our infinite and divine power for the sake of our *self* and each other in this life, and beyond.

Nearby, in the Sistine Chapel, that same collective presence was consuming as the works of some of the most prominent and gifted artists in human history filled the chapel. Scenes depicting the entire realm of humanity through the eyes of Christianity transcended the physical limits of the chapel. The iconic images spanning the beginning of creation, the creation of man, and the last judgement filled the chapel with a presence from beyond. One was immersed in a concentrated intersection of past, present, and future that depicted the timeless quest to inspire and nurture the highest potential in mankind—to create a collective presence for the good of all people to attain a higher state of being.

Immersed in such a powerful presence, one can't help but be held in a space full of contemplation of the unlimited opportunity and infinite potential of mankind. It is simply our choices that determine how far and how quickly we reach that potential. We can choose to step onto paths of destruction, or onto paths of creation and evolution.

The quest to evolve to higher beings can inspire a collective presence and create a binding force that surpasses differences. That quest is not specific to one religion—it can bind peoples across religions. It can build bridges across boundaries. It can reach all people.

Standing in the center of the chapel, I looked up to see one of the most iconic images in human history hovering above me—the hand of God reaching out to touch the hand of Adam in Michelangelo's *Creation of Man*. The image was strikingly symbolic of the potential we each have to reach out and touch humanity with our presence, beyond religions and boundaries. *"How iconic is the touch of our hand on humanity?"* I contemplated, *"What are those touches that allow us all to ascend to a higher place?"*

"As a well-spent day brings happy sleep, so a life well used brings happy death," said Leonardo da Vinci. Our opportunity to use this life well, to spend this day well, is all in the present moment. It is now. It is here. Within the present moment, lie infinite possibilities to create a touch with our presence that allows us to ascend life.

Irrespective of whatever we believe to be the source of our creation, whichever god or gods or higher power in which we believe, we each have an undeniable path and a journey in our present moment. In the present moment, we can each choose how to use our presence to touch our life to become our greatest self, and how to reach out to touch humanity to help nurture a higher state for all people. It is a choice we each have the power to make.

Leaving Rome and exploring areas to the North, I would come upon the wonders of the small but extraordinarily mystical city of Torino. Torino held one of the largest collections of treasures from Egypt in the Museo Egizio, and one of the greatest icons of Christianity—the Shroud of Turin. My *Lonely Planet* had literally fallen open on the page describing Torino. I was drawn to the description of this "magical city," filled with Egyptian treasures, and "top-class" galleries and museums holding Italy's most important art collections. The romantic Baroque architecture of the city, and the "white and black energy" of the good and evil forces that were said to flow through the city attracted me.

Walking through the main square of Piazza Castello on a Sunday morning, I felt a mystical romanticism evoked by the beautiful Baroque buildings that surrounded the square. Water fountains and colorful flower beds of yellow, pink, and orange complemented the vibrancy of the coffee houses and cafes that filled the promenades.

Sunday brunch in the square seemed to be an institution as old and revered as the architecture. Patrons flowed from cafes that were filled with extravagant smorgasbords of appetizers along the windows and countertops, as though royalty was expected to visit. Colorful vermouth martinis, of which Torino was the birthplace, flowed with charm from behind the counters as if noble celebrations were at hand. Yet it seemed that it was simply life that was the cause for celebration, as I strolled from cafe to cafe sampling an endless array of appetizers, and sipping a martini of different kinds here and there.

The energy I felt as I strolled through the square may have been that of the "white heart" of Torino. The Piazza Castello was near the "white heart" of the city, full of the positive energy of the forces of good that were said to be present here. It was possibly not coincidental that amidst the "white heart," I would stumble upon the cathedral that was home to one of the most mysterious and powerful icons of Christianity—the Shroud of Turin.

At first, I didn't know I had arrived at the home of the shroud. I simply followed a path for no other reason than the feeling that drew me to take steps in that particular direction. I had become used to following that feeling without a second thought. After meandering along the quaint and quiet streets beyond the main square, I came upon what seemed to be a modest church, but that emitted an energy much greater than its size.

Stepping inside to explore, I stopped as I stood in front of the life size image of the Shroud of Turin that lay just around the corner from the entrance. The mere reproduction projected an aura of powerful energy. Maybe it was seeing such an iconic image right there, so close, that created such a powerful projection. Maybe it was the energy that resonated from thousands of people who had over time been in this same space, filled with a collective awe and mystery of the shroud. Nonetheless, the energy felt very present.

Walking around the main chapel to the smaller Chapel of the Shroud, the enlarged image of the face from the shroud, the face many believe to be the impression of the face of Jesus Christ, was surreal and haunting. Hanging behind the protective glass of the shrine, the photographic negative of the face from the shroud projected an almost luminescent image that reached out beyond the glass and penetrated every sense of being. It was a consuming interaction that simultaneously created a sense of weightlessness and centeredness—almost hypnotic and trancelike—with the deep-set eyes of the image never seeming to shift away.

Controversy as to whether the shroud was the burial robe of Jesus Christ has surrounded the shroud for many years, yet that controversy seemed insignificant in the presence of such powerful energy. What was most significant and extraordinary was the intensity of the presence, whether that was from the thousands of believers who had projected their collective energy into that space, or whether its source was directly from the image. Either way, it seemed to be an affirmation of the power of the presence that lies here among us, and beyond us.

With the eyes of the image fixed upon me, I was once again captured in awe from the feeling of a powerful presence from "beyond." Looking deep into the eyes of the image, I felt drawn deeper into that presence, until there was no sense of being either present or beyond. The two spaces seemed to naturally and effortlessly merge into one. In those moments, the presence of many became the presence of one, and the presence of one became the presence of many.

Throughout the world, we each have different images that represent the face of all that lies beyond, of a higher power, of another level of consciousness, of the god or gods that we believe represent the presence that draws us to a higher state of being.

They are images that hold us in moments that reveal our greatest potential. They are images that hold us in moments that draw us to the steps we need to take to ascend to our greatest self. They are different images that take us to a common place of contemplation of the purpose and value of our presence in the here and now, and the significance of the present to whatever we believe lies beyond.

Standing in front of the Shroud of Turin, I wondered, *"What is the shroud of our lives in which we are wrapped and from which we need to rise to ascend to a higher place? What do we endure and transcend in this life that is born of a higher purpose? How powerful could be the impact of the image that we leave behind?"*

With each step along my journey, my sense of purpose was resonating more and more strongly. With each new experience, it seemed as though a new light touched all of the darkness that had consumed me for so long. That new light illuminated a power and a presence that had long been buried. The depths of darkness that had seemed endless, the nightmares that had seemed inescapable, the images that had seemed to forever haunt each moment, were now replaced by a purposeful presence infinitely more powerful than any of the darkness.

There were so many moments in my life when I came so close to letting the darkness bury me. In this moment, the power of the presence we have within us to keep us reaching toward something more, despite those things we need to endure, was never so clear. We can find our greatest power, our greatest purpose, our greatest presence through the worst of that which we endure.

As I left the cathedral and strolled by architecture from another time, my thoughts were still with what lies beyond, and the power of the presence from beyond when we allow it to be revealed. Just blocks away from the cathedral, I would come upon another center of energy from beyond—this time emanating from ancient Egypt. The Museo Egizio held the largest collection of Egyptian artifacts outside of Cairo, and stepping into the museum was like stepping into an afterlife.

Standing amidst this afterlife, statues of pharaohs, preserved mummies, and tombs full of ancient artifacts created their own place and time in the present moment as though they were fully sentient here and now. The space between past, present, and beyond seemed once again indistinguishable.

Paintings of funerary scenes along the dimly lit stone walls told the story of the transition to this afterlife. The image of the jackal-headed god that protected the dead, Anubis, seemed to seep from the walls and lurk in the subdued light of the tomb. The breath of the creature-protector seemed to drift closely by with the slight movements of the damp and thick air. It is told that Anubis would accompany the deceased to weigh the heart of the deceased in front of the god Osiris against the feather of the goddess of truth and justice. If the heart was lighter, the deceased had led a righteous life, and could proceed to the afterlife. If not, Osiris would condemn the deceased for eternity. Within these walls, the eyes of the gods of the afterlife seemed to peer into the present from their place beyond.

Yet again, the sense of presence from beyond was penetrating. Maybe that presence is centered in the connection that the Egyptians taught humankind has to the divine essence of the Creator and the Heavens. "The kingdom of heaven is within you; whosoever shall know himself shall find it," tells a central teaching. "Know thyself" was an essential element of living and dying in Egyptian teaching. How one lived, determined how well one died.

Standing by the walls of ancient tombs, alongside statues of great pharaohs, and surrounded by artifacts and frescos with scenes of transition from life to the afterlife, one was transported to the sacred chambers of the enormous pyramids. The pyramids of Egypt were the most visual representation of a life well lived, exemplifying the ascension of the soul up the great staircase to the heavens and the afterlife.

The enormous statues of pharaohs reflected their god-like stature in Egyptian religion. The pyramids of the pharaohs reached to the greatest heights. The pharaohs, believed to be descendants of the gods, were the bridge between the human and the divine realm. The pharaohs were believed to be the powers that could bring people together to coexist and cooperate to maintain what the Egyptians called "maat"—the eternal order of the universe, encompassing truth, justice, balance, and order. Without peoples working together, the eternal order would be destroyed, and disorder and disharmony would exist for all.

From one religion to another, from one philosophy to another, the consequence of the life that one leads is surely a constant that brings us back to the significance of the moment that we have before us. We are brought back to the choices that we can make in each moment as to how to live, and how to use our presence, for the good of the evolution of our own being, and for the benefit of humankind.

On the Tomb of Inherkhawy, *The Harper's Song for Inherkhawy* from 1160 BC, sings to the moments of opportunity we have to live in each day.

> *So seize the day! Hold holiday!*
> *Be unwearied, unceasing, alive*
> *you and your own true love;*
> *Let not the heart be troubled during your*
> *sojourn on Earth,*
> *but seize the day as it passes!*

From the Masters of Paris, to the ancient Gods of Greece, to the great philosophers and legends of Rome, to the iconic images of the Sistine Chapel, to the energy of the Shroud of Turin, and to the presence of the afterlife within tombs from ancient Egypt, the power and significance of the present moment was a connecting force between each. The present moment is *the* connecting force between the past, the present, the future, and that which is beyond.

Our presence in each moment can be a connecting force to create timeless masterpieces. We can live with epic nature, and be iconic in our endeavors. We can leave impressions that compel others to endure and aspire beyond limitations. We can seize each day, and transform every experience into a source of positive power for our *self* and for others.

Our presence can enable us to ascend to our greatest heights. We can transcend all that shrouds us, and reach toward that "something more," beyond anything that can be seen. We can live in each moment to create our most powerful and purposeful presence. We each have that power in each present moment.

## MOMENTS OF PAUSE

1.  When you contemplate how much greater your presence can be than the physical space you fill, what greater presence do you visualize?

2.  How can you make that presence become a reality?

3.  What is the most heroic, epic, and powerful life you can imagine for your *self*?

4.  What are the things that you most need to do to heal your wounds, to allow you to soar to your greatest heights, and to give you the strength and resilience to help others?

5.  Day to day, moment to moment, how do you create the space to pause to be aware of your presence, to tap into the power and infinite potential of your presence, and to pursue your most purposeful presence?

6. As you contemplate that you are the sculptor of the "block of your being," how do you carve out the "angel in the marble and set him free" to enable your *self* to soar toward your most purposeful and powerful presence?

7. What have you endured and transcended in this life that you believe to be born of a higher purpose?

8. How powerful could be the impact of the image that you leave behind?

9. How can you use your most purposeful presence to become part of a collective presence that is of benefit to humanity—for the greater collective good of mankind?

10. How does the thought of creating your most powerful and purposeful presence give rise to choices you need to make in your life now?

## MORE MOMENTS FOR YOU

**Twenty-One**

# Finding Your Bodhi Tree

*"With our thoughts, we make the world."*

—BUDDHA

THE POWER OF OUR THOUGHTS holds the secret to the power of our journey. One and a half years after standing amidst the Greek gods of the Acropolis, the Old City of Rome, the Shroud of Turin, and within the tombs from the pyramids of Egypt, my journey had brought me to India.

In India, I would come to experience just how much the power of our thoughts holds the secret to the power of our journey. My time in India would take me into infinite and timeless moments of pause. In India, I would find a sanctuary within my *self* where I could find infinite refuge, discover purposeful paths, and gain wisdom that was far beyond my *self*. I would come to see how readily we can transform our thinking and our state of being, by sitting quietly in the essence of our greatest and most powerful self. I would immerse my *self* within my *self* and beyond my *self* in endless moments of pause that would make me feel that my journey was only just beginning.

India was a place where I had long wanted to travel to experience the deep spirituality and rich mysticism of the birthplace of Buddhism. Throughout my journey, Buddhist philosophies enabled me to experience life and living with a profoundly positive perspective. Those philosophies enabled me to translate the experiences of life around me into meaningful messages within me. I came to see that how we translate what happens around us determines whether we entrap our *self* in our own prison, or free our *self* to be our greatest self.

The Buddha said, "No one saves us but ourselves. No one can and no one may. We ourselves must walk the path." In each moment, with each step, we choose a path. If we step forward with blindness, and without mindfulness or awareness, we will invariably become lost. Our journey will serve no purpose. If our choice is guided by our greatest self, we can take our *self* along paths beyond our *self*. We become part of "something more." Our path begins with our choice.

Through my journey since leaving Australia, I came to see that throughout my life I had given up my choice in present moments, and given in to demons from the past. I allowed all that happened around me, to command all that happened within me. I allowed the destruction that happened on the outside to poison all that was inside. That negative force became my driving force—the only force I could feel. I allowed that force to direct every step, to determine each path.

Before I left Australia, I had never taken a journey within my *self*. I was traveling as fast as I could in the world around me to avoid the world within me. I wanted to move so quickly through each moment so all that was inside wouldn't have time to emerge. Yet as fast as I was traveling, I was moving nowhere.

My journey had shown me that within us is the force that can transform the world around us. I came to see that our journey through the world around is only as powerful as the journey we take through the world within. I came to discover that the more we venture within our *self*, the more paths emerge around us that take us closer to our most purposeful and powerful self.

The path that led me to India, yet again reinforced to me that the universe has a way of finding us—somewhere, someway, somehow. On different occasions, I had been inspired to journey to India, but the moment hadn't arisen when I had been *compelled* to travel to India. I was in Switzerland when my path to India emerged in the most unlikely way, and compelled me to embark upon that journey with every part of my being.

I was presenting a seminar on global leadership and development at a conference following the World Economic Forum in Davos, Switzerland. In the seminar, I included a quote from the Buddha, alongside quotes from Einstein, Plato, and other philosophers and visionaries that all pointed to a higher purpose for our activities. My professional and personal experiences led me to believe there was no reason that a philosophy of higher purpose for people couldn't extend to organizations.

The enormous inequality I had seen through my travels through some of the richest countries to some of the poorest countries in the world, and from the glamorous corporate head offices in shimmering cities to poverty-stricken marketplaces in remote and forgotten villages, compelled me to try to affect change in this area. My time at Harvard showed me there were well-researched ways and many supremely qualified people all around the world to create that change. Despite this, the inequalities remained for the majority of people on the planet.

Buddhist philosophies particularly inspired my thinking that institutions could thrive on a purpose beyond profits that created positive change for the benefit of all beings around the globe. Through the work I was developing, I was trying to bring together thinking from the east and the west that demonstrated an approach to leadership that created a balance between profits and people that could lead everyone to a higher place. We are more, as a collective people and a collective consciousness, than the sum of our bank accounts.

As I took the podium to start my seminar at the conference, I looked out at the audience. The first person who caught my eye, caused me to wonder if the universe was sending me a message of approval. Amidst the typically western-attired attendees, sat a Buddhist monk in his vibrant orange and burgundy robes.

The Buddhist monk, I would find, was the Chancellor of the Central University of Tibetan Studies in India. The following day, I had the opportunity to speak with the Chancellor. Before I knew it, he asked if I would come to India to present my seminar, and further develop my work. In those moments, I knew it was my time to travel to India. Three months later, I was on my way. I didn't know what my trip to India would bring, I just sensed it was the next step on my journey.

Sarnath, India, is known as the birthplace of Buddhism, and is one of the most significant spiritual centers of Buddhism. It was in Sarnath where the Buddha gave his first teaching after finding enlightenment under the Bodhi tree in nearby Bodh Gaya.

I arrived in Sarnath after traveling from Delhi to Varanasi by plane, and then by car from Varanasi to Sarnath. The contrast between the busyness of Delhi could not have been further from the quiet solitude of Sarnath. Arriving in Sarnath was like stepping back thousands of years in time. At the same time, it felt like a familiar home.

As the car moved through the dusty streets of Sarnath, antique-looking rickshaws pedaled by frail elder men were our most frequent companions. Bicycles occasionally passed by with orange and burgundy robes of monks gently flapping with the rhythm of the steady circular movement of the pedals. The air was thick and rich, and the scent of smoky fires floated in the soft breeze.

Soon enough, we arrived at the unassuming gates of the Central University of Tibetan Studies. The university was one of the "universities in exile" established by the Dalai Lama and the Ministry of Education in India. Its purpose was to continue Tibetan studies and teaching after the destruction of universities and monasteries during the uprising in Tibet in 1959. The university was a place where monks in exile could continue to study the Tibetan and Buddhist texts that were carried by hand across the border to India when Buddhist monks fled the destruction in Tibet. This was a place of refuge and sanctuary for not only the people of Tibet, but also for teachings and philosophies thousands of years old that would otherwise have been lost forever.

An overwhelming sense of humility and reverence filled me as we passed through the entrance gates as though passing through the arms of a great protector. I felt welcomed into a space that vibrated with peaceful and tranquil energy. It was an energy that quickly settled within.

The Chancellor's assistant, Tenzin, met me as the car pulled up to a small guest house not far inside the entrance. The guest house was a quaint two story building with four guest rooms nestled behind a lush courtyard with beautiful and colorful gardens. A small central staircase led up to the balconies outside the two upper guest rooms. Dark wooden doors and shutters were a rustic contrast to the pale yellow and deep red trimmed walls.

Tenzin soon settled me into my room and let me know that I would be meeting with the Professor of Buddhist Philosophy,

Venerable Professor Wangchuk, that afternoon. I had just enough time to freshen up after my trip, and to wander the gardens and explore the surrounding grounds on my way to meet Professor Wangchuk in his teaching room.

The silence and serenity throughout the manicured grounds and gardens was uplifting. There was a sense of freedom that transcended the physical space. Maybe that sense emanated from the thousands of Sanskrit texts that found their home here after the exile—texts that overflowed with the philosophies of freedom of the mind as a path to freedom of the self.

"What we are today comes from our thoughts of yesterday, and our present thoughts build our life of tomorrow: Our life is the creation of our mind," said the Buddha. I contemplated how we each have the power to venture beyond the self we know, to the essential self that is deep within—the self that knows no boundaries, the self that takes us to our greatest self, and that creates a greater world. We are only limited by our most creative thoughts of what our life can be. We can accept the barriers that arise, or we can remove them as we travel along our path.

"He is able who thinks he is able," continued the Buddha. We can tap into the power of our greatest self, transcend our negative thoughts, rise above the worst that has happened to us, and connect with our unique purpose that lies within us. Then, the path ahead becomes illuminated with visions of the greatest life we can create that leads us to a higher place. That path, which can sometimes seem so distant, is as close as a pause in the present moment. That path, which can sometimes seem so inaccessible, becomes a familiar friend when we take the first step, and then take another, and then take more.

As I walked toward the teaching room of Professor Wangchuk, empty sandals lined the wall outside. The image of the dusty sandals was striking. These were the shoes of young Tibetans whose change was forced upon them by violence and destruction, but who sought to change the world through the type of peaceful means relentlessly pursued by their spiritual leader, the Dalai Lama.

Soon enough, a bell chimed through the halls and students emerged from the teaching rooms and quietly moved to their next classes. Here, even the students seemed to flow with a peaceful tranquility through the modest hallways, a vivid contrast to the hurried scurries between the vast auditoriums more typical of their western counterparts. It seemed that with simplicity dwelt serenity.

Peering around the corner of the door into the room, I smiled as I saw Professor Wangchuk rise with a wonderfully cheerful face to greet me. The warmth that emanated from him instantly put me at ease, despite my feeling like a child in front of a great master. His graceful round face and gentle eyes held a presence that was enchanting and endearing. His voice was deep and calm, yet each word seemed illuminated. As we sat, I was on the edge of my seat, anticipating each word as a treasure and a gift. In my imagination, I could never have envisioned this moment.

Ironically, on the pages of my journal in which I was writing of my meeting with Professor Wangchuk, was a quote by Anais Nin, "Each friend represents a world in us, a world not possibly born until they arrive, and it is only by this meeting that a new world is born." In these moments, I felt a new world being born, arising from within, emerging to be revealed with the meeting of my new friend, Wangchuk.

Throughout the years of my journey, I had come to know that there is revelation in every moment, and we befriend it when we pause to experience it. The revelations we experience are our greatest friend, the most significant meeting that births a new world from within us—a world of new life waiting like a child ready to be born from the womb.

We are each born to be all that we can be. "Human existence is the best form of existence," said Wangchuk, "especially if we chose Boddhisattva. This is a state, a choice at the time of death, to return lifetime after lifetime to help end suffering for all sentient beings. Everything else is of no consequence."

Throughout my journey, new life had emerged within me, and filled me with anticipation of the journey ahead. Before my journey, I had no comprehension of the potential of human existence, because my existence was simply survival. I had no sense of being more. I had no sense of being able or worthy to contribute to something more.

My journey had exposed the places where "something more" existed. Those places exist within each of us. Our journey is to befriend all that is within us, so we can become all that we are meant to be.

Everything that surrounded me in the place to where my journey now brought me, was about befriending that "something more" as the most precious part of life, and the most meaningful part of existence. This place, where the Buddha gave his first teaching, represented the "other side" to all that I grew up thinking my existence could be. It represented the "nirvana" in which we can each dwell through each moment of our journey.

The Buddha found his enlightenment, his path to nirvana, under the Bodhi tree. Where can we each find our Bodhi tree? Where can we find our places of pause in every moment that unveil a path to our nirvana? Where can we seek refuge and sanctuary in our darkest times and emerge having found light? Which are the spaces we can create for our *self*, each day, that keep us on a path to our greatest self? Which are the shoes into which we need to change to trek our path?

As I left Wangchuk, I was honored at his invitation to return each day to speak with him. I had so many questions, so many contemplations. I had read many books on Buddhist philosophy and other philosophies of life, but now I had the opportunity to delve into mysteries each day with a great master. With each immersion, I would continue to find that my exploration had only just begun.

It was mid-afternoon as I arrived back to my room after my visit with Wangchuk, and the streets outside called to be explored. After many hours of traveling, I was eager to wander through the paths of the birthplace of Buddhism. Tenzin told me there was a silk maker in the small market at the far end of the road where I could buy some silks and cotton for the hot days throughout my stay, so I set off to explore.

Stepping out through the gates, there was a gentle flow of activity around the dusty street. Across the street, a small row of rustic stores were packed together tightly, as if holding each other upright. They looked as though they had been there for several hundred years. Corrugated iron roofing joined the stores together, and provided shade for the few students, monks, and local villagers who came to buy their essential daily items. Streams of micro-packaged laundry detergents, washing powders, soaps, water, and various snacks hung like small curtains from the iron roofing. Nearby, mothers sat on the ground on straw mats selling freshly picked fruits and vegetables from their small plots of fertile gardens.

Continuing along the road, I felt as if I were continuing back in time. A young bearded man stood beside a wooden cart with large, thin wooden wheels. On top of the cart sat a handmade wooden frame, with corrugated iron nailed all around the frame to create what looked to be some kind of strange vending cart. As I walked by the cart, I noticed the man holding an antique-looking square metal container by a thick wooden handle. Looking more closely, I saw that the metal container was filled with glowing orange coals, as the man moved what became clear to be an iron atop clothes that were laid across the tray of his cart. On the shelves inside the handmade shelter, sat neatly folded clothes. It was a full day's work for this craftsman to continually heat coals, and carefully press the cottons and silks of the town.

Farther along, another vintage craftsman sat inside a small, old concrete structure. The sewing machine in front of which the elder man sat on a simple wooden bench was another hint of the time past into which I had traveled. The steady vertical rhythm of the man's foot on the pedal on the ground rotated the thin, large metal wheel under the base of the table that was connected to a smaller metal wheel of the sewing machine above the table by a thin rubber strap. Like an antique clock ticking, the needle of the machine moved in time with the each rotation of the wheel and another thread weaved through the silk that was flowing from the table onto the dusty ground below. The old man caught my eye as I watched intently, as if captured in the hypnotic rhythm. I smiled as our eyes met and our smiles reflected between us.

Walking on, I came upon a small school. Young children in beautifully laundered and perfectly pressed school uniforms walked by in small groups. It seemed that these children were the pride of the community and the best dressed in town. I had seen similar pride in school children in the mountains beyond mountains in Haiti, in overcrowded inner city slums in the Dominican Republic, and in border towns in Mexico.

It seems universal that the world wants to take care of its children, to dress them proudly, and to give them hope for a future filled with abundant opportunities, even amidst the obvious challenges in the world around. It also seems that when we see each other as children of the universe, we can reach out to each other in the pursuit of abundant opportunities for all.

Despite the simplicity and absence of material wealth, the community seemed rich with pride, contentment, and care for each other. Tidy shelters along the road stood low. They were simply made of thatched bark and tree branches, or a combination of clay, wood, and plastic sheeting. Each shelter was swept at its entrance as if to welcome visitors and neighbors. Pots and pans huddled in the sun beside smoky fireplaces, ready for the next family meal preparation. Each pot glistened in the sunshine, as if new, despite its obvious old age. Along the road, between every few houses, trash had been swept together and burned into tidy piles of ashes, ready to be shoveled up onto a small cart that would take the ashes away and leave a perfectly clean street. The community seemed to be full of diligent caretakers of this spiritual home of the Buddha.

In the background, remnants of temples, stupas, and monasteries hovered like ever-present guardians protecting its community of caretakers. Over thousands of years, it was evident that people had come and gone, yet it seemed that the presence of "something more" was constant and unmoved. Walking through these streets, surrounded by simplicity and bare essentials, I felt more and more like a humble child of the universe. In the absence of "things," noise, hustle, and bustle, there existed an overwhelmingly present space and time to simply *be*.

It was a flashing thought that struck me, and remained with me, as I wandered farther through the community—that we are each caretakers in our time here. We are more than simply consumers of the resources around us in a hurried life of material acquisition. We are caretakers in the places in which we dwell. We are caretakers of our *self*, our soul, our spirit, and our being. When we create the present time and space to simply *be*, our guardians emerge, and our path is cleared to walk with consciousness to higher places.

Ralph Waldo Emerson said, "There is guidance for each of us, and by lowly listening, we shall hear the right word. Certainly there is a right for you that needs no choice on your part. Place yourself in the middle of the stream of power and wisdom which flows into your life. Then, without effort, you are impelled to truth and to perfect contentment."

As I followed the road through the quiet community, I felt as if I were following the flow of a gentle stream, filled with the power and wisdom of spirits and guardians who seemed ever-present.

Each step along the road felt effortless, as though I was following a path that was simply meant to be—nothing more, nothing less. There was no analysis as to whether I was moving in the right direction, or wondering if I would eventually come to the silk store. Those things had become insignificant as I was entranced by the journey through the community. The busyness of my thoughts quieted as the quietness of the community absorbed me.

Almost without noticing, and with time seeming not to pass, I had strayed off the road and walked down a path into a courtyard. As I stopped in the midst of the courtyard, the extraordinarily thick trunk of a tree stood directly in front of me, with its far-reaching branches dwelling over me. A peaceful serenity flowed with the light wind rustling the leaves above. Coming out of what seemed like a trance, I focused on the words that appeared on the plaque on a stone tablet beside the tree. It was then that I realized I was standing right in front of the Bodhi tree, an offspring of the Bodhi tree under which the Buddha found enlightenment in nearby Bodh Gaya thousands of years ago.

I was struck with awe as I stood, captured in a vibration that resonated through every sense within me. The power of this center of spiritual energy thousands of years old was so strong that one could only surrender to its flow, and allow its forces to run throughout, unobstructed, uninhibited.

Many believe energy centers exist throughout the earth, resonating with ancient wisdom and powerful frequencies that connect with our own inner energies. With each breath by the Bodhi tree, I felt the gentle stirring of places deep within. It was as though the energy around was entering with each breath, touching and awakening places deep within my core, causing them to bubble and rise. It felt as though there was no point to resistance, that the unconscious connection between the energies within and around was much more powerful than anything my conscious being could influence.

It seemed as though no time had passed, and that years had passed standing in the energy of the tree. As I looked around, I felt the warm reflection of colorful Buddhist prayer flags hanging all around the courtyard. With the afternoon sun setting, the orange hue of the sun passed through the green, red, blue, yellow, and white prayer flags creating a rainbow of color that gently cast its light upon the tree.

The space within the walls of the courtyard provided a sacred space for the Bodhi tree and the large statues of the Buddha and his first five teachers sitting in circular formation beside the tree. Several monks walked around the courtyard, holding prayer beads and quietly chanting, bowing with reverence each time they passed the sitting Buddha. Other monks sat quietly around the courtyard deep in meditation, gentle vibrations emanating from each. With the afternoon quickly turning into the evening, I quietly left the courtyard, still in the flow of the stream of energy that floated all around, and smiled at the warm and comforting feeling that I had found yet another new home.

Returning to the street, I smiled further as the silk store seemed to emerge from nowhere on the other side of the street, as though I had needed to discover the Bodhi tree before discovering anything else. It seemed the universe was once again conspiring.

The storekeeper returned my smile as I neared his store, and happily motioned me inside. Within minutes, he proceeded to roll out seemingly endless scrolls of silk and cotton across the floor. Soon enough, the floor of the long store resembled a Jackson Pollock piece of art, with color and texture everywhere. I felt as though I had toured an art gallery by the time the storekeeper led me through his store, and helped me choose several silks and cottons. His pride was evident in the way he carefully packaged the silk in thin white paper and placed it gently into a brown bag.

"You go to the tailor," the storekeeper smiled, "And he will take care of you." I had told the storekeeper I was staying at the university and needed some clothes for my stay. As the storekeeper continued, it became apparent that there was an ebb and flow to the community, with each person a part of a greater whole.

The storekeeper explained that I would take the silks to the tailor I had passed working at his sewing machine along the road. The tailor would measure and cut the silks, and they would be ready the next morning. I would need to buy the micro packages of fabric softener and washing powder from the small stores I had walked by to care for the fabrics, and I would need to take the clothes to the ironing cart I had passed along the way for the young bearded man to carefully iron without scorching the delicate silks and cottons.

The storekeeper walked with me outside his store and led me to the street where an elderly gentleman waited on his bicycle-drawn rickshaw. The smiling elderly man took me to the tailor with my new package of fabrics, and then back to the university before dark. There was a perfect order to the ebb and flow in this quiet and content community that seemed to provide all that everyone needed. I felt humbled in the presence of many caretakers.

The next morning, just before dawn, I woke to the warm, sultry air, and headed to the Deer Park where the Bodhi tree stood. Tenzin told me the night before that each morning at 5:30AM, there was prayer and chanting by the monks in the temple beside the courtyard. I was welcome to attend, and I was grateful for the opportunity to be further immersed in the rich vibrations of the energy of the site of the Buddha's first teaching.

This time, as I walked into the Deer Park, I was fully aware of where my steps were taking me. The temple that stood at the end of the pathway, beside the courtyard where the Buddha and the Bodhi tree rested, seemed to be already awake with deep rhythmic chanting from within. The gentle orange glow from candles inside the temple created guiding lights in the dark blue hue of the dawn.

As the magnetism of the orange flicker from within the temple drew stronger with each step, so too did the welcoming arms of the branches of the Bodhi tree. Before entering the temple, I wanted to dwell a little in the energy of the tree and allow its vibrations to settle within me. The energy of the tree reached out beyond its branches, and I was content to be drawn into its arms. The deep chanting from within the temple resonated softly through the court-yard, sounding and feeling like gentle heart beats harmoniously pulsating, and awakening the flow of life all around.

Standing by the tree, I was content to be entranced once more, peaceful in the quiet vibrations. With my eyes closed, the world around disappeared, and I felt the world within awakening with each chant.

My trance was soon broken by the sound of something out of time with the chanting. A rustling, sweeping sound came from nearby. Opening my eyes, I saw a young man in white cottons carefully sweeping around the base of the tree beyond the small gated wall that surrounded the trunk. As I quietly watched him, his care was striking. Each slow and gentle sweeping motion was like a mother tenderly stroking a child.

I had seen the young man the afternoon before. In the late afternoon, he had swept all around the courtyard, which seemed already pristine, and he had cleared incense sticks that had burned down in the small shrine beside the Bodhi tree. When a few visitors came to him as he entered the gate that kept the tree protected, he shook his head from side to side as they motioned to enter to touch the trunk. This young man had a reverent job as the caretaker of the tree.

As he caught my eye, now in the dim morning light, I smiled and motioned my head down in a slow bow, careful not to disturb the vibrations moving throughout. To my surprise, the young man softly motioned to me as he walked to the gate. I understood that he was motioning me to come to him, yet thought I must have mistaken his intention. There was no reason this caretaker would offer me entry into his protected space around the sacred tree. I looked up as if to question his intention as he smiled and once more motioned me to come.

Nearing the gate, I felt again like a small child in the presence of a great master. Yet here, the feeling was so much more powerful than I had felt before. As I moved toward the Bodhi tree, I felt as though I was entering a deep space of spiritual dwelling. This was a space that embodied the enlightenment of the Buddha, and symbolized every philosophy of Buddhism. As the caretaker opened the gate, his deep, welcoming brown eyes felt like an extension of the welcoming branches that reached out from the tree. This was a rich energy center that seemed to welcome and connect life.

Touching the trunk of the Bodhi tree felt like connecting to a life force as ancient and powerful as any I had experienced throughout my journey. As my fingers ran along the course gray bark, tingles ran through every part of me. Those touches opened a passage that led deep beyond—like a key opening a door to places I had not yet discovered. There was no clarity to exactly what lay beyond in those places, just an overwhelming sense of something much more. As my touch left the tree, a flake of gold leaf that decorated the bark from a ceremonial painting clung to my finger and I felt the warmth of its glistening golden light.

The caretaker smiled as he watched me, as though already aware of the doors that would open with each touch of the tree. He seemed proud that the gate he opened to allow me to enter the tree was unlocking new doors, of which he seemed entirely familiar. He lifted a fallen leaf and some pieces of bark from the ground, and gently placed them in my hand, as though he was placing a delicate flower. As I closed my hand to softly embrace the gift from the tree, I felt the presence of thousands of years run through me and settle within. I felt more and more barriers crumble within me, and thousands of passages open. Suddenly, there felt an absolute pointlessness to the walls I had created within me throughout my life. I had cut my *self* off from the sources of power that could lift me up, and isolated my *self* from touches that could fill me with "something more."

Over the weeks I spent in Sarnath, and the many mornings I sat under the Bodhi tree, I started to intimately know those places of something more. I came to find that the key to those places, is always in our hands. We are the caretakers of our worlds within, and our worlds beyond. We build our walls, and we can make them fall. We are the ones who can open the gates that reveal our hidden worlds. We can touch the precious golden light that lies within us. When we think we are able, we become able.

Finding our Bodhi tree is finding the places where we can thoughtfully dwell and reveal the key to those places of "something more." "With our thoughts, we make our world," said the Buddha. Our every step begins with a single thought, and a single thought can change our world.

It was almost pitch black in the early morning when Tenzin took me to the nearby city of Varanasi to experience the sun rising over the River Ganges. Arriving at the river was haunting, as the sounds of animals echoed from the distance, and faint chanting drifted through the darkness. Black silhouettes of gothic-looking Hindu temples, thousands of years old, stood darker than the darkness atop the deep steps leading down to the river. The great temples that stood one beside another, loomed over the sacred river, like more ever-watchful caretakers. In Hindu, Varanasi is one of the most sacred places in the world, and the River Ganges, the holiest of waters.

The Ganges is the river of life and death in India. The presence of millions of people who have flocked to the river over thousands of years, seems to float along with its gentle currents. Many come to the Ganges to bathe in its healing waters, to wash away illnesses, or to vanquish sins. Many others come to receive blessings believed to be bestowed by the touch of the sacred river. Many more come to scatter the ashes of loved ones, so the waters will purify the soul, and provide safe passage to a prosperous afterlife. Others come to pass to the next life, and await the time when their loved ones will burn their body by the river to help their passage into the life beyond. Walking along its shores, one feels on the edge of life and death.

The city is believed to be the oldest city in the world. As the beginning light of the sunrise cast a misty golden hue against the ancient gray architecture of the city, I felt awakened into a time thousands of years old. Slowly, the soft hue turned into a golden light as the rising sun became nearer to the horizon. Life along the river emerged.

Small orange flames flickered every so often, marking the places where bodies were slowly burning along the rivers edge. Loved ones stood by the piles of flame watching as the smoke rose into the misty hue, and the glowing orange mounds burned down into ashes. As more light emerged, light gray piles of ashes could be seen all along the river, some that were still softly smoldering, some that had been long extinguished.

Women and men bathed in the glowing golden waters, cupping the water in their hands and raising it toward the rising orange sun as though in thanks, before casting it over their heads and pouring it over their bodies. Children swam through the water with cheerful chuckles. Beside them, their mothers washed their clothes, beating the garments against the concrete steps in slow rhythmic motion to jolt away every speckle of dirt. In the background, large ripples from long and slender row boats slowly met the shores of the river, connecting all of the activity in a circular spectrum of golden light.

Farther along the river, the flow of activity continued. Rows of young boys in white robes stood on the sandy banks in yoga poses on various colors of mats and towels. Elder men painted in ritual colors and wearing simple robes sat in meditative poses on the large steps of the ghats that led down to the water. Priests stood on small rectangular wooden ceremonial platforms above the waters edge, swinging antique silver bowls. Smoky incense drifted from the bowls and rose into the air, encircling the platform in a veil of wispy, white cloud that peacefully floated out to the river, and met the golden hue of the sunrise.

The river became more and more illuminated in the rich orange-gold light. As the sun continued to rise, the vitality of life along the river seemed to rise with equal richness. The glow of the river reflected the light from the enormous sun onto all that was around. Every part of life was captured in a golden aura of life and death, living and breathing, stillness and movement, ebb and flow, wholeness and oneness. All was connected by the gentle flow of the river, and with that flow, all things came to life.

Within each of us flows a river of life and death. Within each of us flow waters that can heal us, transform us, renew us, and bring new life to us. I reflected back, to walking along the many canals in Venice. Here, the small narrow fishing boats were not so different from the gondolas in Venice. The canals in Venice had brought thoughts of the currents that run through us, that can transform us, that are our life force. This one longest and holiest river in India, was abundant in its life force, and its ability to transform and renew. Yet the Ganges was also known to be one of the most polluted rivers in the world, because of the activity that occurred around and within its waters. Despite that, it remained the holiest, the most spiritually revered, the most healing.

We will each meet those parts of our *self* that have been polluted through our journeys. Those parts of our *self* are a part of the continual ebb and flow of our life. Our suffering, our pain, is inevitable. It flows with us as part of the natural course of our journey. More powerful, however, than our rivers of pain and suffering, are our rivers of healing and transformation. Those rivers run deeper. Those rivers run farther. Those rivers are the sustaining waters of our life.

As we meet with our pain and suffering, we can choose its course in our life. We can choose to be consumed by the pockets of pain that invariably arise on our journey, or we can choose to tap into the transformational waters that fill us, and allow them to move us forward. We have that choice through the power of our thoughts as we meet each experience. If we choose to continually connect to the flow of our positive transformational waters, we can heal our greatest pain and suffering. More so, we can transform our deepest pain and suffering into abundant gifts that take us to our highest places.

"Overcome your uncertainties and free yourself from dwelling on sorrow. When you delight in existence, you will become a guide to those in need, revealing the path to many," said the Buddha.

Sometimes we think we are meant to dwell in continual suffering. We start to feel that we are unworthy of something more. We feel that our imperfections surpass our perfections. We feel we are meant to miss out on abundant happiness. With our thoughts, we start to destroy our world.

Yet we are each created uniquely, with the capacity to experience infinite love and happiness. Often, the greater the search, the more fulfilling is the discovery. Sometimes we wait for others to reveal the path, to relieve our pain, to fill our voids, to provide meaning, purpose, and fulfillment. We need to wait for no one but our *self*.

It is up to us to choose to dwell in the unlimited possibilities of our life, to change our shoes, and to step into that space. The Buddha taught, "Be a lamp for yourselves. Be your own refuge. Seek for no other. All things must pass. Strive on diligently. Don't give up."

We only remain locked out of happiness, until we come to see that only we hold the key to our greatest, most abundant, most purposeful self. Paulo Coelho wrote, "I saw that everything really was written there before me, and that the doors had only been closed before because I hadn't realized that I was the one person in the world with the authority to open them." In every moment, we can turn the key to release happiness into our lives, to allow healing waters to flow through us, and to reveal the path to our greatest self.

Through my journey since leaving Australia, I was able to feel the positive currents that move through each of us, that connect us to the power that lies within and beyond, that guide our *self* to our greatest self. I allowed those currents to move me, to cleanse me, to flow through the darkness, to fill me with "something more."

Along the shores of those currents, the little girl had been able to play, to rest, to be innocent, to breathe, to be free. Holding hands with the universe, the little girl had found safety, and I could take each next step with her peacefully beside me.

Looking far along the River Ganges, and feeling the tight and secure hand of the universe, I knew the river that ran through me held all that I needed to carry me along my path. Yet I still felt like a child, far from mastering all that lay within. Would the touches of the universe fade over time? Ripples of anxiety ran through me as I felt the fear of being ill-equipped to master the length and depths of all that had emerged throughout my journey.

Then, almost unconsciously, a smile filled me as I looked around. I realized that I stood exactly where I needed to be. I stood in the place to where the universe had brought me. Here, every day, I could embark upon the journey to master all that lay within. I could discover how to keep the touches of the universe present in every moment. In this space, I would learn to be the caretaker of all that flowed within.

In each moment, we stand in the place to where the universe has brought us. In that moment, we are exactly where we need to be to take the steps to discover all that is within and beyond. We are each, now, in the moment that is here to take us to all that we have the opportunity to be. We are in the moment where we can be our most diligent caretaker, step onto a path toward our greatest self, and live our greatest life.

Sunrises and sunsets under the Bodhi tree became my closest companion in the home of the Buddha. Each morning the chanting in the temple awakened life into the day, and each evening the chanting settled life into the peaceful darkness. Days and nights became a tranquil rhythm, inhaling and exhaling the life force that dwelt within the moments. With each gentle touch of the breeze, the breath of the universe nurtured its children. I felt cradled in the arms of abundance. I felt passages open to places within and beyond that called me to venture deeper.

In each moment, passages within and beyond await each of us. Our pause opens the door, and our thoughts carry us along rivers that lead us to worlds filled with infinite wisdom and possibilities that are uniquely ours to discover. These are the rivers that lead us to our greatest self. Like wandering through an abundant garden, we can pick the flowers that are the essence of our being and emerge with them. We can illuminate our life in their vibrancy. We can illuminate the world around as their color touches and uplifts others.

As the golden hue of the sunrise drifted through the arms of the Bodhi tree on another mystical morning, my eyes were fixed on the leaves of the tree. I came to find that sitting under the tree, when I paused to rest my eyes on any one thing, and let my thoughts come and go, invariably trance-like moments would come. A passage would open, and the universe would reveal its teaching. These moments of meditative pause became the keys to the passages within and beyond. These moments connected me to the purity of all that lay within, to my perfections amidst my imperfections, to the power each moment of pause holds for us to step beyond all that binds us and into all that frees us.

On this morning, as I remained fixed on the leaves of the Bodhi tree, a leaf floated down and came to rest by my side. Picking up the leaf, I placed it in the palm of my hand, answering its apparent call to observe it more closely. A flake of gold from the tree sat in the middle of the leaf. As I looked into the intricate patterns of the leaf, the image became watery with my unmoved gaze, and the veins of color merged and cascaded like a small ocean weaving and swelling. The golden flake sparkled through the waves of color and swirled beyond the leaf, mixing its palette into the air around. The colors danced through the air and flowed into the gray trunk of the Bodhi tree, meandering through the leaves and then merging back throughout me. Everything in my watery gaze became transitory, flowing, connected, one. There was no distinguishing my hand from the leaf, from the Bodhi tree, from the air that bound us together. My existence became nothing and everything. My space became smaller than an atom and as infinite as the reach of the universe. Every boundary dissolved. Infinite space emerged.

Our physical bodies are infinite vessels of energy. In that field of energy, we are connected to every wisdom and insight of existence. There is no wisdom that we cannot attain. There is no insight that eludes us. We are intimately connected to the highest powers of the universe. We are intricately connected to all that is around us.

In every moment, we are conduits to enable the flow of energy within us, to affect all that is around us. Our ability to affect and transform the energy that flows through us is unlimited, because we are that energy. We can activate every atom of our being with an intentional thought that sparks our transformation.

"It is wrong to think that misfortunes come from the east or from the west; they originate within one's own mind. Therefore, it is foolish to guard against misfortunes from the external world and leave the inner mind uncontrolled," said the Buddha. Despite all that happens around us, we can transform our greatest challenges into integral pieces of our greatest self by transforming our thoughts.

We have the power to control all that we think. We have the power to eliminate our negative thoughts and nurture our positive thoughts. We can walk through the worst things that happen to us and emerge more powerful and more purposeful. We can come to know that when pain and suffering comes upon us, that is part of our natural course. We can stay firmly on our path, learning more about our *self* with each experience, feeling more attuned to our North Star as we dig deeper in order to reach higher. In our depths, we find the pieces of our highest self.

We must be the caretakers of our thoughts in order to nurture our happiness. As soon as we allow negative thoughts to direct how we feel and act, we become destructive to our *self* and to others. We fall back into self-defeating habits that crush our spirit, eliminate our choices, and send us back to our self-created prison that can entrap us.

There is no point to choosing to exist in anything but happiness. There is no point to choosing to be anything less than all that we can be. As we become diligent caretakers of our thoughts, we set our *self* free, in every moment, to soar to our highest self, and to be all that we can be.

Lao Tzu said, "He who controls others may be powerful, but he who has mastered himself is mightier still." When we pause, and peacefully sit under our Bodhi tree, we allow our *self* to dwell in our limitless potential. We allow our thoughts to rise and fall, and we rest in the calm space in between our thoughts. We are no longer pushed and pulled by our untamed minds. In that space of pause, we can allow paths to emerge from the deepest core of our being. We cease to be controlled by the forces around us. We cease to be distracted by meaningless pursuits. We cease to allow our negative thoughts and emotions to misguide us. Instead, we move purposefully forward, as we consciously choose the steps that are inspired by the highest powers that reside in the infinite space within us.

Throughout my daily sessions with Wangchuk, we spoke often of the difficulty of sitting in a state of calm abiding, allowing our thoughts to rise and fall, dwelling in the space of infinite clear light within us. There is no fast path. Like the daily exercise we must do to enable our bodies to endure the physical challenges that confront us each day, so too, must we patiently train our minds each day in order to confront the mental and emotional challenges of our journey. Day by day, our minds become stronger. We are more able to resist the pull and push of daily distractions. We can remain steadfastly on our path. We can remain purposefully focused on the higher pursuits that take us to our greatest self. We become our own master and caretaker.

Entering the courtyard by the temple on another morning to once again sit under the Bodhi tree, I passed a plaque inscribed with a teaching of the Buddha, "Those who know the essential to be the essential, and the unessential to be the unessential, dwelling in right thoughts, do arrive at the essential." As I sat under the Bodhi tree, the words remained with me, as I closed my eyes and attempted to enter that quiet space where the essential was able to arise.

On this particular morning, as I sat quietly, a fly buzzed back and forth around my face. The constant buzz was an annoying distraction that penetrated deep into my ear. The waft of rapidly fluttering wings across my face caused unconscious twitches in my neck with each passing. I spent all of my time and energy focusing on this one tiny fly, which seemed to multiply its effect with each thought. Soon enough, the flutter of wings seemed to build into jet engines. I opened my eyes intent to swipe this fly far into the sky. Yet looking down at me, the branches of the Bodhi tree seemed to be smiling in amusement, perhaps even chuckling with the movement of the morning breeze. Relaxing, I smiled, closed my eyes, and allowed the fly to carry on. Soon enough, as I gave up the fight against the fly, and allowed it to simply be—conscious of it, but without any sense of good or bad—the back and forth flutter disappeared. Quietness and stillness emerged.

Our emotions can be like flies constantly buzzing around us. The more we dwell on them, the more we empower them. When we allow them to simply rise and fall, acknowledge their presence, learn from their passing, and let them go, then they lose their power over us. More so, they help us to train our mind to take care of our thoughts, to be mindful of our words and our actions, so we remain centered and peaceful on our path. If our mind is untamed and uncontrolled, we can't think or act from a place of higher purpose, for the good of our *self*, or for the greater good of those around us.

Each thought, each word, each action, are stepping stones on our path to our greatest self.

*The thought manifests as the word;*
*The word manifests as the deed;*
*The deed develops into habit;*
*And habit hardens into character.*
*So watch the thought and its ways with care,*

*And let it spring from love*
*Born out of concern for all beings.*
*As the shadow follows the body,*
*As we think, so we become.*

—BUDDHA

When we think and act for the good of the many, we find our place as a part of a greater whole, part of a greater quest for collective happiness and fulfillment, part of a greater force. We move beyond the transient material things that only serve to keep us attached to meaningless pursuits. Pursuits that come and go like the wind and the rain. Pursuits so fragile that they shatter with the smallest vibration. Pursuits that keep us perpetually busy, but lead us nowhere. Pursuits that fill our mind, but empty our soul. Pursuits that make us think we can get ahead by leaving others behind, when we are all connected by currents that can only run into an abundant ocean, when they flow in the same direction.

"Fashion your life as a garland of beautiful deeds," taught the Buddha. The world in which we live can be transformed into a beautiful garden, but we each must be a caretaker—nurturing, protecting, thinking, and acting for a life and a world that we each have the power to affect. We do not need to accept anything less than all we want our life and our world to be. It is our choice to accept or our choice to affect.

The Dalai Lama said, "Although it will be undoubtedly difficult to bring about genuine peace and harmony, clearly it can be done. The potential is there. And its foundation is a sense of responsibility on the part of each of us as individuals toward all others."

Sitting under the Bodhi tree, amidst a community of Tibetans living in exile from their home, a reflection became clear. If we don't act for others, who will act for us? As I contemplated, the thought arose, *"Who dares to act?"* and I started to write.

*Tibet is not the struggle of one people.*
*It is not confined to the borders of geography—a country or a*
*region;*
*It is a child of the world,*
*As are we all.*
*And when a child cries,*
*The world must give attention;*
*If not, when any one of us cries,*
*Who dares to hear?*

*The doors of the world must be opened.*
*If not, how will we know if there is light or darkness therein?*
*Whether there is nourishment or starvation?*
*Whether there is hope or despair?*
*Whether there is suffering or freedom?*
*Who dares to look?*

*We are one humanity.*
*Peoples connected by the turning of one planet;*
*The rising of one sun—the same light that touches us all;*
*Rains from the one sky;*
*Oceans that traverse us from the one source;*
*One atmosphere that we all breathe.*
*What happens to the one, will happen to the many.*
*So then, the many must act for the one;*
*And the one must act for the many.*
*Who dares to act?*

Once we see that we are all parts of a connected whole, we see there is nothing we can think or do that doesn't affect another. All things are interconnected. All things are interdependent. In each moment, there is cause and effect. "What we do and think in our own lives, then, becomes of extreme importance as it affects everything we're connected to," wrote the Dalai Lama in his book, *The Universe in a Single Atom.*

"When the universe has evolved to a stage when it can support sentient beings, its fate becomes entangled with the karma of the beings who will inhabit it," continues the Dalai Lama. Through our own journey, we come to see that the search for our greatest self can only be realized when we work toward a world in which all beings have the opportunity to become their greatest self. Then, the whole becomes greater than the sum of its parts. We understand why there are so many of us existing here in this one space, and that is because it takes the collective power of each of us to move all of us forward. With our thoughts and our actions, we can become a humanity flowing in the same direction for the benefit of the one and the many.

The future we create starts with the steps we take in this moment. We must be daring enough to take the step. We must be fearless enough to change our shoes. Throughout our journey, in each moment, we must be attentive to hear the whispers of something more. We must continually pause to open the doors to look deeply into all that is within, around, and beyond. We must be courageous enough to act to pursue our greatest self, and the greatest humanity for all.

When I left Australia, I had no idea what would lie ahead. All I knew was that little voice within that lets us know we need to change our course, had grown from a tiny murmur into a mammoth thunderstorm. All I could do was to start with a first step, and make the change that simply felt right, even if that change felt a little beyond reason (or more so, a lot beyond reason!).

Changing my shoes didn't just change my life, it saved my life. It gave me new life. Until I stepped out and allowed my *self* to feel moments of awe that I had never felt, until I allowed goosebumps to awaken all of my senses, until I ventured into the deepest parts of my *self* and found the light within, until I felt the presence of my North Star and the hand of the universe, I couldn't free my *self* to soar on a path to something more.

I needed to let the little girl within play. I needed to be kind to me. I needed to live, to laugh, and to learn that we are each worthy of happiness. We each deserve to live and to love without compromise. We each have paths that take us from our *self* to our greatest self. Every day those paths emerge. Each present moment provides an opportunity to pause, and to step closer to our most powerful and purposeful self.

Invariably, along our journey, we will have doubts, fears, and insecurities. Yet within us, flows the river that constantly connects us to the highest powers of the universe. In each moment, wherever we stand, we can pause to sit under our Bodhi tree, and connect to the river of enlightenment that flows through us.

We each may believe in a different higher power, but that power, in whichever form we believe it to be, flows through each atom of our being. It is an infinite source of all we need for us to become all that we can be in every moment. It gives us the unlimited ability to expand beyond our imagination, to discover the light through our darkness, to unwrap all of the extraordinary gifts we have within us, and to become our most powerful and purposeful self.

When we let our being fly free, uninhibited, unashamed, and fearless, we can soar beyond any boundaries. We are the only ones who can set our *self* free. We can break away from all that holds us back. We can give voice to our greatest pains and destroy the secrets that hold us in fear. We can thrive through any challenge. We can transform every moment into an opportunity to fly higher. With our thoughts, we can make our world. All that we need is present in every moment. We simply need to pause, and tap into the limitless potential within us. When we tap into that limitless potential, when we discover our greatest self, there is nothing that we cannot do.

In those moments of pause, we can immerse our *self* in the awe of everything that is around us. We can step into magical moments that allow goosebumps to evoke our senses, and bring us closer to humanity and to our *self*. We can see the angel in the marble of our being, and sculpt it until it is free. We can allow paths to be revealed guided by our North Star, and navigate them with the resonance of our compass within. We can walk hand in hand with the universe, intimately connected to the higher powers that flow through us.

Our journeys are only just beginning. In each moment, unimaginable new opportunities emerge. What does this next moment hold for you? Can you close your eyes, pause, and feel the murmur of all that is within, waiting for you to befriend your *self* and embark upon a journey to your greatest self, to live your greatest life?

When we dare to change our shoes, when we are bold enough to step out, when we are brave enough to dig deep, and when we are strong enough to leap high, we can be the change we want to see. We can change our life, we can change another life, we can change the world. It is our choice. Nothing can stop us. We have the power in each moment to choose to reach higher, further, wider, broader. There are no limits. There are no boundaries. There is only infinite space, unimagined opportunities, incomprehensible possibilities, and extraordinary dreams that we can make come true.

So what are you waiting for? Leap up! Take your *self* on a journey to your greatest self. Change your shoes! Live your greatest life!

## MORE MOMENTS FOR YOU

_____

_____

_____

_____

_____

_____

_____

_____

_____

_____

_____

_____

# With Gratitude

*"One looks back with appreciation to the brilliant teachers,
but with gratitude to those who touched our human feelings."*

—CARL JUNG

I T IS WITH THE DEEPEST GRATITUDE that I give thanks to all of
those who have touched my life, and broken through the hard outer
shell of a damaged child to tap into that which we each carry—infinite gifts from the universe. Some of those touches have come from
those near to me, some have come through strangers, some have
come from those who have passed quickly through my life, some
have come from those who remain with me. Others have come from
gentle breezes, warm rays of sunrise, splashes of waterfalls, and
the moments of awe that fill us with goosebumps when we allow
those touches to enter our being and awaken "something more."

Every day, I'm grateful for the lessons in each moment—lessons
that reveal opportunities through challenges, love through pain,

hope through despair, laughter through tears, resilience through loss, belief through doubt, light through darkness, and the knowledge that we are so much more than the worst that happens to us. I'm grateful to those who have given me hope throughout my journey through their words of inspiration and wisdom, such as those included in this book. Those words can save a life.

I'm grateful for the learning that we are the greatest force for the change we want in our life, and the change we want in the world.

My hope is that my gratitude extends far enough to help others embark upon their greatest journey without a moment to spare. It took me half a lifetime to feel that I don't need to go through life alone—that I can live greater. That feeling has only come by allowing the touches of light to outshine the darkness, and by nurturing the belief that we are each here to become our greatest self and to live our greatest life.

Thanks to you.

# References

### Chapter Two
Dr. Seuss, *Oh, the Places You'll Go!* (New York: Random House Inc., 1990).

### Chapter Three
Trek America Travel Limited, Southern Sun Tour Overview http://www.trekamerica.com

Trek America Travel Limited, Canadian Mountie Tour Overview http://www.trekamerica.com/tours/mo.html

Trek America Travel Limited, Pacific Coast Tour Overview http://www.trekamerica.com/tours/pc.html

Walt Whitman, *Song of the Open Road, Leaves of Grass* (The Walt Whitman Archives, 1881–82) http://www.whitmanarchive.org/published/LG/1881/poems/86

### Chapter Four
James Lyon et al., *Lonely Planet USA*, ed. 1. (Melbourne, Australia: Lonely Planet, 1999), p. 1001.

## Chapter Five

Deepak Chopra, *The Seven Spiritual Laws of Success* (New World Library/Allen-Amber Publishing; 1st Edition, 1994), p. 57.

His Holiness The Dalai Lama, *Transforming the Mind: Teachings on Generating Compassion* (London: Thorsons, An Imprint of HarperCollins Publishers, 2000), pp. 77, 82.

James Redfield, *The Celestine Prophecy,* (New York: Warner Books, 1997).

Jean Jenson, *Reclaiming Your Life,* (New York: Penguin Books USA Inc).

## Chapter Six

His Holiness The Dalai Lama, *The Art of Happiness: A Handbook for Living* (Sydney, Australia: Hodder Headline Australia, a member of the Hodder Headline Group, 1998), pp. 38, 191.

## Chapter Seven

Deepak Chopra, *The Seven Spiritual Laws of Success* (New World Library/Allen-Amber Publishing; 1st Edition, 1994), p. 11

Hanna Rion, *Let's Make A Flower Garden* (McBride, Nast & Company, 1912), pp. 6, 197, 200.

Sandra Martz, *If I had my life to live over I would pick more daisies* (Watsonville CA, USA: Papier-Mache Press, 1992).

Steve Zikman, *The Power of Travel: A Passport to Adventure, Discovery, and Growth.* (New York: Tarcher/Putman, a member of Penguin Group (USA) Inc., 1999), p. 109.

## Chapter Eight

"The Ethics of Interdependence: An interview with H.H. The Dalai Lama," *EnlightenNext Magazine* (on-line), accessed June 11, 2011, http://www.enlightennext.org/magazine/j24/DalaiLama.asp

Jane Wagner, "The Search for Signs of Intelligent Life in the Universe," performed by Lily Tomlin at the Repertory Theatre, Seattle, September 27, 2000.

Dr. Martin Luther King Jr., "Letter from Birmingham Jail," April, 1963.

## Chapter Nine

Paulo Coelho, *The Alchemist,* (New York, HarperCollins Publishers, 2nd edition, 2006).

James Redfield, *The Celestine Prophecy,* op. cit.

## Chapter Ten

Pema Chodron, *Comfortable with Uncertainty: 108 Teachings on Cultivating Fearlessness and Compassion* (Boston, MA: Shambhala Publishing, 2003). Lesson 12: The Root of Suffering, p. 23. Lesson 85: Obstacles and Questions, pp.165–166.

Rabindranath Tagore, *Fireflies* (The Macmillan Co, 1928).

## Chapter Eleven

Chester Higgins Jr., *Elder Grace: The Nobility of Aging* (New York: Bulfinch Press, 2000).

Fred Ebb, lyrics. Composed by John Kander, *"New York, New York"* (1977).

William Shakespeare, "As You Like It," Act II, Scene VII.

## Chapter Thirteen

His Holiness The Dalai Lama, *Ethics for the New Millennium* (New York: Riverhead Books, A Division of Penguin Putman, Inc., 1999), pp. 5, 8.

## Chapter Fourteen

Chester Higgins Jr., *Elder Grace,* op. cit.

Maya Angelou, "Still I Rise", from AND STILL I RISE, (New York, Random House, Inc., 2011).

Ronald A. Heifetz and Marty Linsky, *Leadership on the Line: Staying Alive through the Dangers of Leading* (Boston, MA: Harvard Business Publishing, 2002), p. 3.

### Chapter Sixteen
John Berendt, *The City of Falling Angels* (London: Sceptre, Hodder and Stoughton, A division of Hodder Headline, 2005), p. 1.

### Chapter Seventeen
Lonely Planet Greece, ed. 7. Paul Hellander et al., (Melbourne, Australia: Lonely Planet, 2006), p. 504.

"Proverbs of Solomon." *The Living Bible*, Proverbs 11:17

### Chapter Eighteen
James Allen, *From Poverty to Power; or, The Realization of Prosperity and Peace* (1901).

"The Children of Abraham," John 8:32, NIV Study Bible.

Kahlil Gibran, "Self Knowledge," *The Prophet*, (originally published by Alfred A. Knopf, 1923).

Paul Hellander et al., *Lonely Planet Greece*, op. cit.

"Shirley Valentine" (film, 1989). Directed and produced by Lewis Gilbert; written by Willy Russell.

Gary Zukov, *The Seat of the Soul*, (New York: Fireside, A Trademark of Simon & Schuster, Inc., 1990), p. 248.

### Chapter Nineteen
Damien Simonis et al., Lonely Planet Italy, ed. 7. (Melbourne, Australia: Lonely Planet, 2006), pp. 620–621.

**Chapter Twenty**
Damien Simonis et al., *Lonely Planet Italy,* op. cit.
Rabbi Hillel Hazaken, *Pirkei Avot* (The Ethics of the Fathers), Mishnah 14.
William Shakespeare, "Hamlet, Prince of Denmark," Act II, Scene II.

**Chapter Twenty-One**
His Holiness The Dalai Lama, *Ethics for the New Millennium* (New York: Riverhead Books, A Division of Penguin Putman, Inc., 1999), p. 171.
His Holiness The Dalai Lama, *The Universe in a Single Atom: The Convergence of Science and Spirituality* (New York: Broadway Books, an imprint of Doubleday Broadway Publishing Group, a division of Random House, Inc., 2005), pp. 69, 91.
Paulo Coelho, *The Witch of Portobello,* (New York: Harper Perennial, An Imprint of HarperCollins Publishers, 2008), p. 204.

# About the Author

K ATHY ANDERSEN LEFT AUSTRALIA to
take a "break" that turned into a journey
of more than ten years. Changing her corporate high heels to hiking boots started Kathy
on a journey where she would experience the
power we each have to be our greatest self,
and to live our greatest life.

Among other things, Kathy's journey
enabled her to step into the darkness of a
childhood filled with abuse and isolation, and
to step out knowing we are each so much greater than the worst
that happens to us. She discovers the gifts and treasures waiting for
each of us in each moment, and that with them, we can rise above
any obstacles and soar to our greatest heights.

From traveling through some of the richest and poorest countries in the world, from remote villages, to shimmering cities, to
wide open spaces, to ancient ruins, to sitting under the Bodhi Tree

in India where the Buddha gave his first teaching, and even to the hallways of Harvard University, Kathy discovers worlds within, around, and beyond that take us on a journey to our greatest self.

In *Change Your Shoes ~ Live Your Greatest Life*, each chapter of Kathy's journey provides insights and guided reflections to give the reader tools to chart their own journey of discovery, and to make positive decisions for a purposeful life. Kathy reveals a journey that we can each take to live our greatest life, and enables each reader to embark upon their own journey as they turn each page.

> *Once we have within us, the insatiable desire for life; when we have allowed the universe to fill us with its gifts, and unwrapped each one of them; when we are brave enough to live and to love without compromise; when we can leave our demons in the past, and see the future as infinite opportunity to be our greatest self; when we see that our presence in the present is the source of our greatest power; when we know that each moment is filled with choices to change our shoes, and to step onto new paths; then we see that we each hold the power to transform our life, to make our dreams a reality, to create the change we want to see in the world, and to live our greatest life.*

Kathy now lives in Miami Beach, and works to create positive change in the lives of people around the world through consulting, speaking, seminars, workshops, and of course, writing.

You can keep in touch with Kathy at www.kathyandersen.com, where you will also find quotes of the day, messages to contemplate in your moments of pause, and ongoing ways in which you can take your *self* on a journey to live your greatest life!

*www.kathyandersen.com*